W9-AJS-589

Getting What We Need Ourselves

Getting What We Need Ourselves

How Food Has Shaped African American Life

Jennifer Jensen Wallach

ROWMAN & LITTLEFIELD

Lanham · Boulder · New York · London

Published by Rowman & Littlefield
An imprint of The Rowman & Littlefield Publishing Group, Inc.
4501 Forbes Boulevard, Suite 200, Lanham, Maryland 20706
www.rowman.com

6 Tinworth Street, London SE11 5AL, United Kingdom

British Library Cataloguing in Publication Information Available

Library of Congress Cataloging-in-Publication Data

Names: Wallach, Jennifer Jensen, 1974- author.
Title: Getting what we need ourselves : how food has shaped African American life / Jennifer Jensen Wallach.
Other titles: Galley title: Tomorrow I'll be at the table : African American food culture from slavery to the present
Description: Lanham : Rowman & Littlefield, [2019] | Includes bibliographical references and index.
Identifiers: LCCN 2018054674 (print) | LCCN 2019012989 (ebook) | ISBN 9781538125250 (electronic) | ISBN 9781442253902 (cloth : alk. paper)
Subjects: LCSH: African Americans—Food—History. | African American cooking—History. | Food habits—United States—History. | Food—Social aspects—United States.
Classification: LCC GT2853.U5 (ebook) | LCC GT2853.U5 W34 2019 (print) | DDC 394.1/20896073—dc23
LC record available at https://lccn.loc.gov/2018054674

∞™ The paper used in this publication meets the minimum requirements of American National Standard for Information Sciences—Permanence of Paper for Printed Library Materials, ANSI/NISO Z39.48-1992.

For Aaron and Jamie

Contents

Acknowledgments

$\mathscr{I}$ am grateful to Jacqueline M. Moore and Nina Mjagkij for inviting me to write a book for their wonderful African American History Series, also published by Rowman & Littlefield. As I became more deeply involved in the project, I realized that the book I wanted to write would not quite fit the parameters of their series, but without their initial encouragement I never would have been ambitious enough to think that I could write an effective overview of a topic as rich and broad in scope as the history of African American food habits. I am incredibly grateful to my editor, Jon Sisk, for his flexibility in letting me tell this story in a way that made the most sense to me. He is not only an incredibly skilled editor, he is also a wonderful friend. I have spent many happy hours with him (often alongside our dear, mutual friend John David Smith) talking about books and drinking overpriced wine and cocktails at hotel bars during academic conferences. I have learned so much from you, Jon. Thank you.

I worked on this manuscript in fits and starts while I was completing a more detailed study about African American food habits and ideas about nationalism during the twentieth century. This book became a vehicle for distilling some of those ideas for a wider audience as well as a useful exercise in putting that work in a broader historical context. In order to put a broader frame around my own research, I drew upon a wide variety of secondary materials written by scholars of food studies and African American history. My notes and bibliography document my debt of gratitude to those other scholars whose fine work made this book possible. As I write this, I am grieving the recent death of Larry Malley, the former director of the University of Arkansas Press, a dear friend and talented editor who did so much to help nourish (the puns are unavoidable) my interest in food studies. The world feels so much lonelier without his warmth, generosity, and laughter. I am sending love and gratitude to his equally magnificent wife, Maggie Malley.

I wrote the first pages of this study in Nocona, Texas, while on a writer's retreat with the University of North Texas food history mentoring group. Thank you, Kate Imy, Sandra Mendiola Garcia, Rachel Moran, Marilyn Morris, Clark Pomerleau, Nancy Stockdale, and Michael Wise for being such supportive colleagues and friends and for letting me bounce ideas off you over cheap wine at the Red River Station Inn. I owe Mike Wise gratitude in his capacity as not only my colleague but also my husband. Mike, a food studies scholar whose own work I admire so much, read and commented on this manuscript and offered ceaseless moral support and so much more. He not only studies food but also grows and makes it. As I write these words, our kitchen counters are overloaded with jars of sweet and spicy pepper jelly and fermenting cayenne peppers on their way to becoming hot sauce. There is no happier place in the world for me than our kitchen. I know our beloved, wonderful, and terrible two-year-old Augie agrees, although he has not yet learned to appreciate the miracle of the vegetables grown in Daddy's garden.

This book and our happiness would not have been possible without the support of our family. Carolyn and David Briggs and Don and Debbie Wise have been incredibly generous in ways that are too numerous to mention here. I am also very grateful to have Sara and David Jensen, Aage Jensen, Janice Thorson, Cynthia Mann, Brian Wise, Gaby Gollub, and Tristan Mehlin in my life. This book is dedicated to my wonderful siblings, Aaron and Jamie Jensen. Thank you for loving me, supporting me, and for even reading my books. Finally, this one is for you.

Introduction

$\mathcal{A}$s an infant, Michael W. Twitty's first solid food was cornbread crumbled into the liquid left in the pot after cooking dark, leafy greens alongside scraps of cured meat. The sweet, salty, bitter, smoky taste of that first bite encapsulated the essence of a complicated southern cooking tradition to which Twitty, the descendent of enslaved people, was an heir. Generations of his family had been nourished on similar foods, which told a story of frugality, of not wasting, of making do. Although it would be years before Twitty would appreciate it as such, that homemade baby food was also a reflection of the ingenuity and the culinary flair of unknown cooks who had learned how to transform the simple elements of bread and water into a craveable and nutritious meal. Over the course of hundreds of years, this vital knowledge was transferred to millions of southerners and their descendants, including Twitty, a child growing up in Washington, DC, in the late 1970s and 1980s.[1]

Initially Twitty was unimpressed with the value of that inheritance. Southern heritage cooking could not compete with the mass-produced pleasures of fast food, the futuristic appeal of chalky astronaut ice cream, or the lip-staining properties of artificially flavored popsicles.[2] He craved culinary order, uniformity, and homogeneity, cylindrical hot dogs and not pots full of bits of bones and tangles of leaves. Grits were "really bad un-oatmeal." Scraps of pig meat and offal were "horrifying." Okra was "medieval torture . . . snotty and viscous." As a youngster, he "did anything and everything to avoid the smell and savor of 'slave' food."[3]

With the exception of chitterlings, which he never learned to embrace, the power of his family recipes eventually wore down his resistance to these heritage foods, remolding his taste sensibilities. Eventually, he learned to appreciate the idiosyncratic pleasures of food cooked from scratch instead of the identical mediocrity of Pizza Hut and Kentucky Fried Chicken. Soon Twitty began to enjoy helping his grandmother cut out biscuits, snap peas, barbecue ribs, and candy sweet potatoes. He learned to cherish the shared ritual of making what his grandmother described, with satisfaction, as a "good southern meal."[4] After his initial resistance to the foods of his foremothers and fathers faded, Twitty embraced southern cooking with fervor.

Soon just eating these foods was not enough to satisfy him; he had to understand them, to untangle the histories embedded in the recipes. As an adult, his curiosity propelled him southward where he visited places where his ancestors both white and black—created and served (or were served) dishes closely related to what members of his family were still eating in the twentieth century. Embarking on what he labeled as a "Southern Discomfort Tour," he collected family lore, sampled local delicacies, and contemplated the painful histories of slavery and colonialism that resulted in the creation of southern cooking, which combined African, European, and Native American ingredients and food knowledge. During the course of his culinary reeducation, not only did Twitty compile an impressive amount of historical research describing the process of culinary exchange and learn to better understand the ideas about food brought to the table by diverse peoples originating on three different continents, he also learned how to cook using antebellum kitchen technology. He also spent hours in southern fields performing agricultural labor as he worked to combine an intellectual understanding of the past with a visceral one, striving to experience something about how the past actually tasted and felt.[5]

Twitty's fascinating culinary journey from McDonald's to the plantation hearth represents only one facet of his personal food story. His mother, the daughter of southern transplants, "never identified with nor cared for the South." This detachment of both geography and sentiment gave her different culinary reference points than Twitty's grandmother, a southern food partisan. When living in Cincinnati, Twitty's mother learned to savor Jewish challah and began making her own braided loaves. Later she served this sweet, golden bread to her son toasted and topped with blackberry jam.[6] Embedded in Sunday morning breakfasts shared between mother and son was a prophecy, because Twitty became fascinated with the culture that created that delectable bread, eventually converting to Judaism. In the process he added new recipes to his repertoire, dishes like matzo balls and cholent, and Sephardic "soul food" like meat, potato, and spinach-filled pastries called *bourekas*.[7] His embrace of Jewish traditions resonated with his understanding of African American ones, because "both are cuisines where homeland and exile interplay."[8] These foods too became a part of his food story and a reflection of the identity of a man who has described himself as "four time blessed" and as someone who is "large of body, gay, African American and Jewish."[9] As someone with such a multifaceted sense of identity, Twitty has been often stereotyped and misunderstood. He remarks, "When you are all the things I am, it's easy for people to put you in a narrow spot indeed." Undaunted, he calmly notes, that in such a circumstance, "You have to have a way out."[10]

Writing for the *Washington Post*, Manuel Roig-Franzia claims, "Should there ever be a competition to determine the most interesting man in the world, Michael W. Twitty would have to be considered a serious contender."[11] Indeed, Twitty is both remarkable and also unusually skilled at pondering the broader implications of his complex identity; however, Twitty would likely argue that most people are more complicated than outside observers realize. He points out that Africans Americans in general are "so multicultural." To illustrate this point, he uses the example of the black population in Georgia in 1790: "Black people were speaking Ladino—it's the Spanish-Jewish language—Cherokee, Highland Scots, English, Gullah . . . that says something right there. And if they're doing all that, they're obviously mixing the food, too."[12] Twitty's reminder and his own personal example offer a cautionary tale to anyone who might unthinkingly assume that all African Americans share identical culinary sensibilities and relationships to food.

Nigerian novelist Chimamanda Ngozi Adichie's widely circulated 2014 TED Talk, "The Danger of a Single Story," provides a useful template for understanding human, and by extension, culinary diversity. She delivers an apt reminder that all cultures and all people are too complicated to be reduced to a single narrative. Furthermore, she demonstrates that taking one facet of someone's experience, history, or culture without considering it in context with other elements can lead to painful generalizations and cross-cultural or interpersonal misunderstandings. For example, to talk about Twitty's disgust at the thought of eating chitterlings, which he describes as smelling worse than "apes throwing vomit" at the zoo, without mentioning his love for other foods from the southern poverty table, would distort his relationship to his family's food traditions. To write about his affection for foods of the African diaspora without also taking into account his embrace of those from the Jewish one would result in a depiction of only part of who he is. Yet Adichie warns her listeners that it is a very human tendency to do just that, to cling to simple, one-dimensional understandings of both individuals and of entire groups of people, whether out of ignorance or a desire for simplicity.

As a Nigerian who has spent time living in the United States and who travels frequently, Adichie has been repeatedly stigmatized and misunderstood by people who view her from the prism of the single story of a tragic and impoverished Africa. Throughout her life, she has been horrified to discover that people accustomed to watching news footage about famine, illness, and war on her home continent did not have the ability to comprehend the fact that Africa is composed of different nations and manifold personal experiences. Those who had bought into a singular story of African "catastrophe" did not have the framework to understand Adichie or appreciate her memories of a middle-class childhood spent with her nose buried in both English and African novels. As someone who has often been stereotyped, she learned, "The consequence of a single story is this: it robs people of dignity."[13]

This book about African American food history begins with Twitty's example and Adichie's admonition in mind and argues that there is not a single African American food story. Popular ideas about the topic are often embedded in a narrative that traces an uninterrupted line of culinary descent from precolonial West Africa through to the present day. Food writers like Adrian Miller have gone to painstaking lengths to trace ingredients and recipes common on American tables today to West Africa, labeling the region as "the true source" for how many people of African descent living in the United States still eat.[14] Indeed, Miller and others have successfully demonstrated that Africanisms abound in the kitchens of the Americas. In fact, scholars of the black food tradition have demonstrated that it is impossible to study American food culture in general without taking into account deeply rooted African antecedents, which are particularly pronounced in southern regional cooking. This narrative is an accurate one. Perhaps it is even the most important African American food story, yet it is not the only one. If rendered too simply, this account does not always adequately take into account other influences or culinary journeys.

The tendency to privilege African origination stories over other facets of black food history is part of what Paul Gilroy has identified as a larger trend in "black political culture [which] has always been more interested in the relationship of identity to roots and rootedness than in seeing identity as a process of movement and mediation that is more appropriately approached via the homonym routes."[15] Inspired by Gilroy's emphasis on movement and change, this study will attempt to do two things: examine African roots while also emphasizing the routes along which these customs traveled and the transformations that happened along the way. The history of black food traditions can be most accurately conceptualized as a web of ongoing conversations, debates, and reinventions rather than as a single, uninterrupted line leading directly back to the African continent. That line of descent is central, but it is crisscrossed with other memories and experiences that often intersect but sometimes veer off in a different direction. There is not a singular, linear narrative that can be neatly recounted. Instead, there are multiple stories, only some of which this book will begin to unravel.

This book will examine some of the cultural transferences that can be linked back to the continent of Africa alongside more amorphous *ideas* about Africa that inspired many who had no direct experience with the continent.[16] The first generation of enslaved Africans who found themselves clearing forests, curing tobacco, or harvesting sugar in the western hemisphere could draw on concrete memories of the smells and tastes of their homeland. For successive generations, these memories were experienced secondhand, becoming transformed in each re-remembering. In his famous essay, "Imaginary Homelands," Salman Rushdie, an Indian writer who has spent most of his life living elsewhere, compares conjuring up memories of a homeland one no longer resides in to looking at "broken mirrors, some of whose fragments have been irretrievably lost."[17] However, Rushdie suggests that the fragmentary nature of memories is part of what gives them their power: "The shards of memory acquired greater status, greater resonance, because they were *remains*; fragmentation made trivial things seem like symbols, and the mundane acquired numinous qualities."[18] Rushdie's recollections about remembering India from a distance may yield some insights into why the African antecedents of African American foodways matter so much to so many. Displaced Africans had to remember their homeland not only from a distance but also through the lens of the trauma of forced displacement, a reference point that made the remaining shards of mirror all the more precious.

The cultural interactions that took place on the coast of Africa, aboard slave-trading vessels, and in early New World culinary settings led to the creation of a unique style of cooking, particularly in the American South, where the majority of the black population was centered. These new food practices combined African, European, and Native American ideas and ingredients. Over time, pork and corn became the chief cornerstones of this diet. This style of eating became so predominant that it has assumed a central role in most retellings of African American food history. The titles of widely heralded food histories such as Jessica Harris's *High on the Hog: A Culinary Journey from Africa to America* and Frederick Douglass Opie's *Hog and Hominy: Soul Food from Africa to America* capture both the African origination narrative along with some of the key constituent ingredients in this creole cuisine. Furthermore, the subtitle of Opie's book highlights another common interpretive emphasis in most retellings of African American food history. Beginning in the 1960s, the foodways of the plantation South were reframed as an exclusively black food production called "soul food," and eating this style of food became a way to demonstrate race pride. This way of thinking about black food traditions has become the predominant one in American popular culture, so overwhelming, in fact, that in the minds of some, "soul food" has become a single story.

It is important to keep in mind that the now dominant concept of "soul food" has its own history. It emerged within the specific context of the civil rights movement and from within a particular cultural nationalistic framework. As the ensuing chapters of this book will reveal, different generations of eaters thought about the same foods differently. Depending upon the time, place, and subject position of the narrator, the same meal might be described as "soul food," "country food," "southern food," "slave food," or "just food." Thus it is important to remember that although the concept of soul food is descriptive and useful, when looking at the past food sensibilities it can also be distorting. African Americans who came of age before the 1960s used different language and embraced a different set of concepts for thinking about food culture. Furthermore, some did not eat or did not value the foods that later were identified as "soul food."

Throughout history, many, perhaps even most, African Americans embraced southern food traditions. However, alternative food stories reveal the experiences of several generations of African Americans who self-consciously worked to build a set of food practices that were untethered from either African or southern origination stories. For example, during the Progressive Era, some African American eaters sought to eat food that they regarded as sophisticated, modern, and more generically "American" than southern home cooking. In the second half of the twentieth century, many rejected southern regional foods as being unhealthy and as psychologically harmful. Eaters of this ilk rejected pork, a cornerstone of the southern diet, and sometimes all meat. Furthermore, because hunger and poverty were persistent issues throughout African American history, some people were so focused on having enough to eat that their primary concern was never about what kinds of food finally landed on their plates.

Speaking as both a scholar of black food history and a group member, Jessica Harris articulates another of the key ideas undergirding much African American culinary history with her simple but profound claim that "we have our own way with food."[19] The idea that African Americans have innate cooking skills and a shared affinity for food is one that appears, in various guises, in much African American food writing, whether research oriented, celebratory, or instructional in nature. One of the goals of this book is to examine the intellectual history of the pervasive idea that black food traditions are as much inherited as learned and to untangle a tension that sometimes emerges between attempts to uncover shared historical connections and the articulation of ideas that sometimes inadvertently seem to support the idea of essential racial differences. For as James McCann helpfully reminds us, "Combinations of ingredients and structures of cooking are not carried in the genes, but come from historical experiences shared among peoples and across generations."[20]

Assertions of black culinary pride and distinctiveness such as Harris's claim that black people have "our own way with food" or cookbook author Freda De Knight's insistence that whether or not the skill is "acquired or inherent" all African Americans have the ability to turn everyday ingredients into a "gourmet's delight," are, on one hand, empowering celebrations of black culture.[21] Paradoxically, these ideas can also serve as an implicit endorsement of Eurocentric ideas about innate racial characteristics that were used to justify race-based slavery and ongoing black exclusion and debasement postemancipation. Gilroy warns that the "language of absolute cultural difference . . . provides an embarrassing link between the practice of blacks who comprehend racial politics through it and their foresworn opponents—the ethnic absolutists of the racial right."[22] After all, historically white Americans have also believed that black people have an inborn, racialized relationship with food. White supremacists have generally regarded black appetites as outsized and coarse, while paradoxically also claiming—in seeming agreement with Harris and De Knight—that African Americans have innate cooking skills, skills that they depict as being instinctive and bodily, not learned and intellectual. With Gilroy's warning in mind, I am writing from the point of view that black food traditions, like all cultural practices, can be most productively analyzed as the product of cultural hybridity and intellectual exchange rather than as something ineffable and unchanging that only group members can experience and possess.

Twitty hints at something of a middle way of thinking about the problem of essentialism and ideas about innate, racial ways of eating. He acknowledges that there is no "racial" "cooking gene," finding it problematic to "indulge in too much biological essentialism." Yet he wonders if "blood memory . . . contains some clause for the ability not to burn water."[23] Indeed Harris, Miller, Twitty, and others make a powerful argument that African American food culture is unique and that its traditions are enduring. Opie's assertion that African American food expression—both past and present—represents a materialization of a shared "black spirituality and experiential wisdom" is an insight that rings true to many.[24] With this in mind, this book will examine some of the historical, structural, and political reasons that have led chroniclers of black food culture to reify ideas about innate racial differences in the realm of food culture that they have otherwise discarded.

Scholars of black history have frequently suggested that African American cultural expressions have been useful mechanisms for constructing a sustaining sense of community that enabled black people to survive both the psychic and physical traumas of slavery and the uncertainties of freedom.[25] John Blassingame forcefully articulated the idea that culture could be used to insulate practitioners from the totalizing impact of white hegemony in his classic 1972 book *The Slave Community*. Blassingame asserts that enslaved people "created several unique cultural forms" that were designed as a means of "sustaining hope [and] building self-esteem." He further claims that distinctiveness was the key virtue of these cultural expressions, arguing, "The more his cultural forms differed from his master and the more they were immune from the control of whites, the more the slave gained in personal autonomy and positive self-concepts."[26]

This study draws upon Blassingame's core insights, demonstrating that black food expression often served as a means of cementing the bonds of community and of providing a cultural and communal buffer against the forces of white supremacy that sought to weaken and oppress the community. However, although ample food could be a symbol of empowerment, hunger could serve as a painful reminder of racism. Thus, in some chapters of this study, empty plates are as much a part of the discussion as full ones. In addition to highlighting aspects of African American food history that are celebratory and affirming, this book examines food as a weapon of white supremacy, examining, for example, acts such as force-feeding on slave ships and the decision to deprive politically conscious African Americans of food during the civil rights movement. These practices were embedded in an elaborate racist mythology about black culinary difference. Throughout history, African Americans have had to decide whether to ignore, challenge, embrace, or engage racist ideas about essentially different black ways of cooking, eating, and being. One of the core tensions that this book explores is the conflict between the forces of white hegemony that sought to use food as a tool of oppression and African Americans who saw it as a potential vehicle for liberation.

This book is, in part, a book about recipes and ingredients. Among other things, it will overview the kinds of foods that were served on slave-trading vessels and cooked on southern plantations and eaten in segregated restaurants and in the dining halls of black institutions of higher learning. However, this is also a study of *ideas* about food, which is equally interested in uncovering what people thought about their food decisions than in what they actually decided to eat. People of African descent living in the United States, both before and after the creation of the nation-state, have consistently used food both as a means of self-expression and as a political tool. Sometimes black eaters have regarded the contents on their plates as vitally significant; other times they regarded the actual food as more incidental, caring more about economic justice than specific ingredients. With that in mind, the topic of food labor is another important story that this book will address through an examination of the history of African American efforts to produce, purchase, and prepare food both for their own use as well as at the behest of their employers.

The first chapter of the book begins on the continent of Africa with an overview of West African food traditions, which were continually transformed by a process of culinary exchange that began long before the transatlantic slave trade. The chapter looks closely at how ingredients and food knowledge were circulated and then examines how Europeans produced the food needed to support the massive enterprise of the transatlantic slave trade. It closes by considering how Africans used food to resist their captivity, often by simply refusing to eat. Chapter 2 examines the experiences of enslaved people in what is now the United States, contemplating both their attempts to hold onto their native food traditions and their ability to adapt to new ingredients, new knowledge, and the grim new reality of chattel slavery. It also examines the system of slave rationing alongside the various, creative techniques that enslaved people used to increase both the amount and quality of their provisions.

Chapter 3 begins with a discussion about food traditions after emancipation. Because the freedpeople often found that their food supply was actually less secure in freedom than it had been during the era of slavery, hunger is one of the predominate themes in this chapter. White southerners used the issue of food access to help them institutionalize new forms of racial oppression as they demanded subservience and compliance from black employees, including the large number of African American domestic servants who labored preparing food in white households. However, despite the odds against them, some black southerners found ways to resist their oppression, sometimes by using their skills to their advantage, for example, by becoming culinary entrepreneurs. The next chapter begins with an examination of the food practices of the African American elite who did not suffer from food insecurity and instead busied themselves with the cultural work of creating a new set of food practices that they hoped would create a distance between themselves and the painful past of slavery. They generally rejected southern foods. Furthermore, in an attempt to refute white stereotypes about black culinary inferiority and coarseness, they emphasized the importance of middle-class dining etiquette as a way to perform their status as respectable, free citizens. These food reformers often clashed with working-class southerners who saw no need to change their traditional diet. Furthermore, the chapter demonstrates that many middle-class eaters found that their quest to maintain standards of proper behavior became extremely difficult while traveling away from home and concludes with a discussion about how black travelers dealt with the problem of feeding themselves on the road when dining facilities were either segregated or nonexistent.

Chapter 5 looks at the issue of black food habits during the Great Depression, beginning with an examination of the religious figure Father Divine, who amazed his followers by serving bountiful, free feasts to all comers during the biggest economic downturn in US history. Most African Americans could not dine at Divine's table, and the community generally responded to the economic hard times by finding ways to work together, often by forming buying cooperatives to get better prices. Finally, the chapter concludes with a discussion of food practices and World War II, which ended the Great Depression but brought a new set of challenges to African American eaters. Although many black civilians supported the war effort by working to augment national food supplies, black soldiers found that their patriotism did not end differential treatment in the military. Many black soldiers were deeply offended by the fact that they were asked to serve in supporting roles, frequently in the realm of food service, rather than as combatants during the war. Faced with ongoing discrimination, black Americans decided to fight for a Double Victory against racism at home and fascism abroad. Significantly, sometimes the fight for equality on the home front took place at restaurants where African Americans demanded the right to be served as equals alongside white customers.

The last chapter of the book expands upon the discussion of sit-in demonstrations at segregated restaurants, demonstrating that black Americans saw their ability to eat on equal terms with other citizens as a vital civil right. However, many of the poorest African American southerners, who rarely ate at restaurants, showed their support for the growing civil rights movement in other ways, often by sharing what little food they had with visiting civil rights activists. Hunger, a theme explored once again in this chapter, was an ongoing concern for rural southerners who looked for ways to work together to make sure that everyone in the community had enough to eat. This was the moment when many begin to celebrate southern food as racially specific "soul food." However, others emphatically rejected southern cooking, regarding it as both reminiscent of slavery and unhealthful. Finally, the epilogue examines ongoing culinary diversity in the twenty-first century with an examination of the cosmopolitan cooking style of celebrity chef Marcus Samuelsson and a brief discussion of a growing community of African American vegans who have created a robust discussion about race and food politics. Together these chapters tell multiple stories about black food expression. However, they also leave many stories yet untold.

Culinary Origins and Exchanges during the Transatlantic Slave Trade

$\mathcal{A}$ nineteenth-century proverb from what is now the country of Ghana proclaimed maize to be "the Chief among foods."[1] The ubiquitous and tasty grain played such a large part in the local diet that even outsiders who visited the region quickly learned to recognize its significance. Thomas Edward Bowdich, a British writer who traveled throughout the area in the early nineteenth century, raved about the delectability of the food he sampled during his trip. He happily devoured "excellent" local soups and stews and enjoyed exploring abundant markets stocked with an array of fresh meat, salted and dried fish, palm wine, and numerous fruits and vegetables, including not only maize but also things like yams, plantains, and citrus fruit.[2] As he traveled, he studied the agricultural practices used to produce that market bounty and was particularly impressed by the sight of numerous "well cultivated" fields of maize, the prolific and nourishing grain that had become a dietary staple.[3] He observed that Fante people most often prepared their maize by grinding it on a coarse stone, mixing the meal with water, shaping it into loaves, and boiling it until it became a dense porridge he called *cankey*.[4] Bowdich hungrily sampled not only this dish but also other local variations of this "chief" food. He enjoyed eating corn that had been roasted whole on the stalk (a preparation that he thought tasted something like "fresh peas") or drinking the grain after it had been transformed into a "pleasant" beer.[5]

Intriguingly, this abundant food, which had become a culturally resonant symbol to locals, was not actually a product of Africa but was instead an American crop introduced to the region beginning in the sixteenth century. Ironically, this foreign import, which was first brought to the continent by slave traders, was later used to symbolize a very local way of eating and in fact became emblematic of how residents in some areas of Africa, including the

Gold Coast, hoped to eat. The thorough incorporation of maize into some local food systems reveals the obvious, though sometimes forgotten, truth that food culture is never static and that ideas about what is proper or desirable change over time as eaters are exposed to new options. Any attempt to understand the African origins of African American ways of eating must be sensitive to the dynamics of an ongoing set of exchanges of ingredients and ideas, which began on the coast of Africa and continued on the other side of the Atlantic.

The culinary changes that were a by-product of the transatlantic slave trade were but one manifestation of widespread cultural transformations that led to dramatic changes in African societies as well as to the creation of a distinctive African American identity on other side of the ocean. Enslaved people responded to the trauma of being ripped from their home communities in complex ways as they struggled to hold onto existing ethnic identities while also forming new multicultural connections. For the forced migrants who found themselves in chains in the Americas, cultural adaptation was necessary. Over time, members of various ethnic groups became united through trauma and through the tyranny of the European race-making project that used the crude simplicity of ideas about racial sameness to lump culturally diverse people together. Their displacement and forced intermingling meant that their descendants would become members of the social and cultural group that we refer to today as "African American."[6]

Although they managed to form shared social, cultural, and political alliances, it is important to remember that the victims of the brutal transatlantic slave trade did not arrive in the Americas bereft of memories and knowledge specific to their disparate backgrounds. The people whose bodies stocked the holds of the slavers making the voyage across the Atlantic beginning in the sixteenth century represented culturally diverse groups, which historian Gwendolyn Midlo Hall argues deserve "to be rescued from the anonymity of generic Africans and studied as varied, complex peoples."[7] Thus it is important to emphasize that even though the term *African* is used here and in numerous other historical studies for pragmatic reasons, sometimes serving as a placeholder in instances where more precise identifying details are unknown, there was no singular "African" culture that served as a basis for later African American cultural productions. The members of the various ethnic groups who were transformed into African Americans had to transcend the particularity of their own cultural backgrounds as they searched for the basis for amalgamation and compromise. One of the spaces where they found the shared tools they needed to forge a new multicultural identity was the realm of food culture.

During the era of the slave trade, the inhabitants of western Africa spoke diverse languages, governed themselves using a number of forms of political organization, and had various aesthetic traditions. Although these differences were significant, one of the cultural fields where the residents of the vast geographic expanse of West Africa shared the most similarities was in the area of food traditions. Even though there were certainly variations in what filled regional cooking pots, James McCann, author of *Stirring the Pot: A History of African Cuisine*, argues that it was possible to identify "fundamental elements of a common cuisine."[8] Thus, shared taste sensibilities and similar cooking knowledge served as one useful starting place in the creolization process that began on the coast of Africa and was to accelerate in the Americas. Even if the captives could not always initially speak to one another in intelligible languages, this thread of culinary similarity may have fostered a sense of connection.

Like McCann, food studies scholar Jessica Harris makes an expansive case for threads of culinary continuity throughout sub-Saharan Africa. She argues that "traditional dishes tended to be a variation on the theme of a soupy stew over a starch or a grilled or fried animal protein accompanied by a vegetable sauce and/or a starch."[9] Frederick Douglass Opie's research lends additional insights into culinary similarities. He observes that pre-Columbian West Africans tended to use meat and fish sparingly in their cooking as elements to add flavor to a meal without making up the bulk of its substance.[10] James McCann identifies a West African tendency to use meat and fish in the same dish, a practice he identifies as an antecedent to New Orleans creole dishes like jambalaya.[11] Furthermore, the regional ingredient of palm oil gave many West African foods a distinctive color and taste, and palm wine, extracted from a different variety of tree, was often used to wash these meals down.[12] Many West African dishes reflected a local taste for the piquant, and that spiciness was often balanced out by starchy regional staples like *fufu*, a paste made out of pounded and boiled yams, cassavas, or plantains.[13]

Even though enslaved Africans from various ethnic groups initially enjoyed some shared conceptions about what constituted a good and filling meal, it is important to remember that the food traditions that they carried across the Atlantic in the form of memories did not represent timeless, unchanging recipes. For example, *fufu* is a dish that simultaneously represents culinary continuity and change. The texture of the *fufu*, used as an accompaniment to various stewed dishes, has provided people from different parts of West Africa with at least some basis for a shared culinary vocabulary. However, throughout time and across geographic space, the ingredients used to make *fufu* have varied in accordance with local taste and due to the availability of ingredients. The staple ingredients of yam, plantain, and cassava used to make *fufu* tell a story of culinary diversity. Although yams were indigenous to the continent of Africa, plantains are a product of Asia that made their way to West Africa via the trans-Saharan trade sometime before 1000 CE, and cassava is a product of the Americas that arrived on the continent via the same trade routes that transported slaves.[14] Thus, the example of *fufu* reminds students of African American foodways that the quest for food roots is inevitably complicated by the fact that culture is not a fixed and timeless possession but is instead a process that is continually unfolding.

Adaptability was, in fact, one of the cornerstone characteristics of African foodways during this period. James McCann has argued that although "Africa had fewer endowments than other parts of the world in genetic materials of plants and animals available for domestication," inhabitants of the continent never limited themselves to eating only locally available foods. For example, while the earliest Europeans could draw upon fifty-six varieties of large grasses to domesticate in order to create staple crops like wheat, barley, and rye, sub-Saharan Africa contained only four similar species.[15] However, elaborate trade networks across the continent and beyond brought a variety of goods to West Africa before the era of the slave trade. Foods from the Mediterranean or Asia that were incorporated into West African food traditions early on include items such as chickpeas, onions, coconuts, ginger, dates, and domesticated animals like goats and sheep.[16] Pre-Columbian West Africans ate not only a great deal of red rice, which was native to the continent, but many were also familiar with white Asian rice, which had reached east African markets by the ninth century and was being cultivated on the Gold Coast by the time Europeans arrived there.[17]

Some of the most significant changes to African ways of cooking and eating came about after European, initially Portuguese, contact with the continent beginning in the sixteenth century. The European traders seeking slaves to transport to the Americas as well as other African goods initiated an unprecedentedly rapid exchange of biological products that altered the character of the food supply not just in Africa but also around the globe.[18] This circulation of plants, animals, and microbes, which Alfred Crosby memorably labeled the "Columbian Exchange," altered the flora and fauna and, by extension, the cooking pots in Africa so quickly that successive waves of European visitors to the continent and Africans born after the introduction of American foods like maize, cassava, capsicum, and peanuts sometimes interpreted these ingredients as essentially African and not as foreign transplants.

Although American ingredients certainly revolutionized African agriculture, it is important to remember that Africans did not incorporate these items into their diets thoughtlessly. Instead, as J. D. La Fleur points out, they proceeded with caution and "tested the novelties in their kitchen gardens and adapted them to their needs and tastes before eventually adopting as staples the ones they found attractive."[19] By the end of this process of experimentation, New World ingredients had enhanced the food supply of Africa to such a significant extent that the accompanying bonanza led to an increase in the African population. Some historians of the continent have made the dark and ironic observation that the population growth spurred by improved food access may have happened at about the same pace as the population depletion brought about by the labor demands of American plantations.[20]

Maize, the crop that the nineteenth-century ancestors of contemporary Ghanaians regarded as a "chief" food, originated in Mexico. By 1540, less than fifty years after Columbus's historic voyage, it was being cultivated on the Cape Verde Islands off the coast of Africa. By the seventeenth century, supplies of the crop had outpaced native staples like millet and sorghum in many areas along the West African coast. Maize appealed to African farmers because it produced high yields and grew quickly. It rapidly became a key source of food during the "hungry season" when farmers were awaiting the maturation of slower-growing crops.[21] Cassava, another New World plant that many unfamiliar with its biological history assumed was native to Africa, was also widely adopted.[22] This tuber of Brazilian origins is drought tolerant once established and, like maize, has a high yield.[23] Capsicum peppers, native to South America, also played a transformational role in African cooking. The widespread cultivation of peppers gave West Africans a means of amplifying a local taste sensibility that valued hot flavors. This regional preference for spicy food had been previously sated primarily by the native melegueta pepper, also called the "grains of paradise." The seeds of the *Aframomum melegueta* imparted a peppery, though less fiery, flavor to foods than the widely embraced capsicum cultivars.[24]

Peanuts, which originated in South America, became another transformational food in West African diets. The legume soon became part of a crop rotation for farmers in West African river valleys and found its way into cooking pots most commonly in the form of a stew, variations of which remain ubiquitous in West Africa.[25] Interestingly, peanuts were frequently reimported to the Americas along with African slaves, a practice that sometimes obscured the origins of the plant, leading some to believe it was indigenous to Africa. The slang word *goober*, which is still commonly used in the US South to refer to the peanut, may have come from a Bantu word, *nguba*. This term referred to the Bambara groundnut, an African plant similar to the peanut. This nickname highlights the complex history of the peanut and other African dietary staples that traveled great geographical distances before becoming an indispensible ingredient in local cuisines on both sides of the Atlantic.[26]

Ideas were exchanged on Atlantic trade routes alongside human bodies, plants, animals, and other goods as people from different continents observed other ways of being and of eating. Many of the participants in these transactions were unaware of the scale of the transformations that they were playing a part in. For example, slave trader Joseph Hawkins stumbled into his unsavory profession as part of a personal quest to find a way to earn a living. Hawkins was born in Kingsbury, New York, in 1772 into a middling family that Hawkins confesses was "not popular on point of property."²⁷ Because he possessed only a "moderate education" and no family wealth and had failed in an attempt to start a small business, Hawkins made the radical decision to migrate to South Carolina where the institution of slavery was becoming ever more deeply entrenched.²⁸ He made the ironic bet that he could find more freedom and opportunity in a slave society committed to denying those same life chances to a steadily increasing number of human captives.²⁹

Hawkins signed up to serve as the supercargo on a slaver named the *Charleston*.³⁰ The ship left the city's harbor on December 1, 1793, and was docked on a West African river by February of the following year.³¹ As he tramped through the countryside purchasing war captives and transforming human bodies into a global trade commodity, Hawkins became fascinated by the customs of the Igbo people he met, paying attention to details including their style of clothing, religious customs, stage-of-life rituals, and food practices. He filtered his observations, which he published in 1707 as *A History of a Voyage to the Coast of Africa and Travels into the Interior*, through an unabashedly American gaze, certain that his own way of life was at root superior. This travelogue and others like it served as an entryway for Europeans who wished to learn something about African geography and about the lifeways of the people of the continent.

Significantly, much of what we now know about precolonial African foodways comes from the accounts of people like Hawkins, outsiders who journeyed to the continent to deplete it of its resources, individuals who were pillagers first and cultural observers only secondarily. The descriptions of the food habits written by Hawkins, an unlikely and untrained ethnographer, have to be read suspiciously and critically and in conversation with the oral traditions of various West African societies. As James McCann reminds us, during the era of the transatlantic slave trade, "cooking and cuisine in Africa was more fundamentally an oral art."³² Food knowledge and recipes of the various West African peoples who were victimized by the transatlantic slave trade were transferred orally "between neighbor and family" and even "between generations."³³ Scholars of food studies can find echoes of what people ate in the sixteenth and seventeenth centuries, when Europeans first began exploiting African riches, in what people eat today. However, just as it is dangerous to interpret early modern travelers' reports as unmitigated sources of information about African ways of eating, it is also problematic to conflate present-day eating practices with their historical antecedents. Thus, there is much about historical food practices in West Africa that remains unknown.

Hawkins's experiences eating the foods of the continent do, however, give us some insights into how culinary knowledge was transferred between Africans and outsiders during the period. After spending time in West Africa, Hawkins reported being so impressed by the "simplicity and kind manners" of the people he encountered that he felt temporarily tempted to give up the "bustle and cares of enlightened society."[34] Although his romantic fantasies of an easier life far from home were ultimately subsumed by the pressures of his occupational duties, he continued to have minor epiphanies, realizing that some of the stereotypes about African inferiority that he brought with him were unsupported by his face-to-face interactions with the people he met. He was particularly intrigued after he witnessed the process of producing palm oil, a regional food staple that was extracted from the nutlike fruit of the oil palm. West Africans would harvest the fruit, boil it, pound it, strain it, and boil it again to produce a red oil used to cook and flavor food.[35] Hawkins was amazed by the process because, as he later admitted, the procedure "indicates a combination of ideas," a level of sophisticated thinking that he did not think Africans were capable of performing.[36]

Hawkins was initially repelled by the unfamiliar taste of the oil, which he deemed to be "nauseous" to the "palate of the white man." However, repeated sampling of the oil eventually caused him to change his opinion as he implicitly acknowledged that taste sensibilities were not innate traits of races or nations but were instead cultivated. Rethinking his initial response to the reddish oil, he admitted that "habit renders it pleasant."[37] Other Europeans, like Hawkins, not only learned to embrace the culinary possibilities of palm oil, but they soon found other reasons to capitalize upon African knowledge about palm oil production. Eventually Europeans became dependent upon the substance as one that could be used for industrial lubrication, to make soaps and candles, and, as the twentieth century approached, for another culinary purpose: manufacturing margarine.[38] By the mid-nineteenth century, the palm oil trade had replaced the slave trade as the most lucrative European trading venture in regions such as the Bight of Biafra.[39] By the time the slave trade ended, Europeans had learned not only to adapt some of their taste sensibilities, but they had also found a variety of new ways to exploit African resources toward their own ends.

Willem Bosman, a chief merchant for the Dutch West India Company who resided on the Gold Coast from 1688 until 1702, published another widely read account of the culture in the region, which similarly intermingled disdain and admiration while providing a justification for ongoing European interest in African botanical resources.[40] Bosman traveled widely in West Africa, describing the food traditions he encountered by using ingredients and recipes that were familiar to his readers as points of reference. At one point in his journey, he described African yams by comparing the root to European turnips and the leaves to French green beans.[41] When traveling in what is now the nation of Benin, he expressed admiration at the skills of local women who processed New World maize into a beer that he claimed was as strong as those brewed in Holland. He was somewhat more muted in his praise of fried pastries made from beans that although used to make "Oyl-cakes . . . as light as ours in Holland," tasted only "well enough."[42] He was unsure about how to best interpret foods that did not have a handy Dutch analog. Coming from a framework that viewed bread as a dietary staple, he marveled at the fact that Africans did not eat European-style breads. He incredulously proclaimed that "there is not one Oven in this whole Country." He struggled to find a way to describe, for example, the dish of *fufu* that filled a similar niche to European bread in many West African diets. Searching for a language to describe what he found to be a mystifying substance, he decided to think of it as a kind of boiled bread.[43]

Understanding his Dutch frame of reference is vital to interpreting Bosman's description of local dishes. His initial response was always to reject the foods that were the least familiar to him and to devalue African culinary knowledge. At one point he disdainfully claimed that the "*Negroes* eat so poorly and so little."[44] He described a typical meal of a commoner this way:

> Their common food is a pot full of Millet boiled to the consistence of Bread, or instead of that Jambs [yams] and Potatoes; over which they pour a little Palm-Oyle, with a few boiled Herbs, to which they add a stinking fish.[45]

Even though he was outspokenly critical of a diet that he labeled as meager and peculiar, Bosman, like Hawkins decades later, eventually began to savor some African flavors. He learned to enjoy a local stew made of boiled fish, palm oil, and maize, which he begrudgingly admitted was "no very disagreeable food to those who are used to it." Over the course of a long tenure in West Africa, Bosman learned to enjoy foods that he assured his skeptical European readers were "wholesome in this Country."[46]

Europeans like Boswell used the information they gathered about African foodways not only to fuel their bodies and to entertain the readers who would eventually purchase copies of their travelogues but also to support the mechanisms of the slave trade. Although the colorful descriptions of an "exotic" West Africa were designed to satisfy the curiosity of European audiences eager for glimpses into their countries' overseas ventures, men like Bosman and Hawkins were under no illusion about what their true priorities were during their African adventures. They had been sent to the continent not to report and to educate but to enrich their home countries by purchasing slaves. Although food habits were a source of intercultural curiosity, the primary European interest in the foods of the continent was in gathering enough resources and knowledge to keep both themselves and the human capital they were accumulating alive.

Slave traders had to find ways to feed cheaply their human captives from the moment they were purchased until they were sold in New World slave markets. This entire process could take several months, and the task of ensuring the availability of a constant food supply constituted one of the greatest logistical challenges of the trade in human beings. Although the process of enslavement was designed to dehumanize its victims and to convert them to a legal status similar to that of things, unlike inanimate trade goods, people have to be fed. Slave traders had to confront continually the essential humanity of the enslaved by contemplating this biological necessity and in deciding what to feed their human cargo.

According to meticulous research conducted by historian David Eltis, more than twelve million captives were shipped on slavers bound to the Americas between 1501 and 1875. Furthermore, an unknown number of enslaved people perished before embarking on slave ships bound for the Western Hemisphere.[47] Both the captives and crew of the vessels that made this journey had to be fed for as long as two months while at sea. As immense as the challenge was to feed millions on this stage of the journey, the problem of securing a sufficient food supply began long before these individual voyages. European slave traders managed their commercial interests from forts they established on the coast of the continent, and they set up large prisons where enslaved Africans would be housed before the Atlantic journey. European militias accompanied traders on missions into the interior and supervised the forced marches of African captives toward the coast. At each phase of the slave trade and at each location along the way, both the traders and the enslaved had to be fed.

Ultimately their captors ate and in turn fed enslaved people a creolized diet that combined European, American, and African ingredients. Most of the food that they fed enslaved people both on land and at sea was produced in Africa and consisted both of native African foods and of botanical transplants from elsewhere. The Portuguese who set up the first trading posts on the African coast tried, without success, to replicate their food culture on the continent. They failed in early attempts to grow favored foods like barley, wheat, rye, olives, and grapes, which were unsuited to the climate. The Portuguese were able to satisfy some of their food preferences by, for example, importing domestic animals like pigs and chickens, which quickly reproduced themselves, augmenting not only European larders but also African ones in the process.[48] They also successfully grew fruits such as pears and peaches and almonds.[49] Necessity meant that they had to embrace a degree of culinary flexibility and learn to adopt African foods well suited to the climate like sorghum, cowpeas, and yams.[50]

In some areas of the African coast, including the port city of Luanda, a transcontinental creole cuisine had been established by the seventeenth century.[51] Forced to adapt to local growing conditions unfavorable to producing European grains, the Portuguese learned to use flour made from African pearl millet, African grown rice, and transplanted American cassava to make bread, including symbolically significant Communion wafers.[52] Free people, both African and European, who could afford the luxury of culinary choice could enjoy foods like banana cakes that were the end result of the intermingling of a variety of ingredients and cooking customs.[53] On the Gold Coast, enslaved cooks charged with cooking for European personnel began making a hybrid European-style bread using either locally grown maize or millet instead of wheat flour and palm oil instead of butter, milk, or olive oil.[54]

Although captives, too, ate a fusion cuisine, their diets were often monotonous and reflected practical concerns rather than gastronomic ones. When deciding what to feed the enslaved, the first concern of slave traders was that of economy. Although the African captives came from cultural groups with rich cooking traditions and a varied food supply, they were cut off from these food practices as a result of their enslavement. As historian Stephanie Smallwood powerfully observes, "Commodification removed captives from that landscape of abundance and put them into a situation of unmitigated poverty."[55] Dependent upon a limited supply of food rations and the whims of their captors, enslaved people had to learn to live with hunger and uncertainty.

Even when captives were allowed to eat familiar African crops, the ingredients of their homeland were often prepared indifferently and without respect for local culinary traditions. Increasingly, maize and cassava, New World crops with high yields, were cultivated for the specific purpose of providing slave rations. Although these products ultimately revolutionized the way many West Africans ate and were eventually embraced by many local people as beloved, culturally significant foods, Judith Carney and Richard Nicholas Rosomoff emphatically argue that the introduction of these foods on the continent must be interpreted first and foremost within the brutal context of slavery. There was nothing benign or accidental about the introduction of these new foods. They were planted as fuel for the slave system.

When making the decision to plant maize to feed slaves, Europeans chose a grain that they generally did not believe was fit for human consumption and instead was better suited for livestock.[56] In 1597 herbalist John Gerard summarized contemporary English sentiments about the grain when he declared "that it nourisheth but little, and is of hard and evil digestion a more convenient foode for swine than for men."[57] Maize, the stigmatized "animal food" that Europeans fed to human cargo, should, according to Carney and Rosomoff, be interpreted as "a symbol of the dehumanizing condition of chattel slaves, who were no longer able to exercise dietary preferences or choose the type and amount of food they consumed."[58] The Royal African Company capitalized on the availability of the prolific grain by feeding the captives at Cape Coast Castle a meager diet consisting of ground maize that had been made into cakes, boiled, and dressed with melegueta pepper and palm oil.[59]

Although the broad parameters of the argument that maize and other New World crops fortified the institution of slavery is certainly true, it is also important, once again, to remember that individual enslaved people, depending upon when and where they originated, had different associations with the grain. For those who encountered the food for the first time after they were enslaved, the texture and taste of maize must have conjured up the negative associations of the violence and debasement of slavery. However, for those captives already familiar with the crop that the people living in the Kongo referred to as *masa ma Mputu* or "grain of Portutal," the meanings would have been far different.[60] Although Europeans may have used this purportedly inferior grain as a mechanism of dehumanization, West African farmers did not automatically share European prejudices against the grain as being only fit for animals or people of lower social status.[61] For the West Africans who adopted the grain thoughtfully and deliberately, modifying it for use in local recipes, the flavor of maize eventually became reminiscent of the sensations of being at home. Just as the ingredients in cooking pots changed in response to various historical circumstances, so did the connotations of different food items. Maize tasted of home, of slavery, or of both depending upon the experiences of those who consumed it.

Olaudah Equiano, who was enslaved in the mid-seventeenth century, recalled eating maize as a child. In all likelihood he encountered the food again at many different moments during his captivity. Before he was able to purchase his freedom in 1765, Equiano was enslaved in Africa, in the Americas, and as a crewmember aboard several seagoing vessels. He fondly recorded food memories of his native home in what is now the country of Nigeria in his 1789 autobiography, *The Interesting Narrative of the Life of Olaudah Equiano or Gustavus Vassa, the African*. He described his childhood cuisine as being wholesome, "plain," and "unacquainted with those refinements in cookery that debauch the taste." In addition to maize, he described eating an ample diet of beef, goat, poultry, plantains, yams, and beans, foods that were often

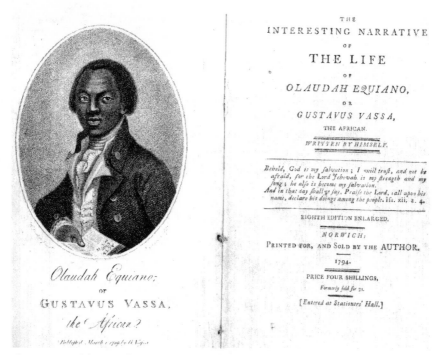

Figure 1.1. Title page from Olaudah Equiano's autobiography, 1794. Library of Congress, LC-USZ62-54026.

washed down with palm wine.[62] Although he does not reveal precisely which European cooking techniques he later learned to disdain, Equiano makes it clear that his captivity compromised his ability to enjoy eating a good meal.

Equiano was captured and enslaved when he was about eleven years old. One day he and his sister were at home in their family compound when a man and woman climbed over the walls surrounding their home, snatched the two children, gagged them, and then sold them into slavery. He recalled that the trauma of being stolen away from their family was so intense that the children were unable to eat in the aftermath. His grief was compounded even further a day or two later when he was separated from his sister. Once again overcome by anguish, his body rebelled against the idea of ingesting the food needed to sustain it. His captors were eager to preserve his life and health before selling him, so they force-fed him, a ritual that happened again after Equiano finally found himself on board a slave ship poised to sail across the Atlantic. After he was forced to go below deck, he was overwhelmed by the stench of the unwashed, chained bodies of the Africans who shared his fate. He again refused to eat, and a member of the crew flogged him mercilessly until he agreed to accept nourishment.[63] Later the young boy was mortified to discover that although his captors regarded eating as mandatory, enslaved people were expected to eat just enough to survive the voyage and not to show a desire for more food. He was horrified anew at the cruelty of his captors when one day they caught a number of fish, ate their fill, and threw the leftovers overboard rather than feeding them to the hungry slaves aboard the vessel. Those captives who tried to salvage scraps of the meal before it was heaved off the side of the ship were beaten for their audacity.[64] Equiano had discovered that food was one of the key tools that the Europeans used to assert their authority over the bodies of the Africans they enslaved as they claimed the right to decide what and when the captives ate.

Both the behavior and the appearance of his European captors were chilling to Equiano, who was initially afraid that the enslaved people would "be eaten by these white men with horrible looks, red faces, and loose hair."[65] He was hardly alone in his suspicions. The habits and the mannerisms of the men employed by the enormous slave-trading apparatus instilled so much fear into their victims that rumors about cannibalism were widespread. At least one eighteenth-century manual for slave traders suggested that they attempt to soothe these anxieties by directly informing their captives that Europeans did not practice cannibalism.[66] Following this general advice, English slave trader William Snelgrave claimed that he gently corrected this misapprehension. He publically, if somewhat unconvincingly, expressed pity for those among his human cargo who feared that they were destined for the dinner pot, noting, "These poor People are generally under terrible Apprehensions upon their being bought by white Men, many being afraid that we design to eat them; which, I have been told, is a story much credited by the inland *Negroes*."[67] Willem Bosman heard similar stories from slaves captured in "a far In-Land Country" who "very innocently persuaded one another, that we buy them only to fatten and afterwards eat them as a Delicacy."[68] The enslaved people soon learned that although their bodies were not to be literally ingested, they would be consumed in other ways by the relentless demands of New World slavery. Although their flesh was not destined to be eaten, their labor would provide the fiscal means for their masters to feed and enrich themselves. Metaphorically then, if not literally, slavery did eat black bodies.

As Equiano discovered through his own bitter experience, the slave traders who thought themselves virtuous for stealing labor instead of ingesting flesh fed their captives food that was both simple and minimal on their trip across the Atlantic. The task of supplying a ship carrying several hundred slaves with even the bare minimum of food needed for a transatlantic journey that generally took between three to six weeks to complete was so overwhelming that ships often had to stop at several port cities seeking supplies before leaving the continent. One seventeenth-century trader claimed that it took more than a hundred thousand yams to feed five hundred slaves throughout the voyage.[69] Another trader purchased eight tons of rice before embarking for Jamaica with 250 slaves in 1793, and a French trader estimated that one ton of food, of whatever variety, was required to sustain ten captives on the voyage.[70]

These supplies were not only difficult to procure in sufficient quantities, but they also took up a great deal of precious cargo space. Slave traders experimented with finding the most profitable ratio of food supplies to human bodies. In the sixteenth and seventeenth centuries, it was not uncommon for profit-obsessed captains to overcrowd their ships so much that they could not bring sufficient food supplies along. When this was the case, the enslaved ate only one daily meal, which might consist of no more than a bowl of maize or millet and a small jar of water.[71] Although food shortages certainly took a toll on the health of many onboard slave-trading vessels, the risk of dehydration on ships undersupplied with water was even more serious. Enslaved people spent much of their time in hot, poorly ventilated spaces below deck, and many suffered from nausea and diarrhea, conditions that intensified the already substantial danger of dehydration.[72]

In light of evidence that skimping on supplies was short-sighted even when the primary motive was profit and not humanitarian concerns, many captains began to embrace the idea that transporting fewer but better-fed enslaved people would actually result in higher profits. Increasingly, the enslaved received two daily meals. The first was generally offered at about ten in the morning followed by a final daily meal at about four in the afternoon.[73] Depending upon the vessel that carried them, enslaved people ate staple foods like yams, rice, legumes, cassava, and maize on their transatlantic voyage.[74] The captives generally received more carbohydrates than proteins, although beans and small portions of meat or fish were commonly served.[75] During the lengthy voyages, all of the food provisions were vulnerable to degeneration and to infestation with insects, and both captives and crew sometimes had to eat tainted food or go hungry.[76]

Male captives, whose labor was highly valued on American plantations, significantly outnumbered enslaved women. Female slaves were generally less tightly constrained on the transatlantic voyage and were often tasked with performing much of the labor of cooking on slave ships.[77] Although they had to work with the ingredients they were given and within the confines of orders they received from the crew, it seems possible that they found ways to infuse what was designed to be functional food with some of the character of their home cuisines.

A common dish served on board ship was called "dab-a-dab," which was a concoction of beans, rice, small scraps of salt meat, palm oil, and melegueta pepper.[78] The melegueta pepper, a familiar taste throughout much of West Africa, was often included in shipboard diets because it was thought to prevent stomach disorders.[79] The palm oil may have actually been something of a concession to the taste sensibilities of the captives. An eighteenth-century French manual designed to give advice to the captains of slave-trading vessels suggested using the familiar substance to liven up dull rations, claiming, "It is healthy and soothing; mix it into each mess tin. *Le nègre* is used to it, and its use is salutary."[80] Although slave traders did not serve traditional West African recipes on board ship and provided only monotonous and limited rations, evidence suggests that some traders made at least passing attempts to appeal to the palates of their captives.

Many of the early modern Europeans engaged in the transatlantic slave trade had a humoral understanding of how the body functioned. They believed that the body was composed of four core substances—black bile, yellow bile, phlegm, and blood—which could become unbalanced and cause illness. They theorized that food could become an important means of restoring bodily equilibrium and that carefully chosen meals could actually correct humoral deficiencies. As a corollary belief, many thought that different categories of bodies had different nutritional needs and that factors such as biological sex, social station, and place of geographical origin should be taken into account when constructing ideal diets.[81] This understanding of how the body functioned worked in combination with newly emerging ideas about innate racial differences to encourage some slave traders to be thoughtful about what they fed people who, increasingly, they began to conceive of as having fundamentally different corporealities.[82]

In keeping with the belief that bodies thrived on foods selected for their own peculiar needs, many slave traders chose the primary ingredient for the morning meal on board ship based upon the place of origin of the majority of the captives it was carrying. They fed rice to captives from Senegambia or the Windward Coast and yams to those from the Bight of Benin or the Bight of Biafra. Those from the Gold Coast could often expect to eat maize.[83] Seventeenth-century trader Jean Barbot explained that he only fed yams to his captives because he had discovered that "the slaves there being of such a constitution, that no other food will keep them; *Indian* corn, bean, and *Mandioca*, disagreeing to their stomach so that they sicken and die apace." Barbot was in fact so convinced that food choices could determine the outcome of a slave-trading mission that he attributed a 1698 mutiny aboard the *Albion* to the fact that the yam supply had run out.[84]

Although these early modern ideas about how food could function as a kind of medicine likely played a role in decisions about how to best provision slave ships, it also seems likely that enslaved people may have found ways to induce their captors to supply them with familiar food. Although slave traders strove to have complete control over what their captives ate, they were forced to contend with the fact that even after being robbed from their homelands, enslaved people still maintained a degree of rudimentary control over their own bodies. One slave trader complained, "We can scarcely make them eat European provisions, much less when they begin to complain & their appetite becomes weak."[85] Slave traders could issue commands and dole out punishments, but individual enslaved people made choices about the degree to which they obeyed them and with what affect. As Equiano discovered after he was taken into captivity as a small child, the arena of food consumption was one place where he could assert his individual will and try to thwart the desires of those who sought to own him completely. It seems plausible that the captains of slave ships knew that they were more likely to coerce their slaves into eating if they fed them familiar foods. Even if the gruel that was ubiquitous aboard slave ships was a far cry from beloved home recipes, the choice of familiar core ingredients such as yams and the use of West African flavoring components like melegueta pepper and palm oil might have been concessions, however small, to the desires of the enslaved.[86]

One of the most common techniques that enslaved people used to resist the will of their captors was by refusing to eat altogether. The practice of declining sustenance was so common that Marcus Rediker has claimed that the "Atlantic slave trade was, in many senses, a four-hundred-year hunger strike."[87] Culinary historian Michael Twitty has speculated that many captives rejected the "sloppily made slurry" served aboard slave ships simply because the indifferently prepared "mixture was so foul" that they could not bring themselves to consume it voluntarily.[88] The act of rejecting food could also be a manifestation of severe illness. Extreme dehydration, which was all too common in the crowded and poorly ventilated slave quarters below deck, lessened the appetite and even impacted the physical ability of those so afflicted to eat.[89] Sometimes the loss of appetite was an unconscious response to the profound trauma of being taken away from all that was familiar by force and by the fear of an uncertain future. In his reminiscences about the slave trade, Jean Barbot noted that it was a common occurrence for enslaved people to "fall into a deep melancholy and despair and refuse all sustenance."[90] The Dutch spoke of "banzo" and the English of "fixed melancholy" to describe despondent behavior among captives, many of whom refused to eat.[91]

The hunger strike could also be used as a conscious means of protesting the entire system of slavery and, for the most determined, as an attempt at exercising an ultimate final act of personal agency. Some slaves who refused food willfully chose death over slavery. In 1783 a Fante man who had been accused of witchcraft and enslaved alongside his entire family made such a decision. After being brought aboard the *Brooks*, he not only refused to eat, he also attempted to commit suicide by more immediate methods by ripping open his throat with his fingernails. An English speaker, he was able to communicate with the crew, and he proclaimed that he would "never go with white men." In the end, he succeeded in achieving his goal, and he died a slow, agonizing death from hunger and his self-inflicted wounds.[92]

The crews of slave-trading vessels became frantic in the face of attempts of their human property to starve themselves. Alexander Falconbridge, who worked as a surgeon on slave-trading vessels, reported on the extreme means that crew members would use to force the enslaved to eat. He recalled:

> Upon the Negroes refusing to take sustenance, I have seen coals of fire, glowing hot, put on a shovel and placed so near their lips as to scorch and burn them. And this has been accompanied with threats of forcing them to swallow the coals if they any longer persisted in refusing to eat. These means have generally had the desired effect. I have also been credibly informed that a certain captain in the slave-trade poured melted lead on such of his Negroes as obstinately refused their food.[93]

The crew also force-fed enslaved people using an instrument called the *speculum oris*, which was designed to pry open the mouth of those who refused to eat. In John Woodall's 1617 instructional manual for maritime medics, *The Surgions Mate*, he suggests using the "*speculum oris with a screw*" to cure "lythargy," a coded way of describing the behavior of enslaved people who refused to eat.[94] Thus, from the beginning of transatlantic African slavery, food became a battleground where captors tried to assert their ownership and their domination, and captives sought to assert their agency and maintain a sense of bodily integrity despite the degradations of chattel slavery.

Of the more than twelve million enslaved people who were forced to embark on transatlantic voyages, slightly more than ten million disembarked in the Americas. The rest succumbed to communicable diseases, dehydration and malnutrition, overt violence, or suicide. Of the number who lived to see the other side of the Atlantic, David Eltis estimates that less than four hundred thousand arrived in what is now the United States.[95] Immediately upon their arrival at slave-trading ports, the captains of the slavers procured fresh food and water. The crew fed the enslaved what was likely the most substantial meal many had had in weeks or months. The caloric infusion would, it was hoped, improve the immediate appearance, if not the overall health, of the enslaved who were headed to market.[96] At the point of sale, the enslaved traded in their maritime masters for new ones and one set of limitations on what and how much they ate for different circumstances.

The culinary encounters that began sometimes on voluntary terms on the coast of West Africa and became overtly coercive during the Middle Passage continued long after landfall. In America, as in Africa, the exchange of knowledge and ingredients took place on a number of different emotional and logistical registers. The next chapter demonstrates that food practices could be coercive and dehumanizing or culturally affirming, enabling the captives to hold onto memories and sometimes even the actual ingredients of home. The sharing of food traditions and new taste experiences also helped them construct new multicultural identities. Finally, the sphere of food practices allowed these forced migrants to have a lasting impact on the culture of the new societies being forged in the Americas.

· 2 ·

Africanisms and Adaptation
during the Era of Slavery

*H*enry C. Pettus was born into slavery in Georgia a decade or so before the end of the Civil War. One of his most vivid childhood memories was of his mother gardening by the light of the moon. After she spent the day working as an unpaid field hand planting and harvesting cotton to enrich her master, she would come home and tend to a small garden plot where she grew watermelons, potatoes, and peanuts to supplement her family's diet. Sometimes her owner bought some of her watermelons, and she would use the money to buy, among other things, a pig for her family to eat each year.[1]

The foods that this enslaved mother produced were emblematic of the creolized foodways of the Americas. The pig that would be consumed down to the smallest scrap was a descendent of the hogs first introduced to the Americas by the Spaniards in the sixteenth century.[2] The potatoes were a product of the New World. Her family's diet also demonstrated an ongoing culinary connection to what their African ancestors ate. The peanuts, which also originated in the Americas, had been a staple food in Africa for centuries by the time the Pettus family was finally freed from bondage.[3] Finally, the watermelons that were transformed into much needed cash had originated in Africa and constituted a material connection to the family's origins on a continent they had never seen.[4]

According to Judith Carney and Nicholas Rosomoff, the slave ships that carried millions of African people to the Americas also became "the unwitting vessels of African's botanical heritage." They carried seeds of African plants alongside human captives.[5] During the era of the slave trade, these tangible traces of Africa gave enslaved people the ability physically to hold onto aspects of their culinary heritage. In general, African crops were transplanted with the greatest success in climates the most similar to West Africa, and African foods were grown with the greatest frequency in the areas with the largest number of enslaved people. In colonial North America, culinary Africanisms became more identifiable in areas with the largest black populations, such as Carolina, than in regions like Massachusetts, which were less dependent upon slave labor. In the American South in particular, African Americans played a tremendous role in the creation of a new multicultural style of eating. Just as many West Africans chose to Americanize their diets after the introduction of crops like maize and cassava to their continent, colonial European Americans also modified their ideas about what constituted good food as they incorporated ingredients and tastes inspired by African food practices.

Enslaved people living in North America had to contend with the fact that some of the tropical plants they were accustomed to cooking with did not thrive in the cooler climate. These West Africans must have keenly felt the loss of key ingredients such as the plantain, a fruit native to Asia that had been widely incorporated into African diets before the Columbian era, and the yam, a tuber native to the continent. While African yams quickly became a Caribbean staple, Africans living in regions farther north tried, with little success, to cultivate the favored food there.[6] In these places the crop endured primarily in the form of memories. The word *yam*, a diminutive of the Wolof word *nyam*, "to eat," soon became used interchangeably to refer both to African yams and to sweet potatoes from the Americas.[7] Although sweet potatoes differ from yams in taste, texture, and color, they share a somewhat similar outward appearance, a fact that inspired some to use them as a substitute food out of a spirit of pragmatism and compromise. However, in other instances, transplanted Africans did not have to rely solely on their imaginations to recreate the foods of home. Other African crops including sesame, sorghum, okra, black-eyed peas, watermelon, and red rice flourished in the more northern climes.

It is important to note that the African ingredients that found their way into North American cooking pots were not necessarily the preferred or most cherished foods of the captives. They were the foods that slave traders chose to carry. They were also plants that were hardy enough to be able to survive a long, transatlantic voyage intact and to thrive in a different climate.[8] These ingredients, whose transplantation was often more serendipitous than deliberate, gave African slaves the means of enjoying some familiar tastes and some of the tools that they would use to help create a new American style of eating.[9]

For the enslaved people who found themselves working against their will in North America, their first concern was, of course, finding strategies to make sure that they had enough to eat. However, in the process of attempting to fill their own stomachs, they helped develop recipes that would also be used to fill other bellies and create a foundational foodways on the continent. While laboring involuntarily in North American fields and kitchens, enslaved Africans transferred agricultural, botanical, and culinary knowledge as they tweaked dishes to suit their own taste memories and preferences. However, at the same time that they tried to hold onto some of the tastes of home, transplanted African cooks and eaters also embraced new culinary ideas, incorporating them into preexisting concepts about what food should look and taste like. Ultimately, culinary change was dramatic in these New World contexts where neither Africans nor their European captors could recreate their former diets.[10]

Africans transformed their food habits because the ingredients they had to work with were different. It is clear that African captives endeavored to retain connections to familiar ways of doing things as a means of maintaining their sense of cultural identity after being involuntarily ripped from their homelands. However, those cultural ties did not stifle either the intercultural curiosity or the practical concerns that would have encouraged the captives to modify their ideas about what and how they would eat. David Eltis, Philip Morgan, and David Richardson advise against assuming that enslaved people were cultural conservatives who held tenaciously to "traditional ways" without realizing that they were also—by both choice and necessity—"experimenters and improvisers."[11]

Regardless of their preferences, these involuntary migrants had to contend with the fact that their captors now claimed ownership over their bodies and the right to influence how and what they ate. Archaeologist Theresa Singleton has made a useful distinction between what she calls "value culture" and the "reality culture" of enslaved people that provides a useful way for thinking about how these first generations of African migrants negotiated between their cultural preferences and the limits on their ability to indulge their predilections. The "value culture" of the enslaved people consisted of their "customs, beliefs, and values presumably influenced by African heritage," while their "reality culture" was the "aspects of slave life influenced by external forces, especially social controls within slave society."[12] An examination of African American food history reveals an ongoing conversation between culinary ideals and constraints. Africans could not eat precisely what and when they wanted, yet they were unwilling completely to give up their traditional practices. Sometimes the cultural compromises that were used to reconcile these tensions yielded surprising results.

The self-proclaimed white prerogative over black bodies sought to limit African choices in every realm, and white colonists hoped to enrich themselves by expropriating both labor and knowledge from their captives.

European Americans developed an ideology of racism that labeled people of African descent as separate and inferior. This belief system was used to justify black debasement and enslavement. However, paradoxically, at the same time that Europeans denigrated African intelligence, arguing that Africans thrived only under white supervision, they also demonstrated an ongoing reliance upon the agricultural and culinary knowledge of enslaved people. African traditions helped shape American foodways, and African agricultural knowledge aided European colonists in their quest to find ways to extract wealth from unfamiliar lands. A close study of the foundational foodways of the British colony of Carolina illustrates that far more than the brute strength of enslaved laborers was used to enrich white settlers.

European colonists relied on concrete skill sets derived from African agricultural traditions when establishing New World farms and plantations. The majority of the white founding population of Carolina was from Barbados, a slave society centered upon the sugar plantation system. When white migrants from the island decided to try their luck in North America in the mid-seventeenth century, they had no idea what resources they would extract from the colony or by what means they would enrich themselves. They did, however, know that slave labor would provide the basis for their new efforts, and they exploited the physical and intellectual assets of African people to reach their goals.

Initial attempts to cultivate almonds, olives, and dates and to produce silk were disappointing. However, in the latter part of the seventeenth century, colonial Carolinians began their most lucrative agricultural undertaking yet when they successfully experimented with raising cattle. Local planters who had been accustomed to growing sugar in Barbados knew little or nothing about caring for large numbers of livestock, so they compensated for this knowledge deficit by relying upon the skills of enslaved people from the Gambia River region who had experience raising cattle. The colonists allowed their cattle free range under the supervision of black herdsmen who had used similar techniques in West Africa. These African workers were considered to be so skilled that they often were entrusted with herds owned by absentee investors.[13] Due in large part to the fact that white colonists allowed their slaves to practice techniques of animal husbandry that were familiar to them, the nascent industry was soon flourishing. By 1750, there were more than one hundred thousand head of cattle in Carolina.[14] The colony's cattle industry was quickly supplying not only the local demand for beef, but it soon became the chief exporter of meat to the West Indies.[15] However, this initial success, as impressive as it was in comparison to earlier wealth-building schemes, did not satisfy the ambitions of local planters who aspired to even greater riches. In their quest for an even more lucrative agricultural undertaking, Carolina colonists once again turned to African agricultural know-how to develop a new get-rich scheme: growing rice.[16]

There is no documentary evidence indicating precisely when and where Carolinians started growing significant quantities of rice, but by 1695 rice cultivation was well established in the colony. It became Carolina's chief export by the middle of the eighteenth century. Intriguingly, though not coincidentally, the black population expanded alongside the rice fields. Slave labor was vital to the expansion of this agricultural undertaking, and Carolina had a black majority by 1708.[17]

There is a long history of rice cultivation in West Africa. *Oryza glaberrima*, African red rice, had been cultivated in the Niger Delta and in Senegambia since at least 1500 BCE.[18] *Oryza sativa*, an Asian variety of rice, had reached the continent via extensive trade networks by the ninth century. Enslaved Africans from rice-growing regions brought knowledge about how to cultivate the grain along with a culinary preference for rice as a dietary staple to the western hemisphere with them. In fact, the first rice grown in Carolina was likely African red rice that was brought to the colony aboard slave ships and then widely cultivated in small subsistence gardens planted by African slaves for their own use.[19] These garden patches may very well have served as sources of inspiration to white Carolinians seeking agricultural products that would thrive in the local environment. Initial experiments soon demonstrated that *sativa* had higher yields than the African variety, and colonists quickly started importing Asian rice and planting it in preference of the African grains that had originally sparked their interest in the plant.[20] Even though the African crop was displaced in favor of a more productive varietal, African knowledge and labor remained essential to the enterprise of rice cultivation.

Many scholars have suggested that local planters sought to purchase slaves who were familiar with how to best nurture the grain, and advertisements announcing slaves for sale sometimes boasted that their human cargo possessed specific sets of agricultural skills. A 1785 advertisement tried to attract buyers with their description of "a choice cargo of windward and gold coast negroes, who have been accustomed to the planting of rice."[21] Scholars have debated without consensus about how many of the slaves imported to Carolina's slave markets may have had direct familiarity with growing rice.[22] Peter Wood argues that at the very least "literally hundreds of black migrants were more familiar with the planting, harvesting, and cooking of rice than were the European settlers who purchased them."[23] Whether or not the majority of the slaves laboring in Carolina rice fields learned how to cultivate the grain in their African homeland or from other enslaved people who trained them, the initial techniques used to process the grain were of distinctly African origin. Enslaved people used African-style mortars and pestles to remove

Figure 2.1.   Engraving of African American workers on a North Carolina rice plantation, 1866. *Frank Leslie's Illustrated Newspaper,* October 20, 1866; Library of Congress,
LC-USZ62-61966.

the hull from the grain. They made large, flat winnowing baskets, which were
inspired by African designs. The planting technique where workers made a
hole in the ground with their heel, dropped a seed into the impression, and
used their foot to cover the seed with dirt also had African antecedents.[24]

Geographer Judith Carney has argued that not only did enslaved Africans introduce the initial techniques that enabled Carolinians to grow this
lucrative staple crop, but African ideas also influenced regional preparations
of rice dishes. In contrast to many Asian cuisines where an ideal pot of cooked
rice is supposed to be sticky to make eating with chopsticks easier, traditional
methods of cooking *glaberrima* favored a method that produced distinctive
and separate grains of rice. This result was achieved by boiling and then
steaming the grain until all the moisture was absorbed. Because Africans
were much more familiar with eating rice than Europeans, they likely trained
their masters about how best to prepare the grain. After all, enslaved people
not only cooked for themselves, they also labored in the kitchens of white
colonists. Eugene Genovese has described African American influences on
the style of eating of their masters as a quietly subversive "culinary despotism"
from below.[25] Despite the restrictions inherent in the system of slavery, these
cooks still found ample opportunities to influence how and what those they
cooked for ate. This African cooking method for rice set the standard for
Carolina rice cookery that is still employed today.[26]

Judith Carney and Nicholas Rosomoff have made a case for African culinary persistence by examining what they have labeled the "memory dishes" of
the African diaspora.[27] One dish that was likely eaten beginning in the earliest

days of rice cultivation in Carolina is "Hoppin' John." In its most basic renditions, the dish is a one-pot meal consisting of combination of rice, black-eyed peas, and small pieces of bacon or another cured pork product. Jessica Harris has argued that this recipe has distinctive African roots as evidenced by strong similarities between it and the contemporary Senegalese recipes for *chiebou niebe*, a dish that utilizes beef instead of pork.[28] Culinary historian Karen Hess agrees that Hoppin' John likely references African food traditions due to the fact that variations of this beans-and-rice dish appear throughout the Caribbean and South America. She speculates that transplanted Africans in each of those regions made efforts to replicate core tastes and techniques of their homeland. Their various efforts resulted in somewhat similar dishes that also display distinctive regional variations.[29]

Recipes for Hoppin' John make direct allusions to Africa through the usage of black-eyed peas, a legume of African origins, alongside more subtle references in the form of the rice cooking technique. However, the inclusion of a cured pork product in the dish is a result of European influence. Europeans had been dining on cured pork since the time of the Romans. The Spanish explorer Hernando de Soto first introduced pigs into North America in 1539, and new European arrivals began following the familiar custom of preserving ham and other cuts of pork by salting, drying, and smoking them.[30] Dishes like this one capture the creative possibilities that emerged when ingredients from various cooking traditions were combined into a single meal.

An example of another southern "memory dish" is gumbo, a strongly seasoned stew containing meat or seafood that is served over rice.[31] Gumbos are most closely associated with Louisiana cuisine, but early versions of the dish can be traced to the southeastern United States as well. The elastic dish, which can contain a variety of proteins, vegetables, and seasonings, likely emerged as a way to use up small portions of leftovers. Gumbo, perhaps more clearly than any other single American dish, represents the multicultural nature of southern, American foodways. The stew is generally thickened with a roux, a combination of butter and flour, which were favored ingredients of European cooks. Gumbo filé includes ground sassafras leaves, an ingredient commonly used by Choctaw living in southern Louisiana. Many gumbos also contain okra, an African ingredient that thickens the stew.[32]

The word *gumbo* reinforces African culinary connections as well. The name of the dish is derived from Bantu words for okra, *ochingombo* or *guingombo*.[33] Africans who grew okra in garden plots inspired Europeans to adopt the vegetable, which thrived in southern summer gardens, into their diets as well. In 1824, white Virginian Mary Randolph published what is likely the first American regional cookbook, *The Virginia Housewife*. Randolph's collection contains two recipes for how to prepare the ingredient, which she describes as "nutritious, and easy of digestion."[34] Her recipe for "Gumbo" calls for okra seasoned with only butter and salt and pepper, but her recipe for "Ochra Soup" bears a stronger resemblance to its Louisiana cousins and clearly reflects African, European, and Native American ingredients and influences. In addition to okra, her soup recipe contains onion, lima beans, squash, tomatoes, veal or chicken, a cured pork product, butter, flour, and is served over rice.[35]

Although the process of deconstructing well-known dishes like Hoppin' John and gumbo might reveal some valuable secrets about their origins, the task of tracing culinary influences is never straightforward. The process sometimes requires making some interpretive leaps. For example, as Karen Hess notes, beans and rice dishes somewhat like Hoppin' John "exist in all rice lands," not just in the African diasporic world.[36] This fact raises possibilities and questions about the precise genesis of this and, by extension, other dishes. Deciphering past culinary conversations between continents and among various groups of people is difficult in part because what might look like culinary transference could be a culinary coincidence instead. Inspiration may have come from multiple sources or from unexpected ones. Sometimes people in different parts of the world simultaneously create similar foods and arrive independently at recipes that have a great deal in common. When faced with the same set of ingredients, it is entirely plausible that cooks living in different locations around the globe may devise similar ways to prepare and eat them.

One common dish that seems to have appeared independently in different geographies and at different moments around the globe is dough made from maize that has been steamed or boiled inside cornhusks or other leaves. Pre-Columbian Aztecs made variations of a dish that has become an iconic regional dish in many locations in Central and South America and that is now known by the Spanish name of *tamales*. The Aztec version utilized ground corn processed with lime that was made into dough and steamed inside cornhusks. Sometimes the resulting breadlike substance was served plain, or it could be stuffed with ingredients such as beans, fish, squash, meat, and chile peppers.[37] Before European contact, Cherokees living in the southeastern regions of what became the United States were making a similar dish that consisted of maize dough infused with ingredients like beans or pumpkins and boiled in cornhusks.[38] On the other side of the Atlantic, an eighteenth-century European traveler to the Gold Coast observed women making something quite similar to the plain Aztec tamal and to the Cherokee dish. The European observer explained that what he regarded as a "tolerable" bread that was "heavy on the Stomach" was made by grinding cornmeal, mixing it into dough, and boiling it "in a large Earthen Pan full of Water, like Dumplins."[39] Culinary historians have demonstrated that contemporaries of these West African women also cooked cornmeal wrapped inside of leaves.[40] The boiled dish was likely a version of the contemporary Ghanaian dish of kenkey, which historian James McCann describes as a "tamale-like lump made from fermented maize paste boiled in husks."[41] Although the maize they used to make their meal originated in what is now Mexico, these African women first received the grain from Portuguese traders and not from the Central Americans who made tamales.

Even though these dishes are hardly identical, they bear a certain amount of resemblance to one another, yet they were created independently. Different groups of people who did not directly interact with each other still came to similar conclusions about how best to transform maize into a portable meal. Although there is no doubt that successive generations of eaters have been influenced by these tamale-like dishes in Africa, the Americas, and beyond, it is sometimes impossible to trace accurately the culinary lineage of even relatively recent incarnations of this meal. For example, in the early twentieth century, African American vendors living in the Mississippi Delta region began to sell yet another variation on this treat, which they began calling "hot tamales." These small, simmered, stuffed treats are made from coarse cornmeal filled with meat and seasoned frequently with chili powder. Did these vendors derive inspiration for this core recipe from Mexican migrant workers they encountered in Mississippi who introduced them to variations upon the original Aztec dish? Are Delta tamales the outgrowth of centuries-old Native American techniques for making steamed or boiled cornbread? Are they the culinary descendants of seventeenth- or eighteenth-century African recipes? Were they influenced by all three traditions? Theories abound, but a definitive answer has continued to elude students of the food culture of the region.[42] The case of these somewhat similar maize preparation techniques serves as a useful illustration for how difficult it can be to trace culinary antecedents and connections. Thus, food historians must proceed with circumspection, realizing that when documentary evidence is scarce, there are often multiple plausible theories for how certain recipes and techniques were created, and a definitive answer may prove to be elusive.

Although the details surrounding culinary creation in the Americas are sometimes murky, when examining foundational foodways in the United States it is still possible to make some useful generalizations. Culinary historian Jessica Harris has observed that when looking for the birth of a distinctive style of eating in the American South, the region where African slavery became the most entrenched and held the longest sway, "three is the magic number." She argues: "The intricate braiding, over/under/over/under mingling and remingling of the three disparate culinary traditions, Native American and European and African, have given us the origins of the food of the American South."[43] Although, as Harris acknowledges, the categories of "Native American," "European," and "African" are convenient but sloppy placeholders that enable us to describe quickly large groups of people who actually represent a variety of distinctive subgroups, it is still possible to extract some valuable insights into the kinds of culinary contributions made by the various peoples who jointly created these foundational foods. Michael W. Twitty points out that the blending of European, African, and Native American styles of cooking was the result of numerous small events and culinary negotiations that took place "across the generations and was never really a singular cultural event."[44]

Native Americans taught Europeans and Africans about edible local plants, giving crash courses about how to cultivate and cook star American agricultural products including numerous varieties of maize, squash, and beans. Native Americans also transferred important knowledge about how to hunt, fish, and forage for local edibles. Without the ability to assemble Indigenous knowledge, Europeans and Africans may not have been able to recognize unfamiliar plants or animals as potential sources of food. For example, Native people taught the new arrivals about how to use uniquely American foods like American chestnuts, the tuber tuckahoe, and persimmons.[45] In addition to transferring information, Native Americans directly fed some of the earliest colonists from stores of food that they donated, traded, or had stolen from them.[46]

Europeans helped usher in a much more carnivorous way of eating to the Americas, sating their appetite for animal flesh by introducing domesticated animals, including pigs and cattle, to their colonial homes.[47] Their taste for meat stood in contrast to the habits of members of many African ethnic groups who traditionally used meat in small portions as a flavoring rather than as a central meal component.[48] These sensibilities, and the increasing availability of livestock, particularly pork, also encouraged some Native people, including the Cherokee, to grant meat from domesticated animals a more central role in their diet.[49] Europeans also introduced a preference for bread and pastries made from wheat flour.[50] Although attaining a sufficient supply of this coveted grain was often an elusive goal for the first European colonists, this preference made a lasting imprint on southern cuisine in the form of baked items like pies and biscuits.[51]

African contributions to a new American style of eating consisted not only of the introduction of a number of African ingredients, but the first generation of African cooks is also credited with a number of other innovations. For example, they spiced up European tastes with their preference for a hotter flavor profile, which had been honed on the home continent through the consumption of melegueta pepper. They also drew upon West African traditions of frying food in palm oil to inspire an ongoing southern preference for fried foods.[52] The southern American taste for bitter leafy greens such as collard, turnip, or mustard greens is likely in part the outgrowth of West African traditions of including similar leafy vegetables in soups and stews.[53]

Although there can be no doubt as to the fundamental truth of this claim that Africans, Europeans, and Natives each played a significant role in creating southern American culinary influences, the cautionary tale of the tamale reminds us that sorting out who learned what from whom and when can be complicated if not impossible to discern at times. What is unambiguously clear, however, is that the historical context of these initial culinary exchanges was one of intense human pain, both physical and psychic. As historian Robert A. Gilmer is careful to point out, sometimes recipes and ingredients were shared willingly as a means of forging intercultural connections, but the opposite was true far more frequently. More often knowledge was exchanged within the contexts of brutality and exploitation. Europeans acquired Native American and African food knowledge as by-products of the processes of colonization and enslavement, and Africans and Natives gained information about each other and about European food preferences while being victimized by these systems. Sometimes African people and Native people formed culinary connections while being enslaved alongside each other and working to enrich the Europeans. At other times the lines between victim and oppressor were less clear. Drawing upon the techniques of chattel slavery utilized by their white colonizers, Native people sometimes enslaved Africans.[54] Regardless of the particular dynamics of intercultural interaction that resulted in food exchanges, as James McWilliams reminds us, "America's culinary history is inextricably linked with suffering."[55]

Food, which was a symbol of suffering, on the one hand, could also function as a useful coping mechanism and as an equally potent symbol of resilience. Beginning in the 1970s, historians from the "slave community school," which sought to describe the institution of slavery from the perspective of its victims rather than its perpetrators, emphasized the significance of food practices in the daily life of enslaved people. In his influential study, *Roll, Jordan, Roll: The World the Slaves Made*, Eugene Genovese argues that by studying food customs we can better understand the slaves' "spiritual power and ability to make a harsh world as pleasurable as possible."[56] Historian Charles Joyner agrees, noting that it is important to understand the food practices of enslaved people simply because eating was "one of the few sources of pleasure they enjoyed."[57]

Realizing that food could serve as a source of solace, North American slaves exerted as much control as they could over the terms under which they cooked and ate. Sometimes enslaved people ate meals prepared in communal kitchens; however, on larger plantations most successfully bargained for the right to cook food in their own homes, a practice frequently employed for at least morning and evening meals.[58] The ability to prepare and to eat foods on a small scale in family units gave individuals a greater degree of control over when they ate and how their food was prepared. In many places, enslaved people also organized to ensure that slaveholders distributed rations on the weekend, a practice that meant they had fresh supplies before Sunday, which was often a day of relative leisure when food might be savored and shared, sometimes in the context of picnics or revival meetings.[59] Food was at the center of celebrations for enslaved people, and masters sometimes doled out items like beef, molasses, sugar, coffee, and liquor as much coveted rewards.[60]

During the antebellum era, food played a central role in what for many enslaved people was the best time of the year—the Christmas season. Not only did custom dictate that they should have as much as a week free from work, but it was often the time of year when they ate the best. Solomon Northrup, who spent twelve years in slavery, recalled the dynamics of the Christmas feasting tradition in antebellum Louisiana:

> The table is spread in the open air, and loaded with varieties of meat and piles of vegetables. Bacon and corn meal at such times are dispensed with. Sometimes the cooking is performed in the kitchen on the plantation, at others in the shade of wide branching trees. In the latter case, a ditch is dug in the ground, and wood laid in and burned until it is filled with glowing coals, over which chickens, ducks, turkeys, pigs, and not unfrequently the entire body of a wild ox, are roasted. They are furnished also with flour, of which biscuits are made, and often with peach and other preserves, with tarts, and every manner and description of pies, except the mince, that being an article of pastry as yet unknown among them. Only the slave who has lived all the years on his scanty allowance of meal and bacon, can appreciate such suppers.[61]

Frederick Douglass, who participated in similar Christmas celebrations while enslaved, argued that there were actually negative implications associated with this ritual of overindulgence. He was particularly concerned about what he regarded as the excessive drinking of alcohol that often accompanied the feast. Douglass argued that this celebration served the interests of the slave masters more so than those of the enslaved, claiming that the "holidays serve as conductors, or safety-valves, to carry off the rebellious spirit of enslaved humanity." Douglass theorized that the sanctioned opportunity to indulge freely the desire for food, drink, and leisure enabled enslaved people to release tensions and resentments that had been building throughout the year. He believed that this annual ritual was such a vital part of the slave regime that enslaved people would allow their anger and frustration to erupt into full-blow rebellions if this privilege was taken away from them.[62]

If Douglass was right that Christmas feasting and revelry ultimately shored up the stability of the institution of slavery, that fact does not diminish the immediate joy felt by those who participated in these annual repasts.

Figure 2.2. Drawing of enslaved people celebrating Christmas, 1863. Drawing by H. L. Stephens, Library of Congress, LC-USZC4-2527.

When trying to capture what these feasts meant to the people who took part in them, Northup describes "eyes roll[ing] in ecstasy" and bodies shaking with laughter.[63] The opportunity to eat for pure gastronomic pleasure and not to fuel their bodies for immediate labor in the fields, kitchens, nurseries, and workshops of North American slavery was personally and communally meaningful and far too rare. The enslaved used the rituals of mealtime to develop and cement patterns of expressive culture that would help psychologically sustain them while also creating a sense of community.

Not only did the Christmas holidays offer a chance to feast at the master's expense, during the holidays enslaved people often had the chance to socialize with family and friends living elsewhere, a custom that helped facilitate the widespread exchange of ideas. They could alternatively choose to trade in the chance to enjoy several days of leisure and could instead spend their time, as Frederick Douglass advised, "hunting opossums, hares, and coons." They could also choose to spend the holiday week augmenting their personal and familial food supplies by foraging or tending gardens.[64] As they traded information, observed other ways of cooking and eating, and found creative ways to add to their own personal larders, enslaved people were developing a food culture that paid homage to shared cultural roots while also solidifying newly emerging customs.

In an often-cited turn of phrase, Charles Joyner suggests that black cooks inevitably utilized an "African culinary grammar" when cooking New World ingredients in these settings. He defines "African" cooking techniques somewhat vaguely as "methods of cooking and spicing, remembered recipes, ancestral tastes."[65] Eugene Genovese more or less agrees with the spirit of Joyner's assessment, making a similar case for culinary distinctiveness. He claims that African Americans were known for "imaginative spicing," which included the use of sesame oil and red pepper, tastes that referenced African food habits. However, unlike Joyner, Genovese is less certain about the source of these cooking techniques. He speculates that they may indeed have been derived from "African conditioning." However, he also offers the alternative possibilities that these ideas emerged from the "need to enliven their plain fare or both."[66] Genovese's acknowledgment that there are multiple possible explanations for these food choices serves as yet another helpful reminder that threads of African culinary continuity have to be interpreted within the broader context of ongoing change and adaptation. While sesame oil eaten in Carolina likely tasted much like sesame oil eaten in West Africa, and red pepper from the Americas likely trigged associations with Africa melegeuta pepper, enslaved Africans also ate things that tasted nothing like the foods they or, in the case of those born into slavery, their ancestors had eaten in West Africa. No mystical and unnamed cooking technique could have made foods that African Americans quickly became familiar with and consumed to greater or lesser degrees such as indigenous American nuts or fruit and cakes and pies made out of wheat flour taste like African foods. However, despite these qualifications, Joyner's speculation that "ancestral taste" may have influenced the way that enslaved African Americans experienced their food is also revelatory.

Eating is an intellectual as well as a physical undertaking. Taste is both a product of biology and of culture. Thus, we can speculate that enslaved people imbued the foods they consumed with specific meanings that influenced the experience of eating them. Some enslaved people likely did taste "Africa" in every bite, interpreting even newly discovered foods within old and familiar paradigms. This approach is certainly evidenced in, for example, the conflation of African yams with American sweet potatoes. However, for others the taste sensations of mealtime would have evoked associations of places, people, and experiences that were much closer to their new homes. Particularly for the generations of enslaved people who had not been born in Africa, the foods of the slave quarters conjured up direct memories of American meals alongside inherited tales about Africa. Before the transatlantic slave trade was banned (and to a lesser extent afterward too), new African arrivals could revitalize these food stories with fresh information about life on the ancestral continent.[67] The slaves' creolized cooking style reflected threads of culinary continuity with an ancestral homeland as well as adaptability, imagination, and change.

Slaveholders noticed and appreciated these black culinary skills. Kelley Fanto Deetz argues that the white, southern elite soon came to regard "the labor and expertise of plantation cooks [as] essential commodities."[68] However, the ideology of racism led them to interpret what Joyner would call "African culinary grammar" as an innate racial trait rather than as the manifestation of the processes of cultural creation and transmission. The talented enslaved people who cooked creolized "memory dishes" like fried chicken in the Chesapeake or jambalaya in Louisiana had learned their cooking skills by direct instruction, observation, and practice. However, European Americans often assumed that people of African descent were born knowing how to cook. A Georgia slaveholder proclaimed, "If there is any one thing for which the African female intellect has natural genius it is cooking." One of his contemporaries agreed, noting simply that "the Negroes are born cooks."[69] At best, these white assessments of black culinary contributions took the form of back-handed compliments. Even if they appreciated the food knowledge and cooking skills of African Americans, they failed to understand that southern recipes were the manifestation of intellect, ingenuity, and extensive trial and error rather than the outgrowth of essential racial traits.

Like all people, the enslaved people who sought the means to please their own palates while also tickling those of the ruling classes had decided preferences about what they ate. However, the nature of the institution of slavery meant than none of its victims could be free from the burden of worrying about the problem of simply having adequate food. In general terms, the diet and living conditions of enslaved people in North America improved across the centuries. For example, historian Ira Berlin paints a bleak picture of the lives of enslaved people living in the Chesapeake in the early eighteenth century. First-generation African transplants in that area lived in barracks segregated by sex and thus generally did not have the opportunity to form families. They performed the backbreaking labor of carving tobacco plantations out of the wilderness and suffered disproportionately from diseases due to lack of immunity and poor living conditions. As dismal as the circumstances were for enslaved people in the Chesapeake, they may have been even worse in Carolina. According to Philip Morgan, enslaved people in that region were actually "more overworked and less healthy than Chesapeake slaves."[70] At this point slaves were relatively inexpensive to purchase and thus, in the cruel financial terms of chattel slavery, were easy enough to replace. Because colonial slaves were considered to be a somewhat expendable commodity, slaveholders took few pains to make sure that those they held captive were adequately clothed, housed, or fed. For example, enslaved people in the Chesapeake regularly received rations of corn but only erratic meat rations, which when issued seldom exceeded half a pound of meat or fish each week. Carolina slaves received even less corn, and their masters rarely or never gave them meat.[71] Conditions improved as the monetary value of enslaved people increased.

Various factors, including the growing profitability of slave-grown cotton and the fact that the transatlantic trade was banned in 1807, led to an increase in the price of slaves throughout the nineteenth century. By the antebellum era, slave capital represented a staggering amount of wealth. In 1850, the market price of a slave averaged about $400, which was the equivalent of about $12,000 in 2016 dollars. In an attempt to establish a measure to help people in the twenty-first century appreciate the level of financial investment slaveholders had made in each enslaved person they claimed to own, Samuel H. Williamson and Louis P. Gain explain that the $400 average price in 1850 was about the same amount that it cost to purchase a home during that era.[72] The prices of slaves had doubled by 1860, when four million enslaved people were collectively valued at $3.5 billion.[73] Not coincidentally, concern for the physical welfare of enslaved people increased alongside their market value. Slaves had become too valuable for their owners carelessly to work them to death, and masters started taking greater pains to make sure their slaves were relatively well fed.[74]

The great African American abolitionist Frederick Douglass speculated that peer pressure sometimes encouraged slaveholders to feed their slaves adequately. In his experience, urban slaves were sometimes better cared for than their rural counterpoints because city-dwelling masters lived under closer scrutiny from nearby neighbors. He observed, "Few are willing to incur the odium attaching to the reputation of being a cruel master; and above all things, they would not be known as not giving a slave enough to eat. Every city slaveholder is anxious to have it known of him, that he feeds his slaves well."[75] Former slave Harriet Jacobs reported that one North Carolina planter was so eager to prove his claim that his slaves had all of their needs met that "if a neighbor brought a charge of theft against any of his slaves, he was browbeaten by the master, who assured him that his slaves had enough of every thing at home, and had no inducement to steal." Later, after this public performance where he proclaimed that he treated his slaves well, "the accused was sought out and whipped."[76] This episode makes clear that slaveholders' public proclamations did not necessarily align with their private behavior.

Negative public opinions about the ethics of slaveholding also encouraged many to improve the material conditions of their slaves or at least to make emphatic public claims about how well enslaved people lived. At the same time that the value of slave bodies was increasing, the abolitionist movement was becoming steadily more vocal in its critique of slavery. To counter this growing challenge and to protect their financial investment, slaveholders went to great lengths to frame the enterprise of slavery as beneficial to the enslaved people themselves, claiming that caring for the needs of their slaves was a sacred, Christian duty.[77] Due to this combination of factors, many began taking greater pains to make sure that enslaved people had enough to eat.

Although slave rations varied throughout time and across the geography of the slaveholding regions of the United States, in the antebellum era pork and cornmeal were the cornerstones of the slave rationing system. The precise amount of each core item allotted differed slightly according the preferences of the slaveholder and depending upon how lean or fatty the pork distribution.[78] Writing in the *De Bow's Review*, a proslavery agricultural journal that gave its readers advice about how to care for slaves while extracting maximum profits from their labor, one slave owner claimed that he allowed each laboring hand (including older children) "three and a half pounds bacon, if middling, or four pounds if shoulder" each week. In addition to this, each allegedly received either a peck of meal a week and some vegetables or a peck and a half if "confined [just] to meat and bread."[79] Historians of slavery have gone to great lengths to discern whether or not a typical slave ration, such as the one this unnamed planter described, was enough to support bodies engaged in relentless, grueling physical labor.[80] The consensus is that most actually received enough calories, though evidence suggests that certain segments of the slave community may not have eaten as well as others. John Blassingame points out that the idea that masters could allot an "'average' amount of food for *all* slaves" was problematic from the outset because different people have different nutritional and caloric needs.[81] Furthermore, even when diets were ample enough, they were not always nutritionally complete.[82]

Because the system of slave rationing was designed to maximize labor output and profits, the amount that enslaved people were allotted was often tied to their productivity.[83] This meant that workers in the prime of their lives were generally issued more food than children. Richard H. Steckel argues that while adult laborers were "remarkably well fed," "nourishment was exceedingly poor for children."[84] Young children generally ate a diet that was higher in carbohydrates and lower in protein than that of their parents, and many likely suffered from vitamin deficiencies.[85] Booker T. Washington's personal experiences reinforce the idea that children on plantations often did not get enough to eat. He recalled competing with farm animals for breakfast as a child. With his characteristic resilience he remembered, "I used to go to the places where the cows and pigs were fed and make my breakfast off the boiled corn, or else go to the place where it was the custom to boil the corn and get my share there before it was taken to the animals. . . . If I was not there at the exact moment of feeding, I could still find enough corn scattered around the fence or the trough to satisfy me."[86] Samuel S. Taylor, who was fifteen at the end of the Civil War, also recalled subsisting mostly on corn. He told an interviewer that enslaved children on his plantation ate milk and mush for breakfast and milk and cornbread for dinner. Sometimes, for a special treat, they were allowed to dip their bread in the juices left over from boiling cabbage, a substance that became known as "pot liquor" or "potlikker."[87]

Frederick Douglass's recollections about the diet of enslaved children are even grimmer. When he was a child living on a Maryland plantation, he was often hungry. Not only was his diet inadequate, no efforts were taken to make sure that all of the children on the plantation received a proportionate share of food. The young people were, he remembers, fed communally like farm animals and had to learn to be assertive in order to get their share:

> We were not regularly allowanced. Our food was coarse corn meal boiled. This was called *mush*. It was put into a large wooden tray or trough, and set down upon the ground. The children were then called, like so many pigs, and like so many pigs they would come and devour the mush; some with oyster-shells, others with pieces of shingle, some with naked hands, and none with spoons. He that ate fastest got most; he that was strongest secured the best place; and few left the trough satisfied.[88]

Although the system of feeding enslaved children as described by Douglass and others was inhumane and shocking, the indifference Douglass's owners showed toward his childhood hunger was actually less cruel and deliberate than their lack of concern for his aging grandmother's well-being. After she was no longer able to bear children or put in rigorous days of physical labor, she was given a small, crude house in the woods and "welcome[d] to the privilege of supporting herself there in perfect loneliness; thus virtually turning her out to die!"[89] In the ledger book of chattel slavery, the nutritional needs of children were deemed worthy of some consideration because their labor could eventually become a source of wealth. However, workers like Douglass's grandmother who had already devoted their lives and their bodies to the institution of slavery could become particularly vulnerable to a system that tied food rations to labor productivity.

Children and the elderly were certainly not the only slaves to go hungry. Some enslaved people subsisted on little more than minimal, allotted rations. Mary Jane Mooreman remembered eating only cornbread, buttermilk, and fat meat when she was enslaved.[90] Especially cruel masters expected slaves to labor incessantly despite being poorly fed. Harriet Jacob recalled the behavior of her mistress Mrs. Flint who "could sit in her easy chair and see a woman whipped, till the blood trickled from every stroke of the lash." Mrs. Flint used food as well as overt violence as a means of dominating and abusing her servants. If her cook displeased her, she would theatrically spit into the pots that had been used for cooking in order to contaminate the leftovers that had been designated to feed the cook and her children. She also measured food provisions so carefully that the hungry people working in her household had no opportunities to extract an extra morsel without her knowledge.[91] Charles Ball, who was born into slavery in Maryland in 1781, believed that he could identify, just by looking at an enslaved person, whether or not she or he had a sufficient amount to eat. He claimed:

> A half-starved negro is a miserable looking creature. His skin becomes dry, and appears to be sprinkled over with whitish husks, or scales; the glossiness of his face vanishes, his hair loses its colour, becomes dry, and when stricken with a rod, the dust flies from it. These signs of bad treatment I perceived to be very common in Virginia; many young girls who would have been beautiful, if they had been allowed enough to eat, had lost all their prettiness through mere starvation; their fine glossy hair had become of a reddish colour, and stood out round their heads like long brown wool.[92]

Researchers differ in their assessments of how widespread this kind of hunger was among the enslaved population. In their widely read and often disputed cliometric study of the living conditions of American slaves, *Time on the Cross: The Economics of American Negro Slavery*, Robert William Fogel and Stanley Engerman conclude that the diet of enslaved people "exceeded recommended daily levels of chief nutrients."[93] In a detailed study of the diet, nutritional needs, and energy expenditures of enslaved people living in Georgia, South Carolina, and Florida in the nineteenth century, medical anthropologists Tyson Gibbs, Kathleen Cargill, Leslie Sue Lieberman, and Elizabeth Reitz reach a similar conclusion. They found that the subjects whose lives they researched ate a well-rounded diet of pork, corn, a variety of garden vegetables, and other sources of meat from both wild and domesticated animals. They reached the overwhelming conclusion that this diet "met the nutrient needs of the population in a manner that permitted continued high work outputs as well as substantial population growth."[94]

Richard Sutch, however, argues that although the slave diet may have been adequate, it was generally not generous. Furthermore, he notes that even a calorically sufficient but monotonous diet should still be interpreted as a diet of deprivation due to the fact that food, for most people, is a source of pleasure as well as nutrients.[95] Sutch also argues that many enslaved people who ate a sufficient number of calories likely suffered from malnutrition.[96] Kenneth F. Kiple and Virgina Himmelsteib King concur, claiming that those who ate the most basic slave diet of pork and cornmeal likely suffered from a number of nutritional deficiencies, including a lack of vitamin C, niacin, and calcium.[97]

These differing historical guesses about the general state of the nutritional well-being of enslaved people may be explained in part by the diversity of the slave experience. Although it is possible to make the case that in general enslaved people ate more adequate diets in the nineteenth century than they had in the sixteenth and seventeenth, it is also possible to find numerous exceptions to this blanket statement. Even if we narrow our focus and analyze only the diets of enslaved people living in the antebellum period, the historical moment that is the most thoroughly documented by the firsthand testimony of many enslaved people, it is clear that some suffered from hunger and others enjoyed a surprising degree of abundance. The average experience may have fallen somewhere in between.

Although it is possible to identify trends and variations and to assemble a great deal of information about what grew in the garden patches of the enslaved and what sizzled over the fires in various slave cabins, the diversity and enormity of an institution that involved millions of people and endured for centuries means that there is much that researchers can never know. Since enslaved people were constrained in various obvious ways when deciding what to eat, each individual also made a seemingly infinite number of small decisions about what to eat, how to obtain food, how to prepare it, and who to eat with. Some of these choices enabled them to transcend their dismal circumstances in small but significant ways. However, most of these strategies are lost to history. Historians looking at existing records can often only guess about the role that individual ingenuity played in shaping the slave diet.

When trying to assess the quality and quantity of the slave diet, there is a danger to be found in focusing too much on the official slave rations that were documented in plantation records. In most instances, these allotments represented only a portion of what enslaved people actually ate. Fogel and Engerman speculate plausibly that corn and pork appear so frequently in these records because they not only formed the core ingredients of the diet, but they were also distributed throughout the year. Other foods, particularly garden vegetables, may have been distributed seasonally as available at the discretion of owners and overseers. The custom that slaves would receive surplus garden vegetables may have been so widespread that it was taken for granted and not noted in official documents. For similar reasons, slaves may have been given items like salt, molasses, coffee, and whiskey more frequently than the written record indicates.[98] For example, Charles Ball recalled living on one plantation where the formal slave rations consisted only of corn and occasional allotments of salt. However, he recalled being allowed to harvest apples, peaches, and figs on the planation and being supplied with beef as a reward for completing a difficult task.[99] In most cases, the enslaved people who transcended the limitations of a minimal slave ration diet did so as a result of their own efforts and not due to occasional planter largesse. Ball claimed that in his experience, "An industrious, managing slave would contrive to gather up a great deal to eat."[100]

Hungry slaves sometimes opportunistically took food that had not been allotted to them, a practice that the slaveholder described as "stealing," but which Frederick Douglass came to think of as a redistribution of resources. Douglass worked for a number of different masters, and there were times in his life when he had enough to eat. However, there were long periods when he described being "wretchedly starved" by cruel owners and driven to distraction by the proximity of bread and meat he was not allowed to consume. Finally, in order to survive, Douglass began to try to stave off the "pitiless pinchings of hunger" by swiping an occasional morsel from the larder. In doing so, he reasoned that since he, like the meat he stole, was the property of the master, the food he ingested was not stolen but had merely been relocated, remaining the property of his owner the whole time. He was outraged both by the indignity of having surreptitiously to gather enough food to keep himself alive and by the cruelty of the fact that although his labor was being stolen he was not given the bare minimum needed to fuel his body.[101] Booker T. Washington agreed that the idea of "theft" should not be applied to the actions of desperate and hungry slaves. He recalled being woken up late one night by his mother offering her sleepy children the rare treat of chicken. Although he did not know where she got the bird, he guessed it must have come from the master's yard. However, given the severity of her family's need, he argued that his mother should be considered a "victim of the system of slavery" and not a thief.[102]

Although enslaved people had no ethical qualms about finding creative ways to feed themselves as they labored for their masters' benefits, slaveholders regarded stealing as a serious offense. Harriet Jacobs recalled that one master beat a hungry enslaved person who stole a pig so severely that "the back of his shirt was one clot of blood." Weak from blood loss, the enslaved man attempted to run away, but when his body gave out he was forced to crawl back to the plantation on his hands and knees. Upon his arrival, a fellow slave used lard to remove gently the garment from his lacerated flesh. Unmoved by the gruesome sight, the slave owner claimed he deserved another hundred lashes for his serious "crime."[103] On one of the plantations where Frederick Douglass was enslaved, the plantation owner kept a vegetable garden that was so large that five people were charged with maintaining it. The abundance of the garden tormented the plantation's poorly fed slaves, and a slave was lashed almost daily for succumbing to his or her biological need for sustenance. To prevent the hungry passersby from surreptitiously harvesting a snack, the owner had the entire garden fence covered in tar and decreed that any enslaved person found with tar on his body was automatically said to be guilty of stealing food.[104]

Slaveholders weary of policing their personal food supplies had a tremendous financial incentive to allow enslaved people opportunities to augment their rations by means other than stealing. Frequently, masters granted enslaved people the "privilege" of cultivating gardens for their own use.[105] Members of the slave community no doubt preferred having the opportunity to augment their diets by growing their own vegetables over going hungry or eating a bland, repetitive diet. However, the decision to spend scant "leisure" time working in individual garden plots benefited the master just as much as the slave. Slaveholders were able to profit from the labor of better-fed and thus healthier workers at the same time that they got to applaud themselves for their beneficence in granting the enslaved people the chance to grow supplemental foods.[106]

Charles Ball, who experienced slavery in Maryland, Georgia, and South Carolina, recalled, "On every plantation, with which I ever had any acquaintance, the people are allowed to make patches, as they are called—that is, gardens, in some remote and unprofitable part of the estate, generally in the woods, in which they plant corn, potatoes, pumpkins, melons, &c. for themselves."[107] Other common crops grown in slave plots included black-eyed peas and a variety of other legumes, collards and other greens, sweet potatoes, okra, peanuts, and green beans.[108] Even when land was not specifically set aside for the purposes of establishing specific garden plots, enterprising enslaved people may have managed to plant food in liminal spaces near their cabins or on the fringes of the plantations system. Enslaved people everywhere certainly learned how to forage for wild edibles. Among other things, enslaved people gathered and ate persimmons, wild berries, hickory nuts, walnuts, pecans, and poke greens.[109] Enslaved people fished in the ocean, rivers, lakes, and streams. They also hunted for a wide range of wild animals including wild hogs, deer, opossums, raccoons, turtles, squirrels, ducks, quail, and geese.[110]

Masters often granted them the right to sell excess food grown in their garden patches, and slaves selling food at market became a common sight in many urban areas in the South.[111] One remarkably successful slave woman, Aletha Turner of Washington, DC, was able to make enough money selling her fresh produce so that was able to buy her own freedom for $1,400 along with that of twenty-two other slaves over a period of twenty-five years.[112] In allowing enslaved people the opportunity to earn money, owners also tried to defend the institution of slavery, claiming that since their basic needs for food, clothing, and shelter were already met, slaves could use their spending money for what their owners regarded as purely frivolous items. Because masters, their protestations aside, did not always adequately provide a subsistence and very little in the way of material comforts, most purchases were modest. Enslaved people frequently bought food items like molasses, coffee, and salt to round out their meals and alcohol that could be used for a medication, a social lubricant, or as a coping mechanism.[113] However, significant research by Philip D. Morgan demonstrates that some Lowcountry slaves working on the "task system" that allowed them to manage their own time after completing assigned jobs were able to acquire fairly significant amounts of personal property. Among other things, some enslaved people managed to purchase domesticated animals including chickens, cows, sheep, and hogs, which they could sell or consume to round out their diets.[114]

A close examination of the foodways of slavery demonstrates a diverse set of food practices and a wide spectrum of variation in terms of whether or not enslaved people had enough to eat. Linda Civitello encapsulates the most widely held popular understanding of antebellum southern foodways with her claim that in the South, "what part of the hog you ate showed your rank in society." She argues that enslaved people ate pork bits that white southerners had discarded—like chitterlings, ears, feet, and tails—while their masters ate more choice cuts. Furthermore, she argues that slaves were not allowed to eat "beef, lamb, mutton, chicken, turkey, and geese," forms of animal proteins that she says graced white tables alone.[115] This way of framing black food history has become pervasive.

There is ample testimony supporting the idea that enslaved people had to contend with minimal and inferior food, particularly castoff or even rotten meat.[116] Slaveholders certainly did give scraps and remainders of food and other items to their slaves, but this is hardly the entire story of what enslaved people ate. Pork may have been the most common meat on the table of both black and white southerners, but it was not the only form of animal protein that many enslaved people tasted.[117] Ultimately, generalizations about enslaved people eating "low on the hog" distort the complex and variegated reality about what enslaved people really ate. As Psyche Williams-Forson makes clear, "Some foods eaten by black people have their origins in the plantation master's leftovers, but not all."[118]

Archeological evidence has proved to be an invaluable resource in demonstrating the inadequacy of the idea that all enslaved people ate a minimal and monotonous diet. It has also helped challenge the popular idea that slaves and their masters always ate radically different things. Archeologists studying the site of an antebellum plantation on Simon's Island, Georgia, in conjunction with existing plantation records discovered that the enslaved people who lived there ate a wide variety of foods. Over the years, their rations consisted of a combination of corn, sweet potatoes, rice, and either salted fish or bacon. Evidence suggests that they also occasionally ate less desirable portions of cattle and sheep that were likely given to them by their masters. To supplement this basic food supply, they hunted and fished. Remnants of lead shot in the area of the slave quarters suggests that in spite of prohibitions against slaves owning firearms, enslaved people on the plantation had guns and used them to hunt for animals including opossums, rabbits, and raccoons. They also kept their own domestic animals including chickens and hogs, which meant that they at least sometimes ate "high on the hog." They also planted corn, sweet potatoes, black-eyed peas, turnips, and greens in their own garden patches. In addition to eating food produced on the plantation, they had access to some items that were purchased. Archeologists found remnants of bottles that once contained alcohol and medications including castor oil and laudanum.[119]

Not only is it clear that slaves on at least this plantation had access to a diverse food supply, archeological evidence gathered elsewhere suggests that sometimes there were greater similarities between what enslaved people ate and what appeared on their masters' dinner tables than has been previously assumed. Faunal remains in Virginia have shown that the local elite actually ate allegedly lower-status cuts of meat, and enslaved people sometimes ate large cuts of higher-quality meat.[120] These studies should not be used to draw conclusions about what all slaves ate, for evidence of hunger and deprivation abounds. However, they do raise questions about the received wisdom that all enslaved people ate only limited quantities of a few sources of food.

Even when enslaved people found ways to augment the rations they received through stealing, hunting, foraging, growing food, and raising animals, their ability to assemble a diverse diet did not and could not make a life of slavery acceptable. As a slave, Frederick Douglass experienced both gnawing hunger and having enough to eat. At one point in his life he was actually grateful for the chance to work under the supervision of a cruel man who prided himself in his ability to "break" slaves. He "made the change gladly; for [he] was sure of getting enough to eat, which is not the smallest consideration to a hungry man."[121] Having enough to eat certainly did make his day-to-day existence more bearable, but it did not make him more willing to accept his captivity. After his escape from bondage, Douglass regarded the ironically named "Mr. Freeland," who also made sure that his slaves had plenty to eat, to be the "best master I ever had, *till I became my own master.*"[122] However, working for a relatively kind master and having a full stomach did not impact his ever-present desire for freedom or stop Douglass from trying to escape. Freedom, whether it came, as in Douglass's case from running away, or as the result of emancipation at the end of the Civil War, brought with it a new set of obstacles as the newly freedpeople struggled to make sure they had enough to eat. As the next chapter demonstrates, some actually suffered more from hunger after emancipation than they had as slaves. Many struggled as they negotiated new working relationships and new strategies for finding sufficient food. However, despite the challenges of the era, it was far superior to the alternative.

Foodways, Resiliency, and
White Supremacy after the Civil War

$\mathcal{D}$uring the Civil War, Union troops raided the larder of the Mississippi plantation where Gabe Emanuel lived as a slave. Outraged at their actions, Emanuel decided that "no Yankee gwina eat all us meat." His hunger outweighed his fear for his physical safety. Daringly, he snuck into the army camp, found the purloined rations, and successfully hid the food from the soldiers.[1] Although enslaved people like Emanuel clearly understood that these invaders were fighting against those who held them in captivity and that the fate of the institution of slavery would be determined by the outcome of the war, their hopes for freedom in the future could not always override the pressing demands of present-day needs.

Lucindy Allison, an Arkansas slave, later remembered that northern soldiers indiscriminately stole provisions from slaves and free people alike, observing, "What they keer 'bout you being white or black? Thing they was after was filling themselves up."[2] Enslaved person Peter Brown resented the fact that although confiscating southern food supplies damaged the cause of the Confederacy, it also hurt the most vulnerable inhabitants of the region. He pointed out that although his master claimed ownership over the food in the plantation storehouse, slaves "helped raise the meat they stole." He complained, "They left us to starve and fed their fat selves on what was our living."[3] When local food supplies were low, enslaved people generally suffered far more than their masters. Spencer Barnett grumbled, "The Yankees starved out more black faces than white at their stealing."[4]

Historian Vincent Harding has remarked about the "terrible irony" of the fact that the Union army that ultimately brought about an end to American slavery was mired in racism that could be as virulent as that of the slaveholders themselves.[5] Although circumstances had cast them in the role of liberators, they did not necessarily have compassion for those whose freedom was at stake, and the enslaved people who "voted for freedom with their feet" by advancing toward the Union lines were often poorly rewarded for their faith in these outsiders. During the war years, tens of thousands of African Americans depended upon irregularly issued army rations for sustenance, and even when food was available, they were often required to earn their subsistence by performing arduous tasks.[6] Because the Union camps set up for fleeing slaves were often overcrowded and woefully undersupplied, many refugees from slavery suffered from malnutrition and disease.[7] For the unluckiest, their experience of "freedom" was also far too brief.

In November 1864, Joseph Miller, his wife, and his four children fled along with approximately five hundred other escaped slaves to Camp Nelson, a union supply depot in Kentucky. Federal authorities promised Miller that if he joined the Union army, his family would receive food and shelter. However, shortly after he enlisted, the army expelled the other refugees, including his family, from the camp. He was left to watch helplessly as his wife and children were driven out into the cold weather without food or shelter. Miller later recalled that a soldier told his family "that if they did not get up into the wagon which he had he would shoot the last one of them. . . . My wife carried her sick child in her arms. When they left the tent the wind was blowing hard and cold and having had to leave much of our clothing when we left our master, my wife with her little one was poorly clad."[8] Their youngest son froze to death the same day they were expelled, and in the coming months Miller's wife and other children died from illness, hunger, and exposure one by one.[9] As historian Jim Downs points out, "The Miller family did not die from complicated medical ailments or unknown diseases; they died because they did not have the basic necessities."[10] Deaths like theirs were preventable but far too common.

Ironically, the Millers would likely have lived longer had they not seized upon the opportunity to claim their freedom. Although the Civil War had a destabilizing impact on the southern food supply, prior to the conflict most slaves were able to count on a dependable, albeit limited, stream of food provisions. In contrast to the experiences of the Miller family, most slaves were not faced with the threat of starvation. However, because slave rations were often inadequate and always monotonous, enslaved people devoted a great deal of energy to the task of augmenting their diets. When they fantasized about freedom, most did not envision the destitution that often accompanied emancipation. Instead, they hoped that after freedom they would be able to eat a more substantial, diverse, and luxurious diet. For example, when Booker T. Washington was a child he recalled watching his young mistress consuming ginger cakes and deciding, "If I ever got free, the height of my ambition would be reached if I could get to the point where I could secure and eat ginger-cakes in the way that I saw those ladies doing."[11]

Washington and others like him soon discovered that the realities of their postbellum diet seldom lived up to these daydreams. Testimony from former slaves reveals that although none longed to return to the strictures of slavery, respondents were often nostalgic about the quality of food they had eaten during the antebellum era. What might have once seemed like a limited and inadequate diet suddenly sounded appealing to impoverished freedpeople attempting to survive on far less. Freedman Jim Allen fondly remembered occasions when he ate "candy by the double han'ful" and a "sight of good things . . . from dat garden and smoke house" while he was an enslaved child.[12] In an interview conducted in the 1930s, former Mississippi slave Gus Clark claimed that although his controlling master would not allow his slaves to attend church, pray, or sing out of pure "meanness," slavery was still "better in some ways" than the present day because "we allus got plen'y ter eat, which we doan now."[13] When recalling the food of slavery from the vantage point of Great Depression scarcity, Charlie Davenport hungrily remembered eating a variety of foods, including, "hot bread, 'lasses, fried salt meat dipped in corn meal, an' fried taters . . . fish an' rabbit meat . . . hot pone, baked taters, corn roasted in the shucks, onion, fried squash, an' b'iled pork . . . buttermilk . . . hoecake . . . sweetmilk and collards."[14] For these former slaves and others like them, memories of a relatively dependable slave diet taunted them as they faced the gnawing hunger of the new era.

Even though the material rewards of freedom were far from certain, the psychic rewards were immense. In the early twentieth century, Booker T. Washington remarked that despite the hardships of the postemancipation period, "I have never seen one who did not want to be free, or one who would return to slavery."[15] One former slave concurred with this sentiment, emphatically proclaiming, "I rather get on with eating once a week on bread and water than be a slave with plenty."[16] However, freedom, as welcome as it was, brought with it a new set of complications. Washington recalled that when the slaves on his plantation learned that the day of their liberation had finally arrived, they responded with "great rejoicing, and thanksgiving, and wild scenes of ecstasy." However, their initial unbridled joy was soon tempered by the realization that freedom was a "serious thing."[17] Their existential quest had suddenly been transformed from chafing against the limitations of slavery into the less clearly defined task of defining the meaning of freedom.

Due to the relentless biological need for food, most did not have the luxury of time for extended contemplation when making this transition. Hunger played an enormous role in dictating how many responded to the dawning of new opportunities. When the war finally ended, some stayed on the plantations where they had been enslaved simply because they relished the certainty of having enough to eat. Cecila Chappell worked for her abusive former owners in Tennessee for several years postemancipation because, as she recalled, "I allus had good clothes and good food and I didn' know how I'd git 'em atter I left."[18] While her former owners likely interpreted her decision to stay put as the outgrowth of loyalty and affection or of a lack of imagination, Chappell's choice was a calculated one that reflected a pragmatic desire to be sure that her basic needs were met.

Those who decided to try their luck elsewhere often had to depend upon the charity of the underfunded Freedom's Bureau as they looked for housing and employment. In the first fifteen months after the war ended, the organization issued thirteen million rations of enough cornmeal, flour, and sugar to feed one person for a week.[19] However, these food distributions were insufficient to meet the needs of four million emancipated people during this vulnerable transitional moment. Despite the fact that many were without homes or livelihoods, the organization often limited aid distributions to those they considered to be the most vulnerable and deserving, such as children or the elderly.[20] Between 1865 and 1871, the Bureau spent a total of $3,168, $325.00 on emergency food and clothing.[21] This relatively paltry sum would have amounted to less than a dollar per freedperson even if destitute whites had not also received emergency aid.

The stinginess with which the organization handed out food was, in part, the outgrowth of the belief that charity could lead to moral corruption. Federal bureaucrats and the leaders of organizations claiming to offer assistance to the freedpeople often harbored suspicions that African Americans would not willingly work as free laborers. Instead of viewing relief distribution as a stopgap measure to be used while the recently emancipated searched for jobs, housing, and displaced loved ones, many suspected that African Americans who received subsistence rations would become idle and would refuse future employment opportunities.[22] In 1865, one missionary articulated this idea when he claimed, "If you wish to make them impudent, fault-finding and lazy, give them clothing and food freely."[23]

Former slave owners, who had their own reasons to doubt that the formerly enslaved could thrive as a free labor force, capitalized on these fears and successfully urged the Freedman's Bureau to withhold rations from African Americans who refused to sign contracts to work as field hands. When the Bureau would not feed them, many became dependent upon their former owners for their subsistence.[24] Deprived of their power as slaveholders, white southerners developed new means to coerce black laborers back into dependency and subservience. Hunger proved to be a powerful tool in the reinstitutionalization of white supremacy. Planters used the hunger of the formerly enslaved people as a means of regaining control over their labor by making sure that food rations were only forthcoming to those who signed labor contracts with terms that were far more favorable to the employer than the employee.

Dire necessity compelled most freedpeople to resume work on the plantations. Most ultimately accepted positions as sharecroppers who worked land they did not own in exchange for a share of the crops they grew. Because most freedpeople left slavery owning few material possessions, they were forced to depend upon the former slaveholding class for not only food but also housing and farm animals and implements. The system of sharecropping, which began as a compromise of sorts between landowners who needed workers and would-be black farmers who did not have access to land, was rife with corruption. Backed by the coercive power of the state, landowners conspired to keep African Americans impoverished and bound to the land through a variety of means. In the worst-case scenarios, croppers were reduced to debt peons trapped by laws that said that they could not leave their employers if they were in debt. The status of debtor was often inescapable due to crooked bookkeeping that ensured that even the most industrious and lucky farmers could never clear a profit.[25]

Sharecropping endured as the primary form of labor organization on southern farms until the 1940s. Because the system lasted for so long, the experiences of sharecroppers varied according to time, place, and individual circumstances. Some managed to overcome the limitations of the system, to accumulate small profits, and eventually ascend a metaphorical "agricultural ladder" from tenancy to land ownership.[26] The idea that a good crop year could radically change a person's financial prospects was a key factor in perpetuating the system. As Michael Dougan explains:

> The ideology of sharecropping taught that economic success, universally regarded as landowning, could be achieved through work, luck, a productive wife, and numerous children. In theory a man could begin with nothing but the labor of himself and his family and then acquire mules, equipment and more land, eventually working his way up to a renter, leasing, and finally buying his own land.[27]

This ideology had a stabilizing effect on the system of land tenure, because the idea that economic mobility was possible gave people hope. In the eyes of many, the sharecroppers who managed to become landowners served as proof that the system could work.

Anthropologist Hortense Powdermaker, who conducted a study of life in Indianola, Mississippi, in the 1930s, recorded the story of a successful local farmer she referred to as "J." J. was a black landowner who had been born into slavery. Ten years after emancipation, when he was twenty-two years old, J. left his parents' household and began renting a farm of his own. Due to luck, hard work, and frugal measures of eating "the simplest food" such as "peas boiled without meat," J. and his wife were able to save up enough money to purchase 150 acres over the course of seven years. By the time of his death in 1915, J. had expanded his holdings to 1,600 acres. Although clearly exceptional, he was not alone in his success. Powdermaker documented the stories of a number of other local black landowners, including a "prosperous and influential" member of the black community who saved enough money while working as a sharecropper so that he was able to purchase his own land, hire ten sharecroppers to work for him, send his father to school, and attend college himself.[28]

Landownership was an important key to economic prosperity because not only did owners have the opportunity to sell their own crops and do their own bookkeeping, they also had the power to decide how to allocate their land usage and thus could produce much of their own food.[29] In the late nineteenth century Anderson and Cora Scales managed to purchase property in North Carolina, which they utilized to make themselves as self-sufficient as possible. They decided not to grow commodity crops for market. Instead, in order to earn cash income, they started a small drayage business. Using manure from the stable as fertilizer, they grew much of their own food including snap beans, tomatoes, Irish potatoes, sweet corn, butterbeans, squash, mustard greens, onions, and turnips. They also maintained a small orchard, foraged for wild strawberries, crab apples, and blackberries in season, and raised cows, pigs, and chickens. They were prosperous enough that later in life Anderson Scales was able to open a small grocery store.[30] Those, like the Scales, who managed to acquire land despite the odds against them, served as sources of inspiration to those who hoped to follow a similar trajectory, but these success stories were also all too rare. In general, the rung of wage laborer or sharecropper was a permanent stop in a system that was designed to benefit white landowners and to keep African Americans impoverished and dependent.

Although planters had financial incentives to make sure that valuable slaves ate well enough to preserve their lives and thus their financial value, they generally viewed sharecroppers as a replaceable and expendable labor force whose physical welfare was no longer a source of major concern. While slaves who could count on the steady distribution of rations could expend extra labor to subsidize what their owners distributed, croppers had to provide for all of their own needs. Sharecroppers were often confronted with the painful irony of the fact that in material terms freedom was often less comfortable than slavery. To buy basic necessities, like the cornmeal and fatty pork that continued to constitute the backbone of the southern working-class

diet, sharecroppers had to borrow against their future harvest at high interest rates and purchase overpriced goods at the stores that would give them
credit.[31]

If they could negotiate for the right to plant a garden or to hunt, sharecroppers could draw upon some familiar strategies from slavery to augment
their diets beyond the staples they purchased on credit at plantation stores.
Although they generally did not have the same degree of access to money
and supplies as landowners like the Scales family, many still found the resources needed to plant small gardens. Sharecroppers with garden plots grew
a variety of crops including black-eyed peas, string beans, greens, cabbages,
sorghum, and turnips. Sweet potatoes played a particularly large role in the
diets of some tenant farmers who often stored large quantities of the tuber
in anticipation of winter food shortages.[32] Some kept livestock, which might
occasionally consist of a cow or, more frequently, of a pig and hens.[33] Mary
Dotson recalled that her father, a Mississippi sharecropper, grew greens year
round, made his own molasses, raised hogs for meat, and kept a cow to supply
the family with milk.[34]

Others supplemented their diets by hunting. After freedom, one Alabama sharecropper worked for a planter who only supplied his laborers with
sorghum syrup and cornmeal on credit and then routinely cheated them out
of their share of the proceeds from the crop at harvest time. However, because
he had hunting privileges, the cropper could make sure his family was well fed
even under these dire circumstances. His son Ned Cobb recalled, "My daddy
was a marksman: killed squirrels, possums, wild turkeys, catch fish and all . . .
I'd seed the day come and pass that'd he'd fed us just on game."[35] Despite the
hardships they endured while working land they did not own and navigating
the capricious demands of a number of white landowners, Cobb recalled that
his family often had enough food to share with other members of the black
community or with "raggedy" poor, white people. When travelers would pass
the family home his father would instruct his mother to "fix 'em a nice meal"
of fish, fried ham, chicken, or eggs, regardless of whether or not they had the
means to pay for it.[36]

Not all sharecroppers had the opportunity to grow their own food, raise
livestock, or to hunt. As many soon discovered, the land usage privileges available to financially valuable human capital did not always apply to this new
class of laborer. While slaves were often permitted to grow gardens, planters
increasingly placed restrictions on what sharecroppers planted.[37] Profit-driven
landowners were reluctant to set aside land that could be used to grow mar-
ketable crops for the animal husbandry or the kitchen gardens needed to feed
hungry black families.[38] In the 1930s, one Arkansas cropper complained, "De
landlord wouldn' give us no land foh a garden . . . we had to plant cotton right

up to the do'."[39] Another grumbled that the landowner he worked for would not let him keep any livestock, including chickens, because "dey bothered the cotton." One year he tried to raise a pig to augment his family's meager larder, and the landowner had the animal shot.[40]

The actions of changeable landowners acting out of greed, spite, or neglect who hindered the ability of their tenants to feed themselves were hard to predict from moment to moment or from year to year. Researchers studying the system of farm tenancy near Natchez, Mississippi, in the 1930s noted that landowners were more likely to allow tenants to plant gardens in years when cotton prices were low and extending them credit to buy food was risky.[41] Because so many circumstances were out of their control, sharecroppers often found it impossible to plan ahead. Subsistence strategies that enabled a family to survive one year might not be feasible the next crop season.

Hungry sharecroppers had to endure the painful irony of struggling to find enough food to eat while living in what researchers conducting a study of cotton tenancy in the 1930s described as "abundant land in the south temperate zone." Despite the fact that the region was capable of producing enough food to feed all of its citizens, the study concluded that "tenant families ha[d] probably the most ill-balanced diet and meager diet of any large group in America."[42] After they had expended their small cash reserves and exhausted their credit, it was not uncommon for sharecroppers to spend several months of the year living in a state of "semistarvation."[43] During the lean times, many had to go to desperate lengths to find enough to eat. One Mississippi planter complained that the sharecroppers who he hired to care for his dogs were so hungry that they ate the food allotted for the animals.[44] As a young child in Mississippi, Robert Cableton too recalled eating scraps of meat and bread that a plantation owner had set aside for the dogs. His mother gave the remnants to her children whose right to food was, she believed, "greater than the dogs'."[45] Those who could not find scraps to salvage sometimes had to learn to go without. When asked what hungry tenants did after they had wiped out their stores of food and could not draw on any more credit, one farm manager explained that they "have to strap it," or tighten their belts over their empty stomachs.[46]

Even when sharecroppers had a reasonable amount to eat, their diet was often limited and nutritionally inadequate. The US Department of Agriculture conducted a study of the diets of rural, black Alabamians in 1895 and 1896 and concluded that the core diet of most consisted of three foods: cornmeal, salt pork, and molasses.[47] This ubiquitous "three m's diet" of meal, meat, and molasses was cheap, monotonous, and vitamin deficient.[48] These ingredients were sometimes supplemented with other foods, including garden vegetables in season, but these three central ingredients were often the

Figure 3.1. Impoverished child drinking "milk" made from flour and water in Texas, 1939. Photo by Russell Lee, Library of Congress, LC-USF34-032703-D.

only consistent foods to appear on the tables of the poorest southerners. In fact, fatty salt pork was so commonly consumed that many rural African Americans referred to it simply as "meat" because it was often the only form of animal protein they were familiar with except for an occasional opossum or rabbit.[49] Cornbread, often made with only meal and water, constituted the other staple item on the menu. Samuel S. Taylor recalled how his grandmother made cornmeal cakes in the fireplace of the family cabin and marveled at her skill in making perfectly round bread with a "good firm crust" without using any equipment besides a fireplace poker and her hands.[50]

Although skilled cooks like Taylor's grandmother could help transform this monotonous set of ingredients into meals that were appetizing enough that her grandson was still longing for them decades later, adhering too closely to this diet could take a toll on the bodies of rural southerners. In extreme cases, the spare sharecropper's diet could be deadly. Rural southerners who ate little more than the "three m's" often suffered from niacin deficiency, which could lead to a disease called pellagra. Pellagra is characterized by a variety of symptoms including skin lesions, diarrhea, dementia, and lethargy. The condition, which killed thousands, could easily have been prevented by a more balanced diet.[51]

The problems of malnutrition and hunger were not confined to the countryside. Richard Wright, who lived in the Mississippi capitol city of Jackson as a child, remembered being tortured by "biting hunger, hunger that made my body aimlessly restless, hunger that kept me on edge, hunger that made my temper flare, hunger that made hate leap out of my heart like the dart of a serpent's tongue." The Wright family generally subsisted on two meals a day: cornmeal mush and gravy made from white flour and lard for breakfast and greens cooked with lard eaten in the late afternoon. Occasionally they ate small quantities of meat or fish and more often a peanut roast shaped to resemble meat, which Wright bitterly recalled "tasted like something else."[52]

While hunger was a real and debilitating problem for many in the decades following emancipation, some former slaves managed not only to feed themselves but also to use their knowledge about food as a means of earning a living in this new era by establishing small food-related businesses. African Americans were aware of the fact that white people often used food, or more precisely the lack of food, as a tool of oppression as they deprived black employees of the means to acquire enough to eat. In response to this situation, black people sometimes found ways to use food as a tool of economic advancement and as a means of thwarting the intentions of the system of white supremacy that was designed to keep them impoverished. African Americans who made their living or subsidized their incomes by selling food were continuing practices begun before emancipation.

Many enslaved people had sold produce, livestock, or items they cooked in their spare time in order to earn precious spending money needed to improve the living conditions of their families.[53] Although slaves marketing food were common sights in southern cities and towns, these entrepreneurial efforts were always circumscribed by the will of masters who set limits on the time and resources slaves could spend at market and the geographical distances they could travel. For these reasons, during the antebellum era free black people were better equipped than slaves to leverage their talents in the kitchen to create small businesses. Kathy Ferguson, who had been born into slavery in New York, became a celebrated baker after obtaining her freedom. She earned enough money from designing special cakes for wealthy clients that she was able to use the proceeds from her sales to support more than forty needy children.[54] Mary A. Lee, a North Carolina baker, managed to acquire property worth $2,750 by 1860, and Rachel Lyon of Philadelphia opened a restaurant in 1808 that stayed open until her retirement in 1850.[55] One of the most successful antebellum culinary entrepreneurs was Sally Seymour, who had been manumitted from slavery in Charleston in 1794. Seymour was able to earn enough money from her pastry business that she went on to purchase four slaves of her own and expand her business into a full-scale catering operation.[56]

In nineteenth-century Philadelphia, black caterers like Thomas J. Dorsey, Henry Jones, Henry Minton, and Robert Bogle were so successful that W. E. B. Du Bois later declared that these men "rule[d] the social world of Philadelphia through its stomach."[57] These culinary professionals prepared elegant dishes like lobster salad, chicken croquettes, and deviled crabs that sold for as much as $50 a plate to members of the city's elite.[58] The black-owned Augustine-Baptiste catering business continued operating into the twentieth century, and the business was worth $60,000 by 1910.[59] These free black entrepreneurs served as examples and sources of inspiration to freed-people who hoped to create similar businesses.

In her groundbreaking book *Building Houses Out of Chicken Legs: Black Women, Food, and Power*, Psyche Williams-Forson resuscitates the forgotten story of a group of African American women in Gordonsville, Virginia, who drew upon similar strategies to help their families advance economically after slavery. These newly emancipated women dubbed themselves "waiter carriers" and established a brisk business selling foods like fried chicken, pies, and biscuits to travelers passing through town on the railroad. They tirelessly plied their wares by standing on the platform and enticing passengers to choose their refreshments instead of those offered by other vendors and restaurant owners. Maria Wallace was a successful enough waiter carrier that she managed to earn enough money to build a new home for her children; waiter carrier Hattie Edwards saved enough money that she was able to establish a small inn.[60]

Other contemporary culinary entrepreneurs made money not only by selling food but also by translating their cooking knowledge into a written form. Malinda Russell published a collection of recipes for decadent desserts in 1866 under the title *Domestic Cook Book: Containing a Careful Selection of Useful Recipes for the Kitchen.*[61] Abby Fisher, who was born into slavery, moved to San Francisco after the Civil War to begin a career as a caterer. She made pickles, jellies, pies, soups, and stews that were so popular with her West Coast clients that they encouraged her to publish her recipes. Fisher, who was illiterate, dictated instructions for making some of her favorite dishes that were published under the title of *What Mrs. Fisher Knows About Old Southern Cooking* in 1881.[62]

Although some African Americans, like the "waiter carriers," were able to use their culinary skills for their financial betterment, and a few cooks, like Russell and Fisher, were so successful that they achieved a modest degree of fame, would-be black culinary entrepreneurs had to contend with the reality that in many respects the postwar climate was actually more hostile to black business than it had been during the era of slavery. During that antebellum period, the free black community was small, and slave owners had been expected to regulate the entrepreneurial activities of slaves. However, during the postemancipation period, new commercial relationships had to be established. Widespread social change bred anxieties about what the new order should look like, and the white establishment was hostile toward black economic advancement that might jeopardize their supply of cheap labor or their place at the top of the racial hierarchy. Because the black community was resource poor and the white community was hostile toward their efforts of self-advancement, would-be black business owners generally had trouble raising the necessary capital to begin operations. If they surpassed that difficult hurdle, they then faced the possibility of reprisals from jealous white business owners should they succeed. As cash poor as the majority of freedpeople were, their collective spending power was significant enough that white merchants sought out their business and resented black competition.[63] For African Americans going into business could mean taking a deadly risk. For example, in 1892 Thomas Moss, Calvin McDowell, and William Stewart, part owners of the cooperative People's Grocery in Memphis, Tennessee, were lynched by an angry mob outraged at the success of their business as well as by the willingness of these men to defend their economic interests.[64]

Despite these obstacles and dangers, African American food-related entrepreneurial activities continued. According to an 1899 Atlanta University study, around the time of the Moss, McDowell, and Stewart lynching there were at least 6,319 black grocers and other merchants in the United States. Although many of their stores were small and contained only a "few hundred dollars worth of shelf goods bought on credit," some were "large ventures."[65] Remarkably, James Tate, the owner of an Atlanta grocery store, was able to accumulate $60,000 worth of property only a year after the end of the Civil War. By the end of the century, Samuel Harris of Williamsburg, Virginia, was bringing in $50,000 a year selling dry goods.[66] However, this notable class of black merchants who sold food to their community represented only a small percentage of those who made their living in a food-related occupation.

Most who worked in food service were not food vendors, caterers, or merchants. The majority worked on a much smaller scale and in a more intimate setting as domestic servants inside white homes. Most enslaved women had at least some cooking experience. Some had worked in the kitchens of their former owners and thus knew how to cook elaborate meals for large gatherings. Most had, at the very least, prepared meals for their own families prior to emancipation. When freedom came, many enslaved cooks hoped to

Figure 3.2. Interior of a black-owned grocery store in Georgia, circa 1900. Photo collected by W. E. B. Du Bois, Library of Congress, LC-USZ62-99056.

cast off their professional aprons so that their lives in the new era would feel distinctively different from their experiences as slaves. In fact, when presented with another option, many black women preferred any other job to that of a cook. In urban areas like Atlanta, many black women decided to take in laundry rather than to work as a cook because they could perform the labor of washing in their own homes free of the direct supervision of white employers.[67] However, the demand for black cooks was large, and domestic service became the only occupational option for many. The pressing problem of their own hunger and that of their families often forced black women, interest or aptitude aside, into becoming professional cooks in white homes.[68]

The wages of black domestic workers were vital in keeping black working-class families afloat until at least the middle of the twentieth century.[69] In her pioneering 1923 study of female, black domestic workers, Elizabeth Ross Haynes noted that almost 30 percent of the workers she studied were married, and thus, she presumed, were likely to be mothers as well as wives. Among this number, approximately a third were the primary wage earners in their families. Numerous unmarried domestic workers also supported dependents. Among the 2,071 "widowed or divorced" women seeking assistance in finding domestic work from the US Employment Administration between 1920 and 1922, 2,056 were financially responsible from between one and ten dependents.[70]

Because the wages of black domestic workers were vital to the sustenance of entire African American families, this poorly remunerated class of workers tirelessly fought to leverage their skills to their best advantage. Some took the dramatic step of migrating away from friends and family in an attempt to secure higher wages and better jobs. During the late nineteenth and early twentieth centuries, black domestic workers immigrated in large numbers from the South to northern cities like Philadelphia seeking to capitalize on a shortage of domestic servants in those areas. Those who were successful in securing positions in spite of fluctuating levels of prejudice against hiring black workers could demand wages up to six times greater than they were paid in the South.[71] Regardless of where they lived, black domestic servants fought with the tools at their disposal to make their work more remunerative and fulfilling. Historian Rebecca Sharpless argues that black domestic servants "constantly risked conflict with their employers" as they negotiated for "shorter hours, better pay, and better quantity and quality of foodstuffs to take home."[72]

Although relatively few southerners had enjoyed the services of a full-time cook during the antebellum period, after emancipation wages for black servants were so low that even working-class whites could aspire to hire domestic help.[73] Astonishingly, during the Great Depression, some whites in Mississippi who were poor enough to receive federal relief monies could still afford to hire black domestic workers.[74] The ability to hire a black cook became a status symbol, and for some white women having the opportunity to purchase black culinary know-how became something of a necessity. Out of all of the domestic tasks that were considered to be "women's work" in the nineteenth and early twentieth centuries, the task of cooking was the one that white women seemed to relish the least.[75] The task was, in fact, so unpopular that some white women did not even know how to cook and could not have performed the gendered task of feeding their families without African American assistance.[76]

Black women working in white households were in a paradoxical position. They were part of a simultaneously exploited and valued group of laborers. Thus, the relationships between African American domestic servants and white employers were frequently characterized by contradictory impulses and fraught dynamics. Even though black servants labored in close physical proximity to whites, their employers often found their bodily presence unsettling. Social anthropologists Allison Davis, Burleigh Gardner, and Mary Gardner spent nearly two years as participant observers studying the inhabitants of

Natchez, Mississippi, beginning in 1933. They noted a general white belief in the "organic inferiority of the Negro." Although African Americans frequently cooked in white kitchens, coming into intimate contact with both the raw ingredients and cooking and serving implements consumed or utilized by their white employers, it was the common practice to provide separate dishes for their use.[77] The practice of being willing to consume food prepared by black hands and, no doubt, also infused with sweat and saliva while also seeking to regulate the separation of white and black bodies in other contexts, is one of the central paradoxes of the system of white supremacy as it emerged after emancipation.

Historian Neil McMillan has attempted to explain the contradictory impulses of white supremacists who sought to keep black bodies in their proper "place" by explaining that in the segregated South, "'place' as whites defined it, was always more behavioral than spatial in nature."[78] Thus, white employers were not frightened of their actual, physical proximity to African Americans as much as they feared implied equality with black bodies. Propinquity during the act of service was a necessity, but the merest hint of interracial fraternization—even an action as far removed as eating in separate spaces from the same set of dishes—was regarded as intolerable. White families wished to take advantage of black culinary skills while still exerting control over black bodies by dictating what, where, and how black employees consumed their own meals. By demanding that black servants eat in separate spaces while using a separate set of implements, white employers could take advantage of black servants while performatively maintaining their separate and superior social position.

White southerners who wanted to eat well without laboring in their own kitchens managed to overcome much of their unease about the black presence in their households.[79] However, even though white southerners depended upon the talents of their black cooks, their pay did not reflect their value to the white households they served. Wages varied according to chronology and location, but they were always low. Around the turn of the twentieth century, a cook from Georgia earned $2.03 a week while another living in Texas earned nearly double her salary at a still meager $4.00 weekly.[80] During the Great Depression, a black cook in Mississippi could expect to be paid from $1.50 to $3.00 a week.[81] A white Mississippian explained that he deliberately underpaid his cook while reasoning that "if he gave her more money, she might soon have so much that she would no longer be willing to work for him."[82] However, even such paltry wages were far from dependable. Sometimes employers insisted on paying wages in kind rather than in cash, forcing their cooks to accept castoff clothing or household items in lieu of their agreed-upon salary.[83]

Figure 3.3. African American domestic servant and her employer, Saint Augustine, Texas, 1943. Photo by John Vachon, Library of Congress, LC-USZ62-112493.

Throughout the South, "pan-toting," which occurred when a cook took leftovers home to feed her own family, was widely practiced, sometimes openly and sometimes more covertly. In either instance, the "service pan" enabled underpaid black cooks a means of subsidizing their incomes and of feeding their hungry families, though they generally had little ability to impact the quality and quantity of these remnants.[84] Flossie Vence recalled that her grandmother, "Big Mama," returned home from her job as a cook each day carrying a "little granite pan" that contained "whatsoever would be left. . . . It wasn't much, like biscuits and hash, fried pig foots, steak, chicken, something like that."[85] Anne Moody, in contrast, remembered that food from the service pan was "the best she had ever eaten." The leftovers served as a lesson in inequality as she learned that "white folks ate different foods." She was astonished at the variety of foods and at the abundance of meat that her mother brought home. Without access to the remnants of white family meals, her family ate only beans and cornbread.[86]

Although they seldom took great pains to make sure that the families of the cooks who worked for them were well fed, white southerners often waxed poetic about the cooking skills of their undercompensated black cooks. In 1913, Martha McCulloch Williams fondly recalled childhood gustatory pleasures made possible by the African American cooks she knew during her childhood, "who not only knew their business but loved it—often with a devotion that raised it to the rank of Art." In her worldview, although African American women possessed incredible culinary skills, black cooks were also generic and interchangeable since each purportedly possessed the "palate of a *gourmet* born."[87] Historian Micki McElya argues that in the white mind the "care-giving labor" of black women was viewed as the outgrowth of "motherly instinct and love." Because black domestic talents were allegedly natural and not learned, the work performed by black cooks was thought of as "not as work at all" and was thus underacknowledged.[88]

Although white southerners typically did not appreciate the amount of labor it took for black cooks to develop a broad culinary skill set, they generally regarded domestic labor performed by white women in a much different light.[89] In the twentieth century, white domestic scientists attempted to reframe the traditionally female job of cooking as a serious intellectual undertaking that required detailed knowledge about fields such as chemistry and nutrition. However, in the southern white imagination, black cooks were incapable of cooking with scientific precision and relied instead on innate racial instincts that enabled them to cook without using written recipes or precise measurements.[90] While excellent white cooks were seen as scientists who were trained, skilled black cooks were viewed as instinctual artists who were born.

Because black cooking skills were imagined as instinctive and meals prepared by black hands were sometimes thought of as gifts rather than as the product of labor, white southerners often failed to respect the profound intellectual contributions that African Americans had made to southern regional cooking. The lack of acknowledgment extended far beyond cultural amnesia about the role enslaved Africans played in creating foundational southern foodways; in many instances white southerners failed to give black cooks proper credit for food that they watched them prepare with their own eyes. When white Florida author Marjorie Kinnan Rawlings decided to write the cookbook that was eventually published as *Cross Creek Cookery* in 1942, she drew upon the assistance of her African American maid Idella Parker. The pair spent months working side by side in the kitchen perfecting recipes, often "fir[ing] up a wood stove on a 100-degree Florida day." When the book came out, not only did Rawlings declare herself the sole author, Parker later complained that although "many of the recipes in the book were mine . . . she only gave me credit for three of them." Although the recipe for "Idella's Biscuits" appeared under its creator's name, Parker bristled at the fact that other dishes, like one for chocolate pie, were published without attribution. Her reward for inventing recipes and for doing the bulk of the recipe testing was merely a signed copy of the cookbook, a gesture that Parker later described as a "crumb that white people let fall."[91]

Parker was hardly the only African American cook whose recipes were stolen by whites who hoped to enhance their own culinary reputations using black intellectual property. In 1922 Emma and William McKinney published *Aunt Caroline's Dixieland Recipes: A Rare Collection of Choice Southern Dishes*, a book that they claimed captured the culinary repertoire of Aunt Caroline Picket, "a famous old Virginia cook." According to the McKinneys, Aunt Caroline cooked with the "'pinch of this' and 'just a smacker of that'" method. In other words, she supposedly cooked from instinct. The McKinneys "carefully and scientifically analyzed" her recipes and in so doing reclaimed them as their own.[92] Similarly, in the 1930s, Eleanor Purcell, a columnist for the *Baltimore Sun*, invented the character of "Aunt Priscilla" and wrote a column issuing advice from the fictional character that she rendered in dialect.[93] In the minds of these white "authors," black culinary knowledge was theirs to appropriate and to capitalize upon.

White employers who presumed that black cooks came into the world knowing how to cook did not understand the challenges involved in learning how to make food to the specifications of people intent upon maintaining their place at the top, not only of the labor hierarchy, but of the racial caste system as well. Those who entered domestic service for lack of better options but without the requisite training had a steep learning curve as they mastered not only basic cooking skills but also figured out how to prepare foods that might not be familiar to them. Yet as Anne Yentsch points out, "The daily journeys of black domestic workers between black and white communities opened a path through which food habits and preferences flowed from one group to another and back again."[94] For example, black cooks working in the homes of Jewish southerners might come home carrying unfamiliar foods like chopped liver, kugel, or gefilte fish for their families to sample.[95] As Marcie Cohen Ferris points out, culinary exchanges like these went both ways. Agnes Jenkins, a black cook working for a Jewish South Carolina family in the 1930s, often adapted traditional Lowcountry dishes to make them kosher, substituting, for example, fish for shellfish in some recipes.[96]

In many cases, black domestic servants did not encounter entirely unfamiliar food in white homes, though they certainly were asked to prepare items that they did not often cook or eat at home. For the majority of southerners, pork and corn were dietary cornerstones that transcended the color line, thus most white and black people had a similar culinary vocabulary.[97] However, middle-class whites were able to enjoy high-quality foods and a wider range of supplements to these core ingredients. The African American respondents in a study of southern, black eating habits in the 1940s explained the differences between racial styles of eating in primarily socioeconomic terms, observing, "Whites eat many things Negroes can't afford."[98] African American cooks were frequently struck by the greater quality, quantity, and variety of food that appeared on white, middle-class tables. They also could not help but to note the contrast between the impoverished dwellings in the black community and the more luxurious accommodations in white, middle-class neighborhoods.

Sometimes African American cook Ella Wright brought her two sons to work with her as she cooked in a white household. Her son Richard later claimed that he often regretted tagging along with his mother as his "nostrils were assailed with the scent of food that did not belong to me and which I was forbidden to eat."[99] Not only was the contrast between the abundance of food on the white table and the bread and tea diet that he subsisted upon painful, he could not help but to notice the differences between his family's one-bedroom tenement in a "bleak and hostile" part of Memphis and the well-appointed household where his mother worked as a cook. One of his earliest lessons about racial inequality took place while his empty stomach grumbled as he watched his mother bustle around a spacious kitchen and then deliver a meal to a separate dining room populated by "white faces gathered around a loaded table, laughing, talking, eating."[100]

Not only did many black cooks, like Wright's mother, have to suffer the pain of cooking food for white children while their own children went hungry, domestic servants were also often overworked and faced other threats and indignities. Cooks who lived on the premises were at the beck and call of their employers night and day. Those who lived in their own homes often spent the largest part of the day cooking and caring for white children while their own children waited for them. Richard Wright recalled that his mother usually left him and his younger brother alone most days while she worked. When she returned home each evening, she was "tired and dispirited and would cry a lot."[101] Furthermore, African American cooks had other reasons to dread the time they spent in white households beyond the painful reality of being separated from their own children. Because they spent so much of their time working in isolated conditions in white homes, black domestic workers were vulnerable to sexual abuse at the hands of the men in the household.[102] Cooks who refused sexual advances risked being fired and of losing their livelihood.[103]

Despite these abuses, black women cooks were not powerless. One cook pragmatically remarked that she expected "a little meanness in her mistress" and would put up with some abuse if she was paid fairly.[104] However, some were pushed beyond their limits. One North Carolina cook took pleasure in surreptitiously punishing "mean white folks" by "spit[ting] in the coffee or pee[ing] in the biscuits."[105] Some managed their on-the-job frustrations by taking time off from work now and again in order to allow their anger to dissipate. Many temporarily left their job, and thus also an unreasonable employer, by feigning illness.[106] Although their economic vulnerability meant that they could not make rash decisions to leave an employer, if pushed to their limit some could, and did, permanently quit unsatisfying jobs. When circumstances allowed, many left the profession of cook altogether. When that was not an option, they could sometimes seek employment under more favorable terms in a different white household.[107]

Sometimes unhappy cooks might leave their jobs abruptly and theatrically, as in the case of Anne Mae Dickinson who walked out on her employer and a room full of luncheon guests after being scolded for the way she arranged the coffee cups on the table.[108] More often, quitting was a passive aggressive action, and the cook had to imagine the pain and consternation her absence was causing from afar. Social scientist John Dollard observed that it was common for disgruntled black cooks simply to disappear, frequently the day after receiving their paltry pay. This maneuver was, he speculated, a way for domestic servants to demonstrate "you do not own my body."[109] Quitting was a particularly effective punitive tool if it was timed to coincide with a big event when a cook's skills were particularly vital. One white woman complained bitterly, "I have known them to leave when invitations were out for dining in the house." Unable to recognize that the timing of an absconded servant was likely deliberate and in response to specific grievances, she complained that servants would "leave without any particular reason at all."[110]

Black domestic workers who were privy to the intimate inner workings of white households generally understood the psychology of their employers far better than their employers understood them. Powdermaker remarked at the irony of the fact that "every white woman feels she knows all about her cook's personality and life, but she seldom does. The servant is quite a different person Across the Tracks."[111] Black servants, on the other hand, were familiar both with their employer's public persona and with details about their private lives. On some level, white employers knew that the access that their black domestic servants had to information about the dynamics of their home lives posed a threat to their ability to maintain control over the terms of their working relationships. In the white community, rumors circulated claiming that black servants detailed the flaws of white employers on blacklists they distributed in the black community.[112] White women often lived in fear of losing their domestic help, and employers who were fearful of being "blacklisted" or of losing a valuable employee might be coerced into making compromises.

Working conditions, though hardly ideal, were certainly preferable to enslavement when captive laborers could not count on regular time off. After emancipation, black cooks had greater opportunities to negotiate reduced working hours. One white Alabama man bitterly complained that domestic servants in his region "won't do a stroke of work after three o'clock. If you want a meal after that hour you have to prepare and serve it yourself."[113] In the 1950s, Anne Moody worked for a white woman doing domestic chores while she was still in high school. Because she was not her family's sole wage earner, she had a certain degree of financial freedom and could insist that the terms of her employment not force her to compromise too much personal dignity. In violation of a custom that stated that servants should enter white homes by the back door, she defiantly knocked on her employer's front door day after day until the woman she worked for finally stopped insisting that she enter at the rear of the house. She recalled, "Soon Mrs. Burke decided to let me do things my way. I would have quit had she not. And I think she knew it."[114]

Although Moody and others like her sometimes won fleeting, individual victories over the indignities inherent in the role of working as a domestic servant, the system was stacked against them. Similarly, some exceptional black culinary entrepreneurs managed to earn a living preparing or serving food even though they lived in a system designed to keep black people dependent and hungry. They too were in the minority. From the moment of emancipation, white southerners used their disproportionate control over the southern food supply and the labor market to rebuild a new system of white supremacy totalizing enough to replace adequately the repressive institution of slavery. Although food was often used as a tool of oppression, there were always African Americans who found ways to use food practices to fight against white supremacy and to make the case that they deserved first-class citizenship.

Renowned culinary historian Jessica Harris has reflected upon the fact that she is heir to two threads of black culinary history, "that of the Big House and that of the rural South."[115] Through the experiences of her impoverished ancestors, Harris claims a linkage in blood to the "tastes of pig meat and cornmeal" discussed in the last chapter as well as to a lesser known legacy of a black middle class who dined on higher-status food like Parker House rolls washed down by lemonade.[116] This second culinary style was promoted by generations of upwardly mobile African Americans who used the table as a space for demonstrating elegance and sophistication. The next chapter will begin by discussing a new set of food practices designed to help partakers dissociate themselves from real and inherited memories of the foodways of slavery and deprivation and to fight against white supremacy in the process.

The Quest to Cook and Eat

$\mathscr{P}$rominent educator Charlotte Hawkins Brown carefully curated the items that appeared on her dinner table, selecting dishes featured in newspaper recipe columns and popular cookbooks. When hosting social events, her menus included items such as stuffed tomatoes in aspic, canapés, frozen fruit salad, and bonbons. Brown chose these items to reflect a regionally unspecific middle-class aesthetic that she hoped would appeal "to the eye as well as to the taste."[1] Her interest in the tasks of food selection and preparation extended beyond her concerns about what would appear on her own table. In addition to making thoughtful choices about what she personally consumed or served, she also instructed other members of the black community about what they should eat.[2]

Between 1902 and 1952, Brown oversaw the education of more than one thousand students ranging from the elementary school to the junior college level at the Alice Palmer Freeman Memorial Institute near Greensboro, North Carolina. As the founder and first president of the institution, she urged her students to challenge the limitations of their station and developed a rigorous college preparatory curriculum at a time when many educational programs for black students were focused primarily on teaching vocational skills. Brown held her pupils to exacting academic and personal standards. Like many of her contemporaries who devoted themselves to the cause of what they labeled "racial uplift," she argued that learning codes of decorum were as important as mastering scholastic subjects.[3] Brown offered her students the hope that they could earn greater societal acceptance and social advancement by virtue of their good behavior.

In 1940 Brown had the opportunity to offer lessons about the rules of social protocol to an even broader audience. That year she appeared on national radio and published an etiquette guide self-assuredly titled *The Correct Thing to Do, to Say, to Wear*. Her lecture "The Negro and Social Graces" was broadcast on the CBS radio program *Wings over Jordan*. The regular show featured choral music, religious instruction, and interviews with prominent African Americans and reached tens of thousands of listeners. Brown used her national pulpit to speak directly to the segment of the greater black community that most resembled her own students: "that group of young Negroes from high schools and colleges whose education is above average." She discouraged members of this privileged group from what she saw as a tendency to "associate all forms of politeness, fine manners, and social graces with slavery-time performance of the maid and butler."[4] Brown argued that instead of being a sign of timidity and servility, the mastery of an elaborate set of rules for social etiquette was evidence of racial advancement. Social graces could, she argued, turn "the wheels of progress with greater velocity on the upward road to equal opportunity and justice."[5]

Listeners to the radio program who needed more guidance could turn to her published etiquette guide, where she gave advice about how to behave in a number of social spaces including the dinner table. She vehemently argued that the purpose of mealtime went far beyond that of providing bodies with nourishment. Meals, she declared, should "foster fellowship expressed in fitting conversation."[6] Tables should be well appointed and attractively arranged. Hosts should be gracious, calm, and carefully put together. Rules should be observed at every stage of the meal and ranged from dictating how food was to be eaten ("slowly and noiselessly") to how utensils should be used ("hold your knife in your right hand") to how much one should consume ("eat a little less of everything than you might").[7] She believed that eating the right foods in the proper fashion was one means of disassociating oneself from the degradation of the history of slavery.

Brown's carefully cultivated vision of proper African American food habits must have seemed far removed from the concerns of the impoverished sharecroppers and black domestic servants who survived on minimal allotments of meal, meat, and molasses or who made do by eating variable leftovers from the service pan. As a descendent of slaves who was also familiar with the living conditions in the contemporary rural South, Brown was not oblivious to the widespread existence of a cuisine of deprivation. However, her public discourse about etiquette was aimed at the tiny, and she hoped influential, African American elite who had transcended the problem of achieving mere subsistence. She devoted herself to performing the cultural work of creating a new narrative for freedom. She emphasized an alternative and lesser-known food history that she hoped would help provide a template for the ongoing project of cultural elevation.

Figure 4.1.   Middle-class family eating dinner in a well-appointed dining room in Washington, DC, 1942. Photo by Marjory Collins, Library of Congress, LC-DIG-fsa-8d20202.

The work of creating an atmosphere where "harmonious social intercourse" could flourish alongside the shared "appreciation of tasty food" was designed not only to ensure that the food practices of the postemancipation era were markedly different from those during the era of slavery, it was also intended to serve as a refutation to ongoing stereotypes about black culinary difference and inferiority.[8] When Brown assured her male students that if they behaved like "well-bred gentlemen" while dining out that they would be treated accordingly, she was holding out hope that carefully choreographed dining performances could, in aggregate, disempower a set of pervasive and disparaging ideas about African American ways of eating and thus destabilize the ideology of white supremacy. When "race woman" Alice Dunbar-Nelson dined on foods she regarded as "dainty" and sophisticated like shrimp salad, chicken croquettes, or custard, or when National Association of Colored Women president Mary Church Terrell agonized over what to serve dinner guests at her Washington, DC, home or Margaret Murray Washington urged the black community to reallocate scarce resources to buy high-quality "fresh fruit, fresh eggs, good meat," they were, like Brown, performing deliberate political acts as they refuted stereotypes about inferior black eating habits.[9]

White Americans who were uneasy about the possibility of black social advancement often soothed their worries by creating representations of amoral and ridiculous African Americans whom they deemed incapable of destabilizing the existing social hierarchy. The material culture of the era was replete with images of distorted black figures dining voraciously, which adorned items as various as postcards, figurines, children's storybooks, and consumer product labels. The most common representations of the era displayed black people devouring watermelons and chickens—foods that African Americans allegedly had an outsized appetite for—with glee. Other depictions showed caricatured African Americans relishing small game like opossums and raccoons, meals that were rejected by most middle-class eaters as being coarse and lower class. Images of enthusiastic black eaters were abundant, for example, in minstrel shows and in vaudeville performances where black characters were frequently represented.[10]

Around the turn of the twentieth century, white singers wearing black face makeup performed wildly popular "coon songs" in music halls throughout the country.[11] Hundreds were published in sheet music form, allowing those who could not attend live performances to recreate something of the music hall experience at home.[12] The published music was always adorned with colorful drawings of mischievous, childlike African Americans. Many depicted African Americans engaged in comical or voracious eating practices. These illustrations along with song titles such as "Auntie Skinner's Chicken Dinner" (1905) and "A Pork Chop Is the Sweetest Flower That Grows" (1903) reinforced derogatory ideas about coarse and enthusiastic black appetites in living rooms across the nation.[13]

The pervasiveness of these distorted images inspired many activists to join Brown in placing a great deal of emphasis upon precisely what foods appeared on black dinner tables. Many stressed African American dignity and discernment as one means of refuting these crude popular representations of black food habits. Booker T. Washington, an educator who became the most preeminent racial spokesperson at the turn of the twentieth century, urged African Americans to form new habits. He warned the black community against what he saw as the limitations of the pork and corn-centric rural, southern diet, referring to the repeated ingestion of these familiar foods, which had been core slave rations, as itself a kind of "slavery." He argued that postemancipation black eaters should "throw off the old habit" and embrace a new, more varied cuisine that he regarded as more fitting for freedpeople.[14]

In my book *Every Nation Has Its Dish: Black Bodies and Black Food in Twentieth-Century America*, I examine Washington's dietary advice to the black community in great detail. In particular, Washington advocated for the right of freedpeople to eat high-status foods like beef and wheat bread in addition to the fatty pork and cornmeal that commonly appeared on working-class tables. During his long tenure as the principal of the Tuskegee Institute in Alabama, Washington paid careful attention to the menus in both the students' and teachers' dining rooms and asked that copies of daily meal plans be sent to him even when he was away on his frequent fundraising trips. He sent letters from places like Boston and New York chastising the staff for not serving enough beef and wheat.[15] Although he was pragmatically willing to serve ubiquitous southern poverty staples when the budget and the larder were particularly low, he also wanted his students to sample more luxurious, less familiar foods.

Since European colonization in the Americas, the core foods of wheat and beef had been used to symbolize American prosperity and vitality. Late nineteenth-century medical professionals and early home economists shared the belief that beef was the healthiest, most sophisticated, and most culturally appropriate form of animal protein. In the United States, beef's status as a preferred food was a preference inherited from British forbearers, and throughout the nation's history beef consumption was used as a status symbol and as a litmus test to measure belonging to an Anglo-accented conception of American culture. Progressive Era food reformers bent on assimilating immigrants from white ethnic groups into the mythical American melting pot often promoted foods like beef tea as tonics of citizenship.[16] Beef eaters were viewed as higher class or as "more American" than those who could not afford the relatively expensive meat or who made different food choices.

Washington's campaign to encourage his students to eat what he labeled "clean, fresh beef" was a particularly unusual and proactive one in the context of the time and place.[17] In the South, beef remained a rarity and a symbol of exclusivity and luxury well into the twentieth century. As late at the mid-1930s, only 12 to 14 percent of the meat consumed by all rural southerners was beef.[18] Thus, for white southerners too, beef was hardly everyday fare.

By feeding his students beef, Washington was advocating for far more than culinary *equality*; he wanted to feed his students a diet superior to that eaten by the institute's white neighbors.

Wheat bread, another item that Washington insisted upon serving at Tuskegee, has often been used as a corollary symbol of US national belonging. The preference for this grain has a long transatlantic history and represented a holdover from the culinary worldview of European colonists who favored light-colored wheat bread over loaves made from darker grains like barley, rye, or, in the New World context, corn.[19] Because the initial European settler colonists struggled to grow wheat, they consumed cornbread out of necessity, and corn remained a predominant dietary staple in the South well into the twentieth century.[20] Yet despite its ubiquity on southern tables, the initial symbolic labeling lingered in the minds of many.

Elizabeth Engelhardt demonstrates that in the early twentieth century food reformers still viewed cornbread as a food choice synonymous with "ignorance, disease and poverty." Cornbread was denigrated, she argues, because it could be made quickly with locally produced meal, unlike wheat flour, which was generally produced outside the South and took more effort to transform into bread.[21] To eat white bread one had to have the means to purchase the flour, the relative leisure to spend time kneading and proofing the bread, or, increasingly, the ability to participate in the market economy by buying loaves of premade, fluffy white bread. Thus, having access to wheat bread became synonymous with privilege and sophistication. In the twentieth century, this historically favored grain also became a symbol of progress. Wheat was the idealized bread of both the past and the future. Andrew Bobrow-Strain argues that industrially produced wheat bread in particular was viewed as "a perfectly shaped, perfectly clean, perfectly white spectacle of modern progress."[22]

When Washington defended his students' right to consume these symbolically significant foods that had been coded as luxurious, high status, and quintessentially American, he was making a quiet but assertive case that they be awarded first-class citizenship in recognition of their ability to perform the culinary rites of belonging. W. E. B. Du Bois, an outspoken critic of Washington's political positions and leadership style, actually agreed with many of his rival's ideas about proper eating habits. He concurred that some aspects of southern food traditions were problematic. For example, in 1918 he argued in the pages of the *Crisis* that pork should assume a far less prominent place on black dinner tables. He urged the black community to make thoughtful food decisions and to defend their right to consume a well-rounded diet.[23] To an even greater extent than Washington, Du Bois emphasized the connection between food choices and bodily health. His desire to unsettle the traditional southern diet was accompanied by a set of alternative dietary suggestions, namely the consumption of fruits, vegetables, and fish, foods he regarded as more nutritious.[24]

Du Bois's interest in the subject of diet can best be understood in the context of the postemancipation moment when white medical professionals and insurance underwriters routinely argued that African Americans born into freedom suffered from a wide variety of health conditions that had not plagued their enslaved ancestors. White Americans intent upon making the argument that black Americans had fared better when under the "care" of white slave owners than in the new era argued that conditions like tuberculosis and other infectious diseases were increasing in the black community. Frederick L. Hoffman, a statistician for the Prudential Life Insurance Company, published a detailed comparative study of black and white mortality rates in 1896. He concluded that black Americans were much more likely to die prematurely than white Americans and were thus a poor life insurance risk. In Hoffman's assessment, higher black mortality rates and health differentials among the living could be explained by inherent "racial traits or tendencies" that rendered black bodies more vulnerable.[25]

Black food reformers who wished to counter the belief that black bodies were inherently different and inferior to those of white Americans had to grapple with the fact that these stereotypes were not only perpetuated in the realm of popular culture, they were also validated in the realm of academic scholarship. Hoffman's claims were bolstered by the work of scientific racists earlier in the century who had claimed that there were indeed physiological differences between black and white bodies.[26] Some of these purported physical differences contributed to the idea that black and white people had different taste sensibilities and attitudes toward food. For example, in the 1830s, French anthropologist Julien-Joseph Virey argued that African-descended people were naturally gluttonous, claiming that "in the negro species, the forehead is retreating, and the mouth projecting, as if he were made rather to eat than to think."[27] More than a century later, similar ideas about black gluttony endured. In a study that appeared in English in 1915, Albert de Gobineau wrote disparagingly about the black appetite, claiming: "All food is good in his eyes, nothing disgusts or repels him. What he desires is to eat, to eat furiously, and to excess."[28] These imaginary black gluttons could, the racist logic that followed argued, only survive if their white superiors helped moderate and control these tendencies.

Du Bois refuted these ideas about an innate black tendency toward gluttony, in part, by demonstrating care and caution in his own dietary choices. Throughout his life he carefully monitored his caloric intake and his waistline.[29] However, he made his most assertive argument against the racist claim that black bodies were inherently different and inferior to white ones in the academic rather than the personal realm. He pointed out statistical errors in studies allegedly documenting black bodily difference and argued that poorer health outcomes for black people could best be explained by the fact that African Americans were far more likely than white Americans to live in poverty.[30] He was quick to point out that impoverished people inevitably ate inferior diets.[31] Better living conditions, including a better food supply, could, Du Bois hoped, improve the health of the entire black community. For Du Bois, good eating habits were primarily a means of shoring up the black body. A black community that ate a better diet would, he hoped, be better equipped for the task of fighting against white supremacy.

In order to disempower erroneous ideas about African American ways of eating, many food reformers felt they had to focus not only on *what* they ate but also upon who prepared and served the food. In the minds of many white Americans, black people constituted a class of perpetual servants.[32] When some white eaters thought about African American food habits at all, they envisioned cheerful and maternal cooks who used their culinary skills primarily for the benefit of white employers. This idea was personified most famously in the figure of Aunt Jemima, the bandana-wearing General Mills advertising symbol used to sell pancake mix beginning in the 1890s. For well over a hundred years she has proved to be an effective marketing tool whose smiling face has been used to sell a fantasy along with a product.

M. M. Manring convincingly argues that when buying Aunt Jemima products, white customers purchased not only the tools necessary to make a quick, convenient breakfast, they were also buying into the idea of black subservience, of "a slave, in a box."[33] The image of a willing black servant helped assuage white fears about black quests for economic advancement and social equality. Aunt Jemima did not seek to challenge the prevailing social order. Instead, her aim was to make life easier and more pleasant for anyone who bought her products. Historian Rebecca Sharpless explains the appeal of this character this way: "The image of Aunt Jemima rooted itself deeply into American consciousness, representing a reassuring tie to the Old South in which cooks worked happily for whatever reward came their way."[34]

The mammy and other distorted representations of black servants were recycled in various forms throughout American restaurant dining culture and beyond in the early decades of the twentieth century. In the 1920s, customers at the Culver City, California, Plantation Club, which was built to resemble a columned "big house," could dine on eclectic dishes like "Plantation Chicken Tamales" that were allegedly prepared by an aproned "mammy" with a tooth-some grin. Guests were invited to wash their food down with drinks prepared by "Rufus," a caricatured antebellum black butler.[35] In the 1930s, customers at Daley's restaurant in Richmond, Virginia, made selections from elaborately illustrated menus advertising dishes such as "Chef's Hammy-Mammy Dinner," a feast that for $1.50 included a cocktail or soup, chicken, gravy, Virginia ham, biscuits, and dessert.[36]

Some white believers in the myth of the mammy were not content to confine these representations to the printed page and sought more dramatic ways to embody her. In 1923, the US Congress voted in favor of a maudlin plan created by the members of the United Daughters of the Confederacy to erect a statue of an antebellum mammy figure in the nation's capital.[37] Although black activists rallied to prevent this white supremacist fantasy from being erected in marble in Washington, DC, they could not prevent some white culinary entrepreneurs from building architectural tributes to these imagined characters. In 1940 restaurateur Henry Gaude took white America's fascination with the idea of the mammy, quite literally, to new heights when he built a roadside restaurant in Natchez, Mississippi, called Mammy's Cupboard. The restaurant was built in the shape of a giant, bandana-clad woman sitting atop a red brick skirt, which served as a dining room. For almost eighty years Mammy's Cupboard has attracted customers intent upon eating chicken salad sandwiches or lemon icebox pie while sitting inside the embodiment of a nostalgia for slavery.[38] When it was erected, this giant figure served as a southern counterpart to four Coon Chicken Inns, which had inscribed white fantasies about perpetual black servility onto the built environment in the American West beginning in the 1920s. Diners entered these restaurants by traveling through the smiling mouth of a grinning black man wearing a porter's cap.[39]

The presence of mammy and her equally fawning and subservient male counterparts on both American cultural and physical landscapes was understandably infuriating to African American activists intent upon challenging these crude representations as part of their quest for racial advancement. Mary Church Terrell clearly articulated collective pain over the travesty of the congressional plan for a mammy memorial statue when she proclaimed that if one was ever erected the black community would "fervently pray that on one stormy night the lightning will strike it and . . . send it crashing to the ground."[40] For her part, Charlotte Hawkins Brown tried to work both with and against the myth of the mammy. She too opposed the Washington, DC, monument, but she also looked for ways to utilize the myth of the one-dimensional mammy to benefit the black community. In 1919 she published a short pamphlet titled "Mammy: An Appeal to the Heart of the South," where she attempted to capitalize on white southern sentimentality in order to advocate for the better treatment of the formerly enslaved.[41] Her larger goal, however, was to make sure that future generations would not find themselves in a situa-

Figure 4.2. Mammy's Cupboard Restaurant in Natchez, Mississippi, 2008. Photo by Carol M. Highsmith, Library of Congress, LC-DIG-highsm-04148.

tion where they were dependent upon the largesse of white employers. She too was frustrated by the fact that African American ascendency was continually challenged by images of black servility both on and off the pancake box.

Black women were conscious of the fact that they were embodied refutations of the mammy stereotype. As a woman who hired servants and had never worked as one herself, Mary Church Terrell's very existence contravened these distorted versions of black domesticity. The daughter of a wealthy businessman, Terrell grew up in a household with a family cook and thus never learned even basic kitchen skills. After her marriage she taught herself to cook by reading domestic science training manuals and attending classes and demonstrations, but she also regularly hired servants to help her manage her home.[42] Although Terrell was able to refute ideas about universal black servility through the class performance of employing servants to aid her, she realized, of course, that her background and her circumstances were unusual. Working-class women could not easily follow her example of using middle-class housekeeping practices as a tool for racial uplift.

As a member of the segment of the black community that W. E. B. Du Bois labeled the "Talented Tenth," which was admonished to use their relative privileges to help lead the less fortunate members of the race, Terrell looked for ways to empower less privileged women who not only did not have the means to hire servants but due to the paucity of other options had to work as domestics themselves. In keeping with the motto of the National Association of Colored Women, "Lifting as We Climb," Terrell's domestic reform strategy was twofold. As a member of the elite, she hired servants to help her model elegant and sophisticated menus in her own home, serving dishes like oyster stew, lamb chops, and homemade ice cream to her guests.[43] However, she understood that the working-class women whom she hoped to "lift" alongside her did not have the luxury of performing their equality and sophistication by drawing upon a wide range of dietary choices. Those who worked as servants themselves were in fact likely to encounter comparable foods to those that appeared on the Terrell table only in the homes of their employers. So, in Terrell's effort to support this group, she had to embrace a different strategy.

For Terrell and other reformers of her ilk, one way to "lift" black domestic workers and to disempower the myth of mammy, a character for whom cooking skills were allegedly innate, was to advocate for greater professional training for servants. Terrell's firsthand experiences managing her household likely helped convince her to reach the conclusion that vocational training programs were needed to improve the skills and thereby potentially also the prestige of black cooks. Although she was an unusually sympathetic employer, Terrell was embarrassed by the lackluster skills of one of her cooks who contaminated a dessert intended for guests with coal oil and another who served "badly curdled" soup and lamb chops "tough as leather" to her friends.[44] Ultimately, however, Terrell was less concerned about her intermittent and peculiarly middle-class problem of hired helpers spoiling her dinner and more alarmed by the fact that black servants were overworked and underpaid. More skilled domestic workers could, she hoped, command higher wages and more respect. Writing in the *Colored American* in 1900, Terrell urged wealthy members of the race to remember the National Association of Colored Women in their wills so that the organization could embark upon the "special work" of establishing a school where "colored girls could be thoroughly trained in all the branches of household art."[45]

Terrell and other African American advocates for what was then known as training in "domestic science" made the calculated bargain that even if they did not have the power to restructure society and remove black women from the position of servant, they could endeavor to elevate the status of servant by offering opportunities for better training. Journalist and civil rights leader T. Thomas Fortune declared that "any school that succeeds in arousing in one of our young women the desire to become a good cook does God and humanity a service."[46]

A variety of black educational institutions and organizations responded to the call to provide domestic science training to black women. Professional servants or homemakers who wanted to elevate the fare that appeared on their family tables could sign up for cooking classes sponsored by churches, women's clubs, or organizations like the National Urban League. Those who were interested in a more intensive course of study could enroll in programs such as that offered by Nannie Helen Burroughs at the National Training School for Women and Girls or at Booker T. Washington's Tuskegee Institute, where they received training on a variety of subjects ranging from menu planning to basic cooking skills to chemistry and biology related to household management.[47]

The dual emphasis on training and professionalism for working-class cooks and of elegance and sophistication for middle-class eaters may have worked to put some occasional dents into white ideas about black culinary inferiority, but these performances of proper food habits had a much greater impact on those who practiced them than on the society they hoped to transform. By thoughtfully comporting themselves, which included making careful decisions about what and how they ate, African Americans worked to create a positive sense of self that was impervious to the stereotypes that surrounded them.[48] The privacy of black homes and institutions providing nurturing

Figure 4.3. Cooking class at the Hampton Institute, circa 1900. Photo by Frances Benjamin Johnston, Library of Congress, LC-USZ62-95109.

spaces where favorable representations of African American culture could flourish. Even black domestic servants who had to suffer from the myriad indignities of working in white households could create an alternative reality and inhabit a different social role in their own homes. However, as they knew all too well, maintaining personal dignity became much more challenging outside of black domestic spaces. One of the places where African Americans faced the most challenges in practicing the lessons in proper food behavior taught by Brown, Terrell, Washington, Du Bois, and others was in the realm of travel when daily routines had to be surrendered for the uncertainty of the unknown.

Beginning right after the Civil War, streetcars and railroads became some of the most contentious public spaces where black and white Americans played out tense dramas designed to establish the dynamics of race relations in the postemancipation period. African Americans steadfastly defended their right to travel in dignity in whatever class of accommodations they could afford, while white Americans leery of black social and economic advancement sought to confine African Americans to inferior accommodations as a means of marking them as inferior. The struggle over segregation in the realm of transportation reached a disappointing culmination in 1896 when the Supreme Court upheld a Louisiana segregation law and ruled in *Plessy v. Ferguson* that separate accommodations for white and black rail passengers were legal as long as the facilities were equal.

Although southern states quickly embraced the principle of legal separation, they did so without embracing the mandate for equality. In the aftermath of the *Plessy* ruling, black Americans could expect to be confined to inferior traveling spaces such as the "smoker" car, which was filled not only with tobacco smoke but also soot and sparks from the locomotive.[49] The indignity of being confined to a space overflowing with environmental toxins was often compounded by rough and uncomfortable seating and by the fact that African American passengers could never reliably depend upon having access to regular food service. The rail companies quickly determined that providing separate dining cars for black passengers would be too costly, and they dealt with the issue of supplying food for black passengers in a haphazard and inconsistent fashion. Sometimes they provided segregated seating or allowed black customers access to the facilities after white consumers had finished eating. Other times waiters would bring food—which was often cold, leftover, served without dishes and cutlery, or even partially spoiled—directly to the colored section. Other times, they denied black passengers the opportunity to avail themselves of food services altogether.[50] During World War II, one black pilot recalled an infuriating ordeal when trying to order a meal when traveling by train from Washington, DC, to his base in Tuskegee, Alabama.

Upon boarding, he discovered that the dining car had only four seats reserved for black customers. Hungry would-be diners had already formed a line that spanned the length of several cars as they waited for a chance to be seated. As a result, the pilot had to stand until the train reached North Carolina while waiting for his turn.[51] These inconsistent and discriminatory policies meant that when traveling by rail African American passengers knew they could not count on having the opportunity to purchase any food at all, let alone a sanitary and appetizing meal. As a result, black travelers had to make elaborate advance preparations to be sure their basic needs would be met.

In the 1920s, frequent traveler Joseph K. Bowler assembled a traveling kit designed to help spare himself as much of the indignity and discomfort of traveling by rail as possible. He brought along overalls so that he could protect his good clothing from the soot, tobacco juice, and animal waste that often soiled Jim Crow coaches. He also brought along a generous supply of canned goods, a small table, and a portable stove that he used to prepare meals for himself while on the road.[52] Although few wanted to risk traveling without taking into account the problem of finding food in advance, most African American travelers made slightly less elaborate preparations than Bowler. Instead of bringing supplies that would enable them to cook fresh meals on the road, many traveled with boxed lunches filled with already prepared, easily portable food. These traveling meals were often packed by loved ones who, as Psyche Williams-Forson points out, "'traveled' vicariously through food provisioning."[53] Family members, often women, who were left behind could help protect the people they cared about from some of the stress and hazards of travel by making sure that their basic need for food and drink were met. Depending upon the budget and inclination of the eater, these meals might include easily portable items such as fried chicken, pie, boiled eggs, and biscuits. One doting South Carolina mother who wanted to be certain that her son had enough food for a journey to a different region of the country packed biscuits, multiple pans of cornbread, rice cakes, a large assortment of both pickled and fresh vegetables, cooked beans, cooked bacon, ham, beef jerky, and dried fruit.[54] These ubiquitous boxed meals were such a common part of the black traveling experience in the early twentieth century that black passengers talked about riding a "chicken bone express," joking that common travel routes were already littered with a trail of chicken bones left behind by those who had preceded them.[55]

Black passengers who did not have the ability to plan ahead often had to go hungry. Ruby Hurley, an organizer for the NAACP who traveled throughout the South, remembered having to deal with the indignities of traveling long distances by bus. Because she was on the road for long periods of time traveling from place to place in support of the civil rights movement, she often did not have the time or resources to pack elaborate portable meals. She recalled that "the places to eat were all segregated, and I was not going to eat in a segregated place. So if I ran out of Hershey Bars, then I didn't eat until I got someplace where I could be fed." Given her hectic schedule and the lack of accommodations for black passengers, she often went without food for twenty-four hours.[56]

After mass-produced automobiles became available in the early twentieth century, those African Americans who could afford them gained a new opportunity to shield themselves from the poor travel conditions on Jim Crow coaches. However, although middle-class passengers could ride in cleanliness and privacy in their own cars, they could not indefinitely insulate themselves inside their vehicles. The need to buy gasoline, relieve themselves, and find safe places to eat and to rest forced black motorists periodically to leave the comfort of their vehicles and to directly confront Jim Crow. As Mia Bay points out, black drivers "traversed a landscape in which not even their money was always welcome."[57] They could not assume that southern gas stations would serve them, and even when they were able to purchase fuel they were often unable to use restroom facilities or purchase food at roadside cafes. For these reasons, black travelers often carried toilet tissue, vessels to urinate in, extra gas, and, of course, ample supplies of food.[58]

In 1959, white southerner John Howard Griffin enlisted the aid of a dermatologist to darken his skin so that he could travel through the South and gain insights into the daily struggles of black people during the era of segregation. During his experiment, he was astonished at how difficult it was to gain access to even the most basic necessities. His days revolved around looking for "a place to eat, or somewhere to find a drink of water, a rest room, somewhere to wash my hands," things that he acknowledged that "all whites take for granted."[59] Soon he learned to eat enormous portions of foods when he had access to provisions, because even though he had money in his pocket he knew that nothing could buy him "a cup of coffee in the lowest greasy-spoon joint." He bitterly observed, "No matter where you are, the nearest Negro café is always far away, it seems."[60] Although Griffin had the luxury of transgressing racial boundaries and of abandoning the burdens of second-class citizenship at will, black Americans who were not in a position to sample the white privileges that Griffin had temporarily abandoned were condemned to a lifetime of navigating the logistical challenges of finding sustenance when away from home.

Between the 1930s and the 1960s, a number of black travel guides appeared, which were designed to help African American travelers find resources and accommodations while traveling.[61] The most enduring title in this genre was *The Green Book*, which was created by New Jersey mail carrier Victor H. Green. Green's guide was published between 1936 and 1967, disappearing only after the passage of the Civil Rights Act of 1964, which outlawed segregation in places of public accommodation and made Jim Crow roadmaps less of a necessity. The annual guide directed travelers to friendly filling stations, restaurants, and boarding houses along their travel routes. The book quickly became an indispensible resource for motorists.

Travelers passing through large cities could hope to find numerous black-owned businesses and a wide variety of dining and lodging options. In 1947, *The Green Book* informed African Americans seeking lodging in Atlanta, Georgia, that they could choose between six hotel options, the local YMCA, and a boarding house. The guidebook directed those looking for meals and entertainment to nine restaurants, taverns, and nightclubs, many of which were clustered on Auburn Avenue in the heart of the black community. Although the guidebook was perhaps the most convenient way to find this kind of information before leaving the comfort of one's own home, black travelers who were less prepared likely would have found the "Sweet Auburn" neighborhood by means of city directories, word of mouth, or signage upon arrival in the city. However, travelers headed toward remote areas that lacked a large cluster of black businesses were especially well served by the guidebook, which gave the names of local black families who were willing to accommodate travelers. Motorists passing through the smaller town of Greensboro, Georgia, in 1947 could not simply check into the Hotel Royal as they could in Atlanta. Instead, they relied on the guidebook's invaluable tip that local residents Mrs. C. Brown, Mrs. E. Jeter, and Mrs. B. Walker might welcome them.[62]

Travel, although potentially exhilarating, could also be destabilizing. For African Americans who had learned to navigate the racial boundaries of their daily lives in one locale, movement to another location with a different set of rules—some clearly articulated and some only understood by the insiders who were privy to them—could be unsettling. During the era of legalized segregation, black Americans who made journeys outside of the home and their region had to look for creative ways to provide for themselves along the way by doing research about dining options on their routes and, most frequently, by bringing items of food from home. While serving to nourish black bodies on the one hand, these foods from home also became transformed into powerful symbols of home when consumed in a different locale. When black travelers permanently settled in destination cities, they made a lasting impact on the culture. Sometimes, they also ruffled the taste sensibilities of local residents.

After he reached adulthood, Chris Jackson, the Harlem-born son of southern transplants, finally admitted what many of his country relatives had suspected all along when he confessed that he had once thought that he was better than his "bama-assed cousins in the South." As a child during the 1970s and 1980s, Jackson was certain of his northern superiority. To his young mind, the urban built environment, beginning with the elevator that transported his family to their seventeenth-floor apartment in a housing project, clearly testified to regional preeminence. He was also certain of his more sophisticated cultural taste, most notably his appreciation for the newly emergent genre of hip hop. A family friend who "played country music in his minivan, ate hogshead cheese right out of the wrapper, and still talked like a black Roscoe P. Coltrane even after decades in New York" had given him reason to distrust the taste sensibilities of southerners. However, neither his southern relatives nor the displaced southerner trying to reclaim some of the sounds and tastes of home were perturbed by Jackson's childish scorn. Instead, his Harlem neighbor chastised the boy for his "clean fingernails and fancy tastes" and, by extension, for his lack of appreciation for his own southern roots.[63]

Jackson was better able to understand this clash of generational and regional sensibilities as an adult than as an impressionable and status-conscious child. He was able to look back with both bemusement and understanding about the cultural politics of that particular era. Later he also understood that his experiences were emblematic of countless other episodes that played out between African Americans who identified strongly with southern culture and those who wanted to disassociate themselves from a region deeply connected with the histories of slavery and Jim Crow. His grandparents had settled in New York in the early decades of the twentieth century, hoping to leave behind the limits imposed by the Jim Crow system in their native states of Florida and North Carolina. In doing so they became part of a massive demographic shift known as the "Great Migration," which took place between 1910 and 1970 when six million African Americans left the South for urban centers in other regions.[64] Southerners heading north or west with their knapsacks, suitcases, or trunks filled with precious belongings and with the food needed to sustain them on what was often a disagreeable if not downright perilous journey also brought a set of food expectations and taste sensibilities that sometimes seemed foreign or repugnant to members of the black community already living in places like New York or Chicago.

The first dramatic surge of migration began during World War I when the flow of European immigrants coming to work in the United States was cut off. The nation's seemingly insatiable demand for industrial labor meant that northern employers were more willing than they had been previously to hire black workers. The southerners who left fleeing grinding poverty, racial violence, disenfranchisement, and the other discriminatory mechanisms that undergirded the Jim Crow system often did find better-paying jobs in the terminus cities of the Great Migration. However, they often discovered that food and housing were more expensive, and living conditions were often squalid.

In his 1941 photo essay *12 Million Black Voices*, Richard Wright, who had migrated northward to Chicago from Mississippi, complained about the unscrupulous practices of landlords who subdivided what had once been sizable and comfortable apartments into multiple "kitchenettes." Each tiny unit contained a small stove and a sink. Migrating black families who were limited in their housing options by customs of residential segregation often even more entrenched than in the South had no choice but to rent these units, often for exorbitant rates. According to Wright, the "Bosses of the Buildings" renting out each room of a subdivided seven-room apartment for $6 a week could make a total of $42 a week, an astonishing sum when one considered that a white family living in a different neighborhood could rent a multiroom apartment for $50 a month.[65] To make matters worse, Wright explained, local municipalities neglected already overcrowded black neighborhoods, which were plagued by inadequately lit streets, piles of garbage, and roads and sidewalks in disrepair. Isolated in these islands of segregation, black customers shopping at local stores were often forced to choose between "stale and rotten food" sold at prices as high as those charged for "first-rate and grade-A commodities . . . in other sections of the city."[66] For southern migrants, procuring sufficient and sanitary food was an ongoing problem that was solved only by communal effort and ingenuity.

Researchers for the Chicago Commission on Race Relations (CCRR) who were seeking to understand the living conditions in Chicago in 1919, a year when a violent conflict between black and white Chicagoans led to thirty-eight deaths and more than five hundred injuries, concluded that local residents often had trouble making ends meet. The CCRR studied the cost of living for 179 African American households and concluded that most of these families paid one-half to one-third of the primary wage earner's income in rent. To make up for budget shortfalls, most households relied not only on a family wage, where all able members of the family worked at least part time, but also upon taking in lodgers and charging them room and board. The father in one household earned $22.50 a week, and the family spent $55 a month on rent. In order to supplement their income, they housed three lodgers and served daily meals to seventeen other people in order to earn an extra $26 a week.[67]

"Mr. and Mrs. J." migrated to Chicago from Henry County, Georgia, in 1917. Upon their arrival in the north, they traded in a four-room cottage with a garden and space to keep livestock for a dingy rooming house and later for a "warm, but dark and poorly ventilated flat" that they shared with their married daughter, her husband, and a nephew. Their $25-a-month rent was five

Figure 4.4.   Crowded kitchen in Chicago tenement, 1941. Photo by Russell Lee, Library of Congress, LC-USF34-038642-D.

times more than what they paid in the South, but their wages were higher. While living in Georgia, the husband earned about $1 a day for agricultural labor, and the wife earned from fifty to seventy-five cents a day performing the same tasks. After migration, Mr. J.'s first job was in the Chicago Stock Yards, which commonly employed black workers to aid in the transformation of cattle into meat. He earned $3 a day for that gruesome job before finding better employment in an iron casting company for $30 a week. Mrs. J. supplemented the family income by occasionally doing laundry for $4 a day. Even though their collective earning power was much greater than it had been in the South, the costs of daily living—which included gas, coal, insurance, clothing, transportation, and food—absorbed all their income, leaving them little or no money to spend on healthcare or recreation.

Mrs. J. complained that although the couple gained many things by moving North, including the right to vote and better treatment by their employers, in many ways life was harder. She remarked, "In the South you could rest occasionally, but here, where food is so high and one must pay cash, it is hard to come out even." She missed having a garden and the ability to raise her own food and mourned the fact that the changed system of procuring food had also negatively impacted her social life. She missed the warmth of communal dining experiences in the South, complaining that in Chicago "one is never invited to dine at a friend's house . . . they cannot afford it with food so high." Although her husband had once worked in the meat-processing industry, the family subsisted on a largely vegetarian diet of greens, potatoes, cabbage, and bread subsidized occasionally by milk, meat, and eggs.[68]

Although in many respects, their life was dramatically different in Chicago than it had been in Georgia, the core of their diet remained remarkably similar to the typical southern, working-class diet. Even though the CCRR researchers who recorded their story did not give specific details about what kind of meat and bread they were eating, it seems likely that the meat they ate a few times a week was pork. Furthermore, the bread that Mrs. J. baked daily was probably made from cornmeal. In her Pulitzer Prize–winning study *The Warmth of Other Suns: The Epic Story of America's Great Migration*, Isabel Wilkerson provides evidence to suggest that the J. family was not alone. She noted that even decades after leaving their southern homes, many migrants were still serving "the same southern peasant food, the same turnip greens, ham hocks, and corn bread" in places like Chicago or New York that they would have eaten in places like Georgia or Mississippi.[69] Those who were able to establish a degree of financial stability often used some of their resources—both in terms of time and of money—to prepare elaborate meals that reminded them of home. In the 1950s, Harlem residents George and Inez Starling and Babe and Hallie Q. Blye took pride in feeding both themselves and a steady stream of southern visitors well. Sometimes this meant going to the supermarket to purchase supplies and then grilling ribs. Other times Babe would go to such great lengths to recreate the foods of his Florida home that he would devote some of his scant leisure time to opossum hunting in upstate New York or Connecticut. When he returned from a successful hunt, Inez and Hallie would then cook up the rural delicacy and serve it alongside chitterlings and collard greens.[70]

Some southern transplants were able to capitalize on their appreciation for the foods of their childhood by starting small businesses selling things like fried chicken, catfish, or barbecue to other migrants who took comfort in their ability to patronize businesses that promoted their southern identification with place names like "Georgia Food and Fish Hut" or "Dixie Fish."[71] Food businesses were relatively easy to start up because many would-be culinary entrepreneurs already had cooking experience, not only from cooking for themselves and their families but often from working as domestic servants. Those who could raise the necessary start-up capital might open small grocery stores, lunch counters, or other restaurants. Others with fewer resources soon discovered that it was relatively inexpensive to set up a barbecue cart or another kind of food vending stall on a city street. Most small food-oriented businesses were relatively short-lived due to the fact that not all would-be restaurateurs had either the requisite cooking or bookkeeping skills to succeed or the ability to outperform better-funded businesses owned by individual white people or, increasingly, by corporations. Despite the odds against them, some managed to establish stable, if not lucrative, small businesses. For example, "Pig Foot Mary" became wealthy by selling southern, working-class food on the streets of New York in the early twentieth century.

Lillian Harris Dean migrated to New York from Mississippi in 1901 to work as a domestic servant, but her larger ambition was to own her own business selling iconic southern foods. She saved some of her wages and bought a baby carriage, which she repurposed to use as a vending cart. Dean then made an arrangement with a local saloon to use their stove to cook her food, rigged up a heater to keep her wares warm in her cart, and started selling pigs' feet in the San Juan Hill neighborhood of Manhattan. In 1917, she relocated her business to the corner of 135th Street and Lenox Avenue in Harlem, and she soon became a local fixture who was known for her commanding presence, for her collection of starched gingham dresses, and for unforgettable renditions of not only pigs' feet but also foods like chitterlings and fried chicken. She patiently saved her profits until she had sufficient funds to purchase a five-story apartment house at the corner of Seventh Avenue and 137th Street for $42,000. She bought other buildings in New York as well as houses in Pasadena, California, beginning a second career as a landlord. When she died in 1929, her estate was valued at an astonishing $375,000.[72]

Dean's remarkable story speaks to one individual's tenacity, skill, and luck, but it also demonstrates that the community that made Dean wealthy had a tremendous appetite for the food she was selling. Ironically, many southern migrants actually became more fond of the foods they had left behind when they arrived in their new destinations. Items that had once been unremarkable, everyday fare took on a new resonance when transplanted to an environment where a different set of food traditions were predominant. Ralph Ellison famously captured the power that food had to conjure up memories of home in his novel *Invisible Man*. His unnamed protagonist buys a baked sweet potato from a vendor on the streets of Harlem and is "overcome with such a surge of homesickness that I turned away to keep my control."[73] Migrants could feel reconnected to family left behind and transported back to fondly remembered experiences of their childhood when savoring similar taste sensations.

Many worked hard to maintain access to beloved southern foods and to keep cherished recipes alive. In the 1910s southern migrants living in the

South Side of Chicago celebrated southern food traditions by frequenting the numerous "pig ankle joints" that sprang up throughout the neighborhood. They tried to transfer the pleasures of a down-home summer to their equally stifling urban neighborhoods as they cooled off by eating watermelon when the temperatures soared.[74] Cash-strapped New Yorkers sometimes raised the money they needed to pay the rent on their big-city apartments by charging admission to parties where they served foods like pork chops, Hoppin' John, chitterlings, and fried fish to community members who were hungry for a taste of the South.[75] People with southern origins living in places like Oakland, California, could be easily spotted by the collard and turnip greens growing and chickens roosting in tiny, urban backyards.[76]

Members of the black community who were already established in Great Migration terminus cities like Chicago often watched these unabashed displays of black working-class gastronomic delight with a sense of horror. Many among this group had tenuous cultural ties to the South. Others had self-consciously worked to sever those connections and to adopt food practices that they deemed respectable and generically "American." As Tracy Poe argues, "For urbanized people, eating proper foods in a sanitary, civilized setting such as the home or a restaurant was a social ritual that indicated one's level of respectability."[77] The *Chicago Defender* captured the ethos of both the already established and the aspirational middle classes through articles that urged readers to eat quietly, thoughtfully, and moderately.[78]

Self-consciously middle-class, respectable eaters were afraid that the food sensibilities of the new arrivals who ate things like offal that they bought from vendors on the street instead of packaged and canned goods purchased from indoor shops would reflect badly upon the entire race. In the first few decades of the twentieth century, already established black residents of Chicago prided themselves on the high degree of integration in the local restaurant scene, a state of affairs they attributed to their refinement and good taste.[79] Local African American physician George Cleveland Hall worried that the "shiftless, dissolute and immoral" working class might behave in such a way that they would close tenuously opened doors and foreclose other potential opportunities for middle-class advancement.[80] However, holding to middle-class social norms and using food practices as a marker of social status were not mutually exclusive. Sociologists St. Clair Drake and Horace Cayton noted that so-called Gentleman Racketeers in Chicago liked to demonstrate their cultural refinement at the dinner table, serving "wild duck and pheasant in season, chicken and turkey in season and out, and always plenty of the finest spirits and champagne."[81]

Although they were sometimes characterized as both uncouth and intractable, newcomers all had to make some cultural adjustments. Dietary studies sponsored by the US Department of Agriculture in the late nineteenth and early twentieth centuries reveal that African Americans who left the South tended to give pork and corn a somewhat less prominent place in their diet and were more likely to eat a much wider variety of foods, including greater quantities of beef and wheat.[82] In doing so, they followed the same pattern of many European immigrants who took advantage of American food abundance and increased earning power to purchase more luxurious foods than they had been able to eat in their home countries.[83] African American migrants who lived in close proximity to people from around the globe were exposed to new tastes that they began to incorporate into their diets.[84] For example, black Americans were often frequent and enthusiastic customers at the inexpensive, desegregated chop suey joints that sprang up in urban centers throughout the country.[85] In 1926, race woman Alice Dunbar-Nelson went to watch Ethel Waters perform on Broadway, had cocktails with a friend, and, like many other urbanites, ended her evening out at a "chop suey place" where she ate what she described as a "sobering dish."[86]

Like working-class people everywhere, African American transplants balanced competing interests when making food decisions. They often vacillated between a desire for novelty and deep feelings of nostalgia, affective states that they had to moderate with concerns about the economy and availability of particular foods. However, although they added to and subtracted from their baseline southern diets, most never completely discarded the food culture of their youth. As James R. Grossman argues, on the whole "migrants refused to blend inconspicuously into a cultural landscape defined by middle-class sensibilities and imperatives."[87]

Ultimately, the millions of southerners who were part of the Great Migration southernized the foodscape of whatever cities they arrived in in large numbers. Soon visitors to African American neighborhoods in any part of the country could expect to find foods that closely resembled their southern counterparts. Paul Freedman argues that eventually many black urbanities who had once derided this food as "country" cuisine began to embrace it as a "common cultural possession" of all black people, "even for those who had not grown up on a farm in the South."[88] However, many members of the black community were too absorbed with the daily task of making a living to become permanently embroiled in the politics of dietary selection. Inevitably, much of the community's collective energy was channeled toward the task of simply finding enough to eat, a problem that was exacerbated when the Great Depression led to a surge in unemployment.

The Search for a Common Table during the Great Depression and World War II

$\mathcal{O}$n September 24, 1939, hundreds gathered for full day of singing, fellowshipping, and feasting at the Rockland Palace, a Harlem event space. The guests arrived hungry, knowing that the culmination of the event would be a formal 6 p.m. dinner where, astonishingly, more than two hundred distinctive dishes would be served.[1] Many of the African Americans in attendance had been financially devastated by the Great Depression and were likely in desperate need of a satisfying meal. Nonetheless, for some, the chance to enjoy a mind-bogglingly decadent repast was secondary to their desire to hear the host of the event, Reverend Major Jealous Divine, speak. The chance to be in his presence offered its own form of sustenance.

Although this particular feast was unusually spectacular, Divine regularly hosted meals where at least fifty dishes were served throughout the 1930s. Few New Yorkers, of whatever background, had not heard about these banquets, which were open to all comers. Intriguingly, in spite of his current fame, few knew much, if anything, about where Divine had come from. His physical appearance and accent suggested that he was an African American from the rural South. Divine, however, vehemently eschewed racial labels, referring to himself instead as "dark complected." Furthermore, he was hardly forthcoming about his origins.[2] Rumors circulated claiming that he had been born in Virginia, Georgia, the Carolinas, or possibly the Sea Islands.[3] One of his biographers, Jill Watts, has worked to untangle the lingering mystery, arguing that in all likelihood he was born George Baker Jr., in Rockville, Maryland, in 1879 and that his mother, Nancy Miller, was a former slave.[4]

This commonplace origination story did not suit the mysterious image Divine hoped to cultivate. According to the thousands or, by his own count, the millions who followed him, "Father Divine," sometimes also known as "the Messenger," was God incarnate. Worshippers awaiting his arrival at this meal or others like it would swing, sway, and clap, declaring in song, "Father Divine is all I need, all I need" or "Just give me sweet Father Divine." For some the ecstasy of knowing that they would soon be in the presence of a deity was so great that they threw kisses in the direction of their leader's portrait, shrieked, danced wildly, collapsed in reverie, or even seemed to have sexual orgasms in anticipation of his arrival.[5]

Astonishingly, when it was time to eat, the enthralled crowd managed to contain their excitement and follow a prescribed protocol that dictated that seating at the table was to be segregated by sex but integrated by race. The Messenger asked his adherents to follow a rigid moral code, forbidding them from using profanity, smoking, drinking, or having sex. His insistence on chastity was so strong that he allowed men and women to interact with one another only in limited and restricted terms, and they were forbidden from sitting side by side at ritual meals.[6] Although he was adamant about social separation in that sphere, he was equally insistent that his white followers, who were less numerous though no less ardent than black believers, be dispersed throughout the dining room. Race, he argued, was a false category, and his movement was designed, in part, to destabilize the concept and to fight the evil of racism.[7]

Those assembled for the 1939 feast were guided through the culinary aspects of the experience by elaborate red and purple, rose-covered menus that were designed to help them navigate what promised to be an overwhelming dining experience. Charles Braden, a student of religious studies, attended a similar gathering several years later, during World War II. He was astonished to encounter an abundant feast despite wartime rationing. Initially Braden took a small amount of every steaming dish that appeared, but when he realized that the rice, green beans, peas, cabbage, corn, tomatoes, lima beans, greens, and carrots were soon to be followed by roast beef, ham, fried chicken, duck, turkey, and a vast array of other side dishes, he realized that a better strategy was to become "more selective" about which items he would sample.[8] Diners at the 1939 gathering who had the chance to look through the menu had an advantage over Braden when deciding how to fill their plates.

When it was time to eat, Father Divine would greet the crowd, making it clear that all who were hungry were welcome. He then rang a shiny, silver dinner bell, signaling that it was time to begin. At the 1939 banquet and scores of others like it, Father Divine handled every plate of food that emerged from the kitchen as a way of conferring his blessing upon the food and upon those who would consume it.[9] Diners passed plates to one another, never letting a platter rest on the table, and in doing so performed the group ethos of sharing.[10] One by one, platters containing forty-five different vegetable dishes were followed by numerous kinds of meat. If they had room left on their plates, diners could choose from seventeen varieties of bread, ten different kinds of salad, numerous sauces, relishes, and cheeses. The meal was to be washed down by a choice of seven varieties of cold drinks or five hot ones. Finally, if anyone could bear to eat more, twenty-four different dessert offerings completed the meal.[11]

The food selections were designed to appeal to every taste sensibility. The menu ranged from foods that referenced the rural South such as cornbread, black-eyed peas, and a variety of pork products including feet, tails, snouts, and ears, to those associated with the diets of European immigrants, such as pumpernickel bread, or with contemporary health food movements, such as the roasted grain coffee substitute Postum. However, even if menu items were standard fare, the names of the dishes were sometimes unfamiliar to newcomers. One guest had to decipher the reference to "stuffed angel eggs" for a baffled reporter for the *New York Times*, explaining that the label was an attempt to give a holier-sounding name to the familiar favorite picnic dish of deviled eggs.[12]

Readers of the *New York Times* who were treated to a detailed description of the 1939 feast were likely already acquainted with the phenomenon of "Holy Communion Banquets" being held at private homes, churches, and community spaces, primarily in Harlem, but also elsewhere in the New York metropolitan area. The *Times* regularly covered Divine's activities, including a spectacular Easter Parade in Harlem in 1934. On April 2, thousands of New Yorkers lined the streets to watch worshippers dancing and singing to music provided by instrumentalists standing on trucks. Women wearing white sweaters and emerald skirts sang, "He is God, God, God," while Father Divine himself flew over their heads, looking down upon the spectacle from a red airplane. The parade culminated at a large banquet hall where waiters wearing uniforms adorned with the embroidered words *Father* and *Peace* were waiting, ready to distribute Easter eggs, cake, and cold meats to the needy.[13]

Spectacles such as this one must have seemed particularly surreal in the context of the mass deprivation of the 1930s. During the Great Depression, many survived in large part thanks to food charity programs administered by the government, churches, and other organizations. Even middle-class people who were accustomed to earning enough money to provide for themselves often had to learn to accept handouts. Felix Goodwin, the son of a Kansas schoolteacher, remembered that when the school system temporarily stopped paying black teachers, his mother become eligible for food relief. Although she was too proud to accept the assistance, her hungry children were not. While she was at work, Goodwin and his brother went to the local food distribution center and filled a wagon with butter, flour, sugar, potatoes, and canned beef, which they took home and transformed into a savory pie. When their mother returned to the smell of cooked food, she cried, claiming that they had disgraced the family by accepting charity. Fearing hunger more than shame, the boys returned to the food distribution center each time the larder was low. The also learned to bring a hatchet to guard their supplies from the other neighborhood children after they learned the sad reality that "not everybody had even what we had."[14]

By 1931, hundreds of breadlines serving tens of thousands each day had sprung up in New York City alone.[15] That year, Harlem's Abyssinian Baptist Church soup kitchen gave out more than thirty thousand free meals between Christmas and Easter alone.[16] Soup, because it was made with scraps and could be stretched with water, was a relatively affordable way to feed a crowd. Frequently relief officials distributed food supplies that the needy could cook in their own homes; however, these rations were chosen with economy and nutrition in mind but not flavor. In fact, culinary historian Andrew Coe argues that relief organizations sometimes deliberately gave out foods without seasonings or condiments precisely because they did not want hungry people to become too comfortable or eat too well on the basis of these handouts.[17] In the late 1930s, a hungry family of four living in Chicago might be eligible to receive a box of food containing prunes, butter, dried beans, rice, celery, oranges, and cabbage, which would ensure survival but certainly not luxury.[18] Oatmeal, evaporated milk, carrots, turnips, and canned tomatoes were other items commonly dispensed to the needy.[19] Relief boxes sometimes included concoctions created by home economists that were designed to pack as many nutrients as possible into one ingredient. For example, in New York, the needy might receive Milkorno, a substance designed by nutritionists at Cornell University, which contained cornmeal, powdered milk, and salt.[20] Megan Elias points out that although foods like Milkorno could certainly keep people alive, they did not necessarily fulfill cultural expectations for what food should look and taste like. Thus, many of the hungry suffered from what Elias calls a "double displacement" because not only did they have to cope with constant food shortages, when they finally did get something to eat it might not be the "*right*" food as they define it."[21]

Father Divine's decadent banquets stood in stark contrast to the thin soups, stale bread, and random surplus ingredients that many hungry New Yorkers had become accustomed to relying upon. Anyone was welcome to participate in his love feasts and could either eat their fill for free or give a small donation if they could afford it. Significantly, they could also expect to dine on well-prepared food and, given the number of items served at even Divine's most modest feasts, they had the luxury of making choices. They could, in that unusual setting, be *both* beggars and choosers who could expect to eat familiar, culturally resonant foods at his table. Dorothy Evelyn, who was born in Harlem in 1924, experienced both the breadline and the banquet table. She remembered eating soup and what she and her friends called "prison bread" covered with peanut butter and jelly that was dispensed by St. Mark's Catholic Church. That experience stood in unfavorable contrast to her memories of eating as much fried fish as she wanted at Father Divine's table.[22]

Believers struggled to explain how Divine managed regularly to feed hundreds of hungry people not just subsistence rations but multicourse meals of preferred foods. Some claimed that their god could make money materialize out of thin air and then use those funds to feed the hungry. Others argued that he had the ability to multiply existing resources and could, for example, pour endless cups of coffee out of a small pot.[23] Historians have offered other explanations for these overflowing larders, which are less mystical but in some ways equally profound.

Divine's followers exported the traditions of this organization, which became known as the International Peace Mission Movement, beyond New York to Philadelphia and then to various West Coast cities as well as to Canada, Western Europe, and Australia.[24] The most ardent believers lived communally in Peace Mission "heavens," contributing their wages to the entire religious community. Divine cultivated a communal ethos, and members were encouraged to think of themselves not as individuals but as members of a mighty collective. This primarily African American, working class, and majority female movement combined their collective earning power not only to host decadent meals, they also bought real estate, founded businesses, and created an agricultural cooperative.[25]

By the mid-1930s, the Peace Mission movement owned three apartment buildings, approximately thirty single-family homes or apartments, and several large meeting spaces in Harlem alone.[26] Followers ran numerous cooperatively owned restaurants, markets, and other businesses. Peace Mission restaurants served ample meals for the low cost of five or ten cents, and servers were forbidden from taking tips. Hotels and rooming houses offered similarly low rates, making Divine's businesses popular with cash-strapped Americans from all walks of life.[27] In addition to these urban enterprises, the Peace Mission Movement established a rural cooperative called the "Promised Land" in Ulster County, New York. By 1935, the Promised Land consisted of two thousand acres containing farms, hotels, stores, and other small businesses. The rural outposts of the Peace Mission provided their agricultural products for the communion feasts and supplied the organization's food-related businesses in urban areas, creating an impressive and self-sustaining system of provisioning.[28]

It is not a coincidence that Divine attracted such a large and passionate following during the Great Depression, a moment when the majority of the black population was in need of a solution to the dire problem of finding sustenance. African Americans in urban areas who were long accustomed to being the "last hired and the first fired" suddenly had to compete with unemployed white people for even the dirtiest, dangerous, and least desirable jobs, positions black workers had monopolized during better economic times. Throughout the Depression, black unemployment rates were generally twice that of whites, reaching at least 50 percent, and sometimes even higher. In the rural South, black tenant farmers struggled to survive on a food supply that was more precarious than ever as the pressure increased to use tillable land to grow the inedible cash crop of cotton. Cash-poor landowners and merchants reduced the supply of credit that many depended upon to purchase supplies and, in the worst-case scenario, evicted surplus laborers from the land altogether.[29] For many, their misery was overwhelming, and the bounty at Father Divine's tables seemed fantastical when contrasted with the palpable aura of widespread hunger. Furthermore, the Peace Mission movement offered dignity in the form of a freely offered seat at the banquet table rather than the humiliation of standing in a breadline or of begging for relief.

Writer Richard Wright remembered the humiliation of asking for financial assistance from local relief administrators as a young man living in Chicago during the Great Depression. After he showed up at his appointed time to field questions from a middle-class social worker, Wright resented having to make "a public confession of my hunger." Although he secured a promise that food supplies would be delivered after his interview, he left feeling condescended to, with "the knowledge that the relief officials had not wanted to give it to me."[30] In 1941, after he had become an internationally famous writer no longer condemned to begging for food, Wright had the opportunity to take part in a Peace Mission banquet in New York alongside a white friend. A deeply secular person, Wright found the emotional worship scene that accompanied the banquet unsettling. Other members of the black intelligentsia generally shared Wright's disapproval of Father Divine, a figure Wright later satirized in the form of a charlatan called "Daddly Goodness" who preyed upon the vulnerable in order to make himself rich.[31] However, many who lacked Wright's ability and opportunity to write his way out of poverty found far more hope at the banquet table than in the welfare line. For those who struggled to feed themselves, the seemingly endless supply of food seemed like nothing short of a miracle. In the 1930s, many were in need of just that. Divine told his believers, "We are going to manifest this mighty love right here in this dining room and from here we are going to manifest this Truth from shore to shore and from land to land."[32]

The Messenger inspired his followers to believe in the power of positive thinking. His beliefs were a variant of New Thought theology first associated with Phineas B. Quimby in the early nineteenth century and then famously adapted by Mary Baker Eddy, founder of the Christian Science Church. Both argued that the mind had the power to heal the body. Building upon this idea, Divine believed that thought was a powerful force that could be harnessed for social good, or conversely, could cause great social damage if misused. He regarded poverty and racism, two of the chief problems affecting the black community, as the outgrowth of negative thinking.[33] In his world-view, the Great Depression itself was the result of a collective failure to accentuate the positive. He inspired his followers to believe that they had agency, and that they could, by shared force of will, end a global economic crisis and create a better world simply by thinking the right kind of thoughts. In order to demonstrate their belief in him and in the power of optimism, adherents changed their names, shedding birth monikers for titles like "Lovely Life" or "Sweetness Love."[34] These whimsical-sounding new names were a first step in changing their reality.

The Peace Mission strove to utilize the structure of capitalism to create the businesses that would sustain their community outreach and their communal living spaces (as well as fund an opulent standard of living for the movement's founder) without absorbing the individualistic and competitive ethos of the system. At a moment when radical critiques of capitalism were resonant among many dispossessed Americans, the idea of combining forces to form a collective where everyone contributed what they could and no one went hungry held obvious appeal for many. For thousands, the Peace Mission Movement helped make up for the shortfalls of the growing, but still inadequate, federal welfare state.

Franklin D. Roosevelt's enormous New Deal programs demonstrated that the federal government had accepted an unprecedented degree of responsibility for assuring the financial stability of the nation's citizens. Those who designed this federal initiative searched for creative ways to feed, house, and employ the citizenry while also building up the nation's infrastructure and restoring faith in institutions such as the troubled banking system. Due to their overwhelming need, African Americans benefited from some New Deal programs in disproportionate numbers. For example, African American city dwellers were twice as likely to receive some form of financial aid or food relief than white citizens.[35] Many benefited from initiatives like the Works Progress Administration, a massive job creation program, which was required to hire African Americans in numbers proportionate to their percentage of the population. Black employees of the WPA were hired in relatively large numbers for even high visibility jobs. Five thousand worked for the WPA Education Program, offering classes to a quarter million African Americans. Others worked as artists, writers, and researchers, receiving government funds to support their creative and intellectual contributions.[36] A variety of other initiatives helped needy members of the black community not only to eat or find employment, but also assisted them with other necessities including securing housing, childcare, and job training.[37] However, despite these gains, many programs deliberately excluded or unrepresented black Americans.

For example, New Deal bureaucrats notoriously betrayed the interests of black citizens with the passage of the 1935 Social Security Act. This foundational program was designed first and foremost to provide a guaranteed pension for retirees. However, both domestic servants and agricultural workers were explicitly excluded from the program. Because such a large percentage of the black community worked in one of these occupations, this exclusion was deliberately discriminatory.[38] Black Americans also received a "Raw Deal" from local officials, particularly in the South, who distributed relief monies unequally to black people when they were not excluded altogether. For example, the state of Arkansas paid white families who were eligible for financial assistance an average of $12 a month while black families typically received half that amount.[39] When they received government jobs, African Americans were often forced to work in segregated conditions for lower wages than white workers.[40] The Tennessee Valley Authority, which provided jobs, housing, and electricity to some of the nation's poorest rural citizens, only hired African Americans for menial and temporary jobs and never for supervisory positions.[41] Only 1 percent of the organization's enormous payroll went to black workers. Furthermore, black people were excluded from many of the organization's innovative housing initiatives. For example, white TVA workers in Norris, Tennessee, were able to rent comfortable, affordable homes in a "model village" while African Americans were housed in poorly constructed barracks a distance away from the pristine, new homes because they allegedly "did not fit into the program."[42]

Throughout the nation, many black Americans were dependent upon this flawed but vital welfare system; however, Divine made sure that his followers relied upon him rather than the state to meet their needs. Members of the Peace Mission movement were forbidden from accepting charity in any form. In 1938, Divine told Hattie Read that she had to repay $148.80 she had received from a relief fund in Baltimore, Maryland, if she hoped to take up residence in a Peace Mission "heaven." The eager convert astonished a local judge by repaying the money in full and then asking for a receipt, which she planned to use as her "passport to Paradise."[43] The particular "heaven" Read had her heart set upon entering was at Krum Elbow, an estate owned by twenty of Divine's followers, which was located near FDR's Hyde Park mansion. The Krum Elbow estate contained twenty-eight buildings and sprawled over two hundred acres of farmland, orchards, and vineyards.[44] It is clear that such an environment would indeed seem otherworldly to a working-class person like Read who was accustomed to just scraping by. Given the unequal distribution of New Deal resources, her decision to put her faith in Divine and not in the government seems like a reasonable gamble. Instead of a "New Deal," Divine offered her what Benjamin Kahan has labeled a "Divine Deal." Divine's programs, though open to anyone regardless of race, gender, or social class, held the most obvious appeal to those who had been the most disadvantaged by the current economic, political, and social systems.[45]

The idea of developing a collective economy where resources were shared among group members who severed ties with the world outside was one that predated Divine's movement. His program resonated with many of the same members of the black community who had been attracted to Marcus Garvey, whose Universal Negro Improvement Association (UNIA) was also headquartered in Harlem. The Jamaican-born Garvey's admiration for Booker T. Washington, the founder of the Tuskegee Institute and a booster for black business ventures, first led him to visit the United States in 1916. Sadly, Garvey never had the opportunity to meet his hero; however, he took core Tuskegee ideas about black economic nationalism and radically amplified them. He urged African diasporic people throughout the globe not only to dream of pulling themselves up by their bootstraps as entrepreneurs in white-dominated societies but also to aspire to create an independent black nation-state. Garvey soon led what Robert A. Hill calls "the largest organized mass movement in black history," declaring himself the provisional president of a future African state.[46] In 1920 the UNIA announced that they hoped to build a "Black House" to serve as an analog to the White House in Washington, DC, and to symbolize the fact that black Americans were part of a separate nation.[47]

Garvey inspired millions of African-descended people around the globe to contemplate the possibility of uniting against racial domination and, in varying degrees, to embark on a program of nation-building. His greatest sphere of influence and the location where he made the most progress toward actualizing his program was in the United States. In Harlem, male UNIA members drilled in elaborate military uniforms, which were inspired by imperial European designs. Black women marched wearing the chaste uniforms of the Black Cross nursing corps, demonstrating their readiness to support their troops.[48] Despite their martial attire, Garvey's soldiers did not fight any actual wars; instead they focused upon the political unification and economic advancement of the black community. They founded numerous businesses, some of which were designed to make sure that members of the black community had enough to eat.

Whereas Father Divine set a common table, the UNIA advocated for separatism, setting up food-related businesses run exclusively by and for the black community. Most famously, the organization's ill-fated Black Star Line was conceptualized as a means of facilitating trade among people of African descent throughout the globe. In 1919, the UNIA agreed to pay $165,000 for a ship named the *Yartmouth* that eventually proved to be so unseaworthy that she was later sold as scrap metal for a mere $1,650. After purchasing the ship, Garvey optimistically accepted a contract to deliver liquor to Cuba prior to the beginning of Prohibition in the United States, but the cargo had to be quickly offloaded to prevent the struggling ship from sinking. Nonetheless, the UNIA managed to make the vessel temporarily seaworthy, making a trip to the Caribbean where locals came out in large numbers to admire the black-owned ship. The *Yartmouth* picked up a cargo of seven hundred tons of coconuts in Jamaica, but by the time it returned to the United States, the coconuts had rotted.[49] Sadly, the *Yartmouth*'s misadventures were a preview of what was to come. Garvey's dream of creating a black-controlled global trading network ultimately remained just that. Closer to home, the UNIA worked to feed the black population by opening grocery stores and restaurants that were, temporarily at least, more successful than the Black Star Line. Furthermore, Garvey not only strove to provide his followers with access to black-produced food, he also gave them instructions about how to eat it.

While Father Divine encouraged his followers to view the act of eating as a spiritual one and to punctuate ritual meals with hymn singing and worship, Garvey emphasized the need for bodily discipline. He told UNIA members that they should never eat in the street or chew gum in public. He warned that if they did so, they would "lose respect immediately for not having regular meals hours" and for "having . . . meals in an improper place."[50] Savvy, race-conscious consumers could be assured of having a meal in a proper setting if they chose to eat at Universal Restaurant #1, housed in Liberty Hall, the organization's headquarters. Diners at the restaurant could eat cuisine prepared under the supervision of Mary Lawrence, a food chemist and hospital dietician who was well versed in the latest scientific information about nutrition.[51] UNIA members were to exhibit manners that would exemplify racial pride and personal dignity, and they were also to eat superior food that had been deemed pure and healthful according to the standards of the day. Furthermore, Garvey not only gave diners the opportunity to demonstrate dignity and a regard for their health, he also utilized mealtime as an opportunity to perform a ritual demonstration of race pride. For example, on August 21, 1921, five hundred guests were treated to a banquet at Liberty Hall designed to do just that. The room was lavishly decorated with ferns and flowers, and gold-embossed menus advertised familiar dishes reframed as at least nominally "African." Attendees were invited to consume "Punch Africanos," "Liberian chicken," "Liberty special ice cream," and "Black Cross macaroons."[52] In the act of eating foods that had been given place and race-conscious labels, guests were also performing a unified, transnational black identity.

The rituals and business enterprises that sought to make Garvey's vision tangible were appealing to many. US officials were alarmed by the explosive growth of the UNIA, which could soon boast having established one thousand divisions of the organization worldwide. Garvey, who was a far better propagandist than bookkeeper, did a poor job managing the finances of the enormous organization, inadvertently opening the door for federal officials who indicted the charismatic leader for irregularities in the finances of the Black Star Line. Garvey was convicted of fraud, briefly imprisoned, and finally deported from the country in 1927.[53] He continued his political activities from Jamaica and London, but without his charismatic presence nearby, UNIA businesses in the United States began to crumble. Signs of trouble had loomed even before his departure. Garvey complained that the grocery stores and restaurants were mismanaged by employees who stole funds, bemoaning the fact that "we simply could not get the men of our race to realize that they were doing themselves a great injury in not working for Negro corporations as honestly as they worked for white ones."[54] The advent of the Great Depression further destabilized the organization's businesses, signaling the end of the heyday of the Garvey movement.[55]

To the surprise of some, many displaced Garveyites found their way to Father Divine's tables.[56] From exile, an enraged Garvey informed those he saw as defectors that Divine was "just a man" and a "mad or wicked" one at that.[57] At a 1936 UNIA convention in Toronto, Canada, members passed a resolution condemning Divine as being a "blasphemist" and urged all "sane, intelligent, and self-respecting Negroes" to stay away from his movement.[58] Garvey's sense of confusion about the fact that people who had once operated in the orbit of the UNIA could find Divine's ministry appealing is understandable. Although both Garvey and Divine thought that one of their obligations was to help feed the black community and each formed an impressive network of business ventures designed to do just that, Divine hoped to assemble his followers around an integrated table while Garvey was a staunch separatist. Yet beyond that core difference, Divine and Garvey had many similarities that neither seemed to recognize.

They drew followers in with their personal charisma, insisting that all members of their organization were worthy of respect. Although they reached different conclusions about the nature of God, neither worshipped a deity who was white.[59] Furthermore, Robert Weisbrot argues that many African Americans could transition easily from one group to the next because both movements were all consuming, providing "a vital center of existence" for converts. Anyone who "offered total devotion" received "absolute security" from an insulated group that promised to serve as a buffer between them and a hostile outside world.[60] Garvey and Divine both appealed to people who, due to the difficulties of navigating a racist society, had difficulty making sure that their basic bodily needs were met.

The appeal of combating the Great Depression as a member of a group rather than as an all-too-vulnerable individual appealed even to members of the black community who were unlikely to get swept up in the emotional fervor of a mass political or religious movement.[61] Black journalist George Schuyler and civil rights activist Ella Baker founded the Young Negroes' Co-operative League (YNCL) in 1930, encouraging African Americans throughout the country to form consumer education study groups, to found buying clubs and cooperative stores, and to jointly negotiate for lower prices.[62] Race leader W. E. B. Du Bois shared their enthusiasm for the idea of economic cooperation, a concept in which he had a longstanding interest. As early as 1907 Du Bois had sponsored an Atlanta University study titled *Economic Co-Operation among Negro Americans* that, among other things, documented numerous attempts to sustain black-owned cooperative groceries.[63] In 1919, Du Bois founded the short-lived Negro Cooperative Guild in an effort to promote new collective possibilities. At least one member of the organization enacted the group's theoretical commitment to developing jointly owned businesses, founding first a study group and then later a collective meat market in his hometown of Memphis.[64] In Du Bois's mind, the urgency of developing community-owned businesses had increased dramatically by the era of the Great Depression.

Although he was one of the most prominent members of the National Association of the Advancement of Colored People, an organization devoted to the goal of creating an integrated society, Du Bois's vision for financial collaboration was a purely intraracial one. On January 1934, he published an editorial in the organization's organ, the *Crisis*, bluntly titled "Segregation." Du Bois firmly argued, "It is the race-conscious black man cooperating together in his own institutions who will eventually emancipate the colored race, and the great step ahead today is for the American Negro to accomplish his economic emancipation through voluntary determined cooperative effort."[65] Although Du Bois was publically scornful of the cult of personality surrounding Marcus Garvey, whom he regarded as "the most dangerous enemy of the Negro race in the world" and as "either a lunatic or a traitor," the essence of their economic prescription for the black community was the same.[66]

African Americans throughout the nation responded positively both to the idea of harnessing their collective bargaining power as well as to the resurgent desire to create and support black-owned businesses. African Americans opened cooperatively owned grocery stores in all regions of the country.[67] Cooperatives were particularly widespread in Harlem and included Harlem's Pure Food Co-Operative Grocery, the Modern Cooperative Association, and Harlem's Own Cooperative.[68] Harlem's Own sold memberships for $5 each, and members could shop for milk, meat, vegetables, and canned goods at low prices.[69] Thus it was not only political leaders like Du Bois and Garvey or religious figures such as Father Divine that played a leadership role in fighting the ravages of the Great Depression. Ordinary people pooled their resources in the hopes that together they could pool enough to ensure group survival.

Despite the grandeur of these dreams and the fervor of proponents of cooperation, most collectively owned businesses were relatively small and short-lived. These efforts, though valiant, were ultimately no match for the overwhelming need of black Americans. Due to their limited access to capital, black Americans simply could not complete with other racial and ethnic groups in establishing enough businesses to meet the needs of their community. For example, Chicago had 815 black-owned retail stores in 1929, the largest number of any city in the United States. Although that number is impressive, particularly given the obstacles that black business owners faced whether as individuals or even as part of a collective, Lizabeth Cohen notes that black Chicagoans had only managed to open one store for every 287 black residents of the city. In comparison, there was one Italian-owned store for every forty Italians and one Polish-owned store for every thirty-nine Polish people residing in Chicago.[70]

Given the reality that most African Americans were, by necessity, forced to patronize white-owned businesses, many mobilized to seek better treatment from these companies throughout the 1920s and 1930s. In 1927, the *Chicago Whip* advocated for a "Don't Spend Your Money Where You Can't Work" boycott of local businesses, a concept that was soon adopted by activists throughout the nation.[71] For example, in 1933, the New Negro Alliance (NNA) successfully pressured the Temple Luncheonette and Drug Company, which operated in a black neighborhood in Washington, DC, to improve wages for black waitresses and to hire African Americans for managerial positions.[72] On an even larger scale, the NNA led a boycott and staged demonstrations designed to get the A&P grocery store chain to hire black workers as clerks rather than as lower-paid janitors, particularly in black neighborhoods. They won major concessions from the company, which agreed to hire black clerical staff in a variety of locations in the northwestern part of the city and to give black employees greater opportunities for career advancement.[73]

Although these collective efforts helped ameliorate some of the harshness of the era as the black community worked together to fight for better

Figure 5.1.   The Perfect Eat Shop, a black-owned restaurant in Chicago, 1942. Photo by Jack Delano, Library of Congress, LC-USW3-001469-D.

jobs, higher wages, and lower prices on consumer goods, it was ultimately the US mobilization for World War II that pulled the entire nation out of the grips of the Depression and improved the economic circumstances of black citizens. Black financial prospects increased along with the rest of the nation. However, the differential between white and black earning power, though decreasing, remained substantial. Prior to the war, African Americans earned, on average, about 40 percent as much as white workers. They earned an improved, but still meager, 60 percent after the conflict ended.[74] Part of the increase in wages was linked to the fact that during the war years black Americans had greater access to industrial jobs, which paid substantially higher wages than agricultural work. During the 1940s, 1.5 million southern African Americans migrated north or west looking for better opportunities, and they often found them.[75] Due to wartime labor shortages and federal policies prohibiting discrimination in defense industries, African Americans, who made up 10 percent of the US population, held 8 percent of the jobs in the war industry in 1945. Furthermore, the number of black Americans working in skilled or managerial positions doubled during the war years.[76]

Even long-exploited southern domestic workers were able to use the labor shortages of the era to negotiate for better wages. For example, Anna Mae Dickson managed to quadruple her pay after leaving her job as a domestic servant in a small Texas town to work performing similar tasks at a boarding house in Houston, Texas.[77] Faced with the prospect of losing their black servants, terrified white employers spread rumors about the existence of "Eleanor Clubs," purportedly named after the First Lady who had been outspoken in support of civil rights. Allegedly, these clubs were composed of militant black women determined to agitate for better wages and working conditions or, in more extreme cases, to encourage black women to leave their domestic posts altogether. This ultimate scenario inspired terror in the hearts of the ruling class who knew that the departure of black employees would force southern white women back into the kitchen.[78] Although there is no evidence substantiating the existence of organized clubs of this kind, the availability of better-paying war industry jobs actually did free many black women from the drudgery of domestic service, making it much harder for middle-class white women to hire help.

Writing in the National Urban League's *Opportunity* magazine, George E. Demar explained that by 1943 for "many Negro women the idea of a 'career' outside the 'cook kitchen' loom[ed] for the first time as a reality."[79] The percentage of working African American women employed as domestic workers fell from 60 percent to 44 percent between 1940 and 1944.[80] In the aftermath of this transformation, one black women famously quipped that "it took Hitler to get me out of Miss Anne's kitchen."[81] Indeed, World War II represented a turning point in the cultural and culinary landscape of the South as white women could no longer count on benefiting from the skills of an underpaid black woman to help feed her family.[82] Increasingly, only the wealthy could afford to hire domestic servants, and those who did so began, by necessity, to treat their coveted employees with a greater degree of respect than before.[83]

Although black domestic workers sometimes found that they had greater bargaining power than ever before, black, female agricultural workers found that their labor, long vital to the southern economy, was undervalued and sometimes even spurned. During the war years, the shortage of agricultural workers was severe due to the deployment of men overseas, the allure of high-paying war jobs in urban areas, and increased agricultural output.[84] To fill this shortage, secretary of agriculture Claude Wickard, at the encouragement of Eleanor Roosevelt, agreed to support the formation of a Women's Land Army, which placed 1.5 million nonfarm women in agricultural jobs between 1943 and 1945.[85]

WLA recruitment materials were aimed at white, middle-class women who could afford the luxury of serving their country this way. Recruits had to purchase their own uniforms, which consisted of overalls, a hat with a visor, and a denim jacket.[86] WLA pay was far lower than that for other wartime work, paying about half the wages of an average factory worker.[87] Despite these limitations, some black women formally signed up for the program, working, for example, harvesting tobacco in Maryland.[88] However, even black women who had the resources to purchase their own uniforms and the financial ability and willingness to work for low wages were often turned away. Officials in South Carolina deliberately decided to recruit only white women because they feared that if the WLA became known as a "[N]egro program" no white women would be willing to join. Virginia also opted against hiring black women, and Texas refused to participate in the WLA altogether. In that state, officials were unwilling to recruit white women for the low-status jobs that they associated with the nonwhite laborers who continued to work in the state's fields throughout the war.[89] In most southern states, black women made up a large portion of the agricultural labor force, yet they were denied the status of the predominately white WLA members who were celebrated as patriots.[90] White women who worked on farms were lauded for their personal sacrifices as they supposedly gave "up organdy for denim" and left "thoughts of long red fingernails and lacy dresses behind."[91] However, black women doing agricultural labor were generally not perceived as having sacrificed their femininity for the national cause. Instead, many white Americans regarded backbreaking, physical work as befitting of their lowly station in society and regarded their agricultural contributions as unremarkable.

Despite often having their labor in the agricultural sector taken for granted or disregarded, African Americans sought other ways to support the "food front" of the war. In order to increase the amount of food that could be sent to troops and to US allies, the federal government instituted a compulsory food-rationing program while also asking citizens to participate in voluntary activities designed to increase the food supply. Patriotic Americans were to grow "victory gardens" and then can their surplus harvest for delayed consumption. Officials working for the US Department of Agriculture and other government offices aimed at increasing the domestic food supply were frequently surprised to discover how commonplace gardens were in black communities.[92] In the context of the time, some black gardeners had become accidental patriots by doing what they had always done. Some earned plaudits for working as "victory gardeners" even though many gardens predated the war. The backyard plots that had enabled many African Americans to feed themselves since emancipation were suddenly reframed as patriotic undertakings rather than being recognized for what they were: longstanding mechanisms of survival used by underpaid and undervalued black workers who had no choice but to find enterprising ways to feed themselves.

Although gardens were widespread in the black community, they certainly were not universal, particularly in densely populated urban areas. Data collected by the US Bureau of Labor and the Department of Agriculture reveal that African Americans living on southern farms were able to produce as much as two-thirds of the food they ate at home, while black residents of New York City produced less than 8 percent of what they consumed.[93] Some African Americans who had not gardened before took up the challenge of starting victory gardens as a way to support the war effort. One Harlem resident remembered that her neighbors started a garden in a vacant lot and that "everybody on the block took care of the garden."[94] In 1943, the *Detroit Tribune*, an African American newspaper, sponsored a "Yard Victory Garden Contest," asking their readers to plant small gardens using whatever outdoor space—no matter how small—that surrounded their homes. Those who participated in the contest were promised that not only would they be supporting the troops and the nation's allies, they could also enjoy the benefits of exercise and "vitamins absorbed from the sun's rays" and would gain the ability to access fresh food without having to "ask the price or anybody's permission." The newspaper assured interested readers that "no great outlay of money is needed, only a few packages of seeds and a few plants." In an at least partial acknowledgment of the cost associated with starting a garden from scratch, the editors recommended that cost-conscious families economize by sharing gardening tools among neighbors.[95] In the coming months, the periodical supported those who took them up on the challenge by offering a steady stream of gardening advice.[96]

Community initiatives like this one were empowering to members of the black community who often could participate in white-controlled initiatives only on unequal terms. For example, would-be black gardeners in Baltimore interested in taking part in a community gardening project at public school no. 29 could only cultivate a section of ground specifically designated for "colored" farmers. Furthermore, accomplished African American gardeners who wanted to compete for prizes in annual harvest shows not only in Baltimore but throughout the American South could compete only in a separate "colored" category. Historian Amy Bentley points out that although such practices may have seemed like "nothing more than a benign societal tradition to most whites" they were "virulent" for black participants who were constantly reminded of their status as second-class citizens, even as they attempted to support shared national priorities.[97]

Those who found the necessary time and resources to start a garden sometimes found that they lacked the means and support needed to preserve their harvest for out-of-season consumption. African Americans who had never gardened before or who ate seasonally and had never canned their

Figure 5.2. African American man tending his victory garden in Arlington, Virginia, 1942. Photo by Marjory Collins, Library of Congress, LC-DIG-fsa-8c34636.

produce soon discovered that the supplies needed to preserve food were expensive. Particularly for city dwellers and first-time gardeners, canning was a middle-class undertaking accessible only to those who could afford to purchase the necessary tools. Furthermore, African Americans who hoped to learn how to preserve food soon found that community canning centers and classes were often segregated and that the black community was vastly underserved by these initiatives. For example, in 1943 white residents of Baltimore who wished to learn how to can their produce could enroll in any of fourteen classes, while black residents could choose from among only four options.[98]

While black civilians sometimes struggled for the right to participate on equal terms in the effort to augment the national larders, African Americans in the military often struggled to get away from food service. Ultimately a million African Americans served in the military during World War II; however, they often did so under demeaning and overtly discriminatory circumstances. When war broke out, African Americans could not join the marines or the air corps, could join the army only in noncombatant support positions, and could enroll in the navy only as cooks or as messmen who served food and cleared tables.[99] Amy Bentley argues that being assigned to kitchen duties was deeply humiliating for men who resented being placed in a "decidedly subordinate and traditionally female position."[100]

Living in a sexist and white supremacist society that sought to deny them many of the perquisites of midcentury male gender roles, black troops were often eager to demonstrate their manliness by engaging in combat. They were sometimes successful in agitating for the right to fight. For example, World War II veteran Allen Thompson recalled taking part in a hunger strike designed to protest the relegation of black men to supporting roles in the military. The men in his unit resented being trained to drive army trucks rather than tanks. To show their dissatisfaction, he remembered, "We refused to eat. We did not go to the mess hall. We did it as a whole unit. There were a couple of lawyers in the group, and they got us organized. We just did not eat." Remarkably, their protest was successful. Not only did they avoid the dreaded fate of being consigned to the tasks of transporting and loading supplies, they won a second demand: "We even got black cooks because we complained that the white guys didn't know how to cook for us."[101]

Roland Fallin wrote a poem demonstrating the frustration of black men relegated to KP ("kitchen police") duty, most of whom were unable to change the nature of their assignment:

> I'd like to sail the seven seas,
> And wear an officer's cap,
> And chase the Germans and the Jap;
> Not serve the soup or fix the bunk
> On which other men may nap.[102]

As of 1943, there were 26,909 black men enlisted in the navy, two-thirds working as messmen.[103] One navy messman remembered feeling dehumanized in his role, more like an object than a person. "I worked in the mess hall, washed dishes, did the dirty jobs. I mean you were just a 'boot.'"[104] Many resented being sent to segregated cooking and baking classes run by "white petty officers and chiefs . . . [who] knew less than the [messman] who went there."[105] Most suffered from the humiliation of being seen as an interchangeable servant. William Welch Dancy recalls that the messmen who waited on officers not only cooked, served meals, and cleared dishes, they also did other intimate chores. As was the case with female domestic servants working in white homes, black men working in a similar capacity often learned unsavory secrets about the people they served. Dancy remembered, "We knew each officer's habits. We'd read their mail. We'd do their laundry and see the gonorrhea stains in an officer's skivvies. . . . We also listened in on discussions of strategy and tactics."[106]

Although many men understandably bristled at being asked to serve insensitive officers who did not respect them enough to shield them from either personal secrets or sensitive military ones or at being "trained" by white officers less skilled than they were, others found ways to find personal satisfaction in their role. Chester Wright, a navy cook, regarded himself as a "frustrated artist" who used his skills in the kitchen as a means of expressing his creativity. He spent his free time at port working in professional kitchens and refining his skills. A French chef named Pierre gave him a transformational lesson when he told him that in Europe excellent cooks or servers were respected as skilled professionals. Wright learned to blame the "rednecks" in the United States for making black people believe there was something "low about serving," concluding, "'subservience' is a self-inflicted wound—a trip the white man put on you."[107]

William Henry also gained an appreciation for well-cooked food during his time in the navy. While waiting to go on leave, he spent some time with a cousin serving in the army and was appalled by the quality of the food he was served. An army cook complained, "These old sailors come down here, they've been eating steaks and chickens . . . and they think they're going to get that around here." Henry agreed that the ingredients in army meals were inferior to those he was accustomed to eating in the navy, but he also blamed the difference in the quality of the food on the skills of those preparing it, claiming, "you guys are just nasty cooks!"[108] He preferred the food eaten and prepared by locals in the South Pacific to that served by the US military. He regarded the islanders he met as "regular blacks, 'Negroes'—like myself" who knew how to eat well. He recalled stuffing himself on bananas and other local foods and becoming "forty pounds overweight" as a result of his indulgence.[109]

Although some found ways to use food as a means of expressing or enjoying themselves, many African American members of the military continued to experience food customs as tools of discrimination and humiliation. The War Department forbade discriminatory treatment in military base facilities starting in 1943, but African American soldiers could not be sure that the official policy would be respected.[110] While being treated in a US

Army hospital in Alabama, Bill Perry was mortified to find out that he had to wait until the white soldiers finished eating before he could have his meal.[111] When attending Officer Candidate School in Camp Barclay, Texas, Jim Williams recalled that everyone would go to the PX to get a snack between classes. He made a point of rushing to get to the head of the line each day only to discover that the white waitresses served the white soldiers before him regardless of his position in line. When he complained about his ill treatment, he was confined to his barracks for a week as a punishment.[112] Perhaps most appallingly of all, African Americans were horrified to discover that German prisoners of war often had access to segregated dining rooms that excluded black soldiers.[113]

These humiliating experiences were also galvanizing ones. Black soldiers asked to fight for their country became more adamant than ever that they deserved full citizenship rights upon their return. Civilians supporting the war on the home front grew similarly outraged at being asked to support the cause of democracy, the fruits of which were denied. Muriel Rand, the African American actress who starred in the Broadway production of *Carmen Jones*, experienced these contradictions acutely. She accepted an invitation from the US Treasury Department to go on tour to sell war bonds, an event the press celebrated, announcing, "Carmen Jones off on Bond Tour." However, neither her fame nor the fact that she was traveling on behalf of the federal government could spare her the humiliation that awaited her when she deplaned in Atlanta, Georgia. Forgetting for a moment that she had landed in the segregated South, she strolled with the rest of the passengers to the airport lunch counter. Before she could place an order for coffee and sandwiches, she was rebuffed by a waiter, who pointed, yelling, "You can't eat nothin' here!" Her appetite destroyed, she returned to the plane, refusing the offer of a white passenger to bring her refreshments. Afterward, Rand traveled to New Orleans where she helped sell $1,000,000 in war bonds as she "wondered whether it was worthwhile" to support the country that condoned her mistreatment.[114]

Enraged by episodes like that one, in 1942, James G. Thompson, a black cafeteria worker from Wichita, Kansas, wrote a letter to the editor of the *Pittsburgh Courier* suggesting that African Americans supporting the war effort fight a "Double Victory" campaign against both external and internal enemies, against both fascism abroad and racism at home.[115] The newspaper quickly adopted his idea and developed a "Double V" logo that it utilized frequently to remind black Americans of the scope of their struggle. In 1943, students at Howard University similarly made the linkage between the cause of the war and of civil rights clear when they formed a Civil Rights Committee under the auspices of the university chapter of the NAACP and set out to protest segregation in the nation's capitol. They decided to begin by targeting businesses in the predominately black U Street area that discriminated against African Americans in their own neighborhood, causing continual "embarrassment and mortification." Four students entered the Little Palace Cafeteria, placed their orders, and responded calmly when the waitresses refused to serve them. They pulled out schoolwork and refused to budge. More black students trickled in in groups of three until the cafeteria was half filled. The managers closed the restaurant, and the protestors calmly moved outside where they picketed for three days, holding signs that said, "We die together—Why Can't We Eat Together?"[116] In at least this one small instance, their campaign for "victory at home" was successful. The management agreed to change its policy and serve black customers.

The militancy exhibited by these students and others who engaged in similar protests signaled the beginning of a new chapter in US history. Although African Americans had been chafing against the limits of the system of white supremacy since the era of slavery, by World War II the struggle had reached a new level of urgency. Furthermore, the changing political climate seemed to signal that change might be possible. As the next chapter demonstrates, restaurants were to become one of the most significant staging areas in the coming full-fledged battle for civil rights.

· 6 ·

Food as Politics during the Black Freedom Struggle

$\mathcal{O}$n May 28, 1963, Anne Moody, Pearleana Lewis, and Memphis Norman, students at historically black Tougaloo College in Jackson, Mississippi, walked up to the white's-only lunch counter at a Woolworth's five-and-dime store and politely asked to be served. The waitress on duty told them to move to the counter at the back of the store reserved for black customers, but they refused to budge. Sensing their resolve, the waitress panicked, flipped off the lights, and, along with her coworkers, abandoned not only the black would-be customers but also the white diners. The white waitresses had almost certainly seen images of protests like the one that was unfolding before them in the newspapers. After a 1960 lunch counter sit-in staged by four black college students in Greensboro, North Carolina, successfully led to the desegregation of some dining facilities in that city, thousands of young people throughout the South engaged in similar activities, unifying to create a wave of protests against restaurant segregation on an unprecedented scale.[1] The white waitresses in Jackson surely knew what they were in for. Not wanting to be in the crosshairs of the struggle for civil rights, they fled. The protestors, however, stayed put for what was to become one of the most terrifying and infamous sit-ins of the decade.

Somehow the three young people managed to stay serene as the store filled with white students from a nearby high school who began heckling them. The belligerent counter-protestors quickly found a rope, fashioned it into a noose, and began attempting to lasso it over the activists' heads. Someone threw Norman, the only male member of the group, to the ground, kicking him until he lost consciousness. Joan Trumpauer, a white Tougaloo student, quickly made her way through the crowd to take Norman's place. The mob responded by chanting "white nigger" and knocking her off her stool. They then yanked Moody from her perch, dragging her thirty feet toward the door by her hair. After somehow fighting their way back onto their seats, Trumpauer and Moody were joined by three white Tougaloo faculty members, an African American civil rights activist, and a black student from a local high school. This biracial group willingly submitted to three hours of unremitting abuse. Someone punched sociology professor John Salter in the face with brass knuckles and cut him with a broken sugar container. The crowd burned them with cigarettes and doused them with anything they could put their hands on, including ketchup, mustard, vinegar, salt, sugar, and spray paint. Marcie Cohen Ferris points out the painful irony of the fact that "the very food the protestors had peacefully demanded the right to order and be served was used to humiliate and hurt them."[2]

Although they were covered with food, burns, and blood, the protestors refused to leave no matter how abusive the crowd became. Finally, the management decided to close the store. A. D. Beitel, the president of Tougaloo, arrived and escorted the battered group outside where they were met by an even larger crowd of white protestors who had been encouraged by local radio stations to come to the scene and by dozens of police who begrudgingly offered them only minimal protection from the surging, angry crowd.[3] In the aftermath, Anne Moody was in stunned disbelief at "how sick Mississippi whites where." She was chilled at the unfolding realization that "they believed so much in the southern way of life, they would kill to preserve it."[4] Heartbroken and coated with mustard, sugar, and ketchup, she stumbled, dazed and shoeless, into a local beauty shop. Craving calm, normalcy, and soothing hands, Moody asked to have her hair washed. An empathetic beautician rushed her to the head of the line and not only scrubbed her hair but also removed her sodden stockings and wiped the smeared food from her legs.[5]

The central theme recited again and again by participants in the sit-in movement as an explanation for their actions was the desire to preserve their sense of personal dignity. Those who participated in demonstrations at restaurants throughout the country often talked about how humiliating it was to be denied access to dining venues or to be given differential, inferior service. Ironically, their fight for dignity made them subject to a host of other humiliating experiences, such as those suffered by the group in Jackson and elsewhere who faced physical and verbal abuse and sometimes arrest and imprisonment. Yet as Christopher Schmidt observes, "Even efforts to embarrass and demean them became, in the eyes of the students, new opportunities to display and demand recognition of their inalienable dignity" as they calmly and serenely ignored white violence and abuse.[6]

Ella Baker, a mentor to many of the young activists involved in this movement, famously reminded observers that nothing less than "human rights" was at stake in these confrontations, something "much bigger than a hamburger or even a giant sized Coke."[7] It is clear that the thousands who participated in the sit-ins were not putting their bodies on the line merely for the right to consume American junk food. However, the food sold at the lunch counters, diners, and drive-ins targeted by southern protestors was not incidental either. Cokes and hamburgers were, and still are, powerful symbols of American culture and affluence. Being denied the right to consume them on equal terms amounted to an assault on the black protestors' claims of national belonging.[8] Esther Terry, a student at Bennett College in Greensboro, recalled, "We went downtown wearing hats, and we wore gloves, and we were Bennett ladies . . . it was such a jarring thing to be told, 'Well, Bennett Lady, guess what? You can't sit down here and have a cherry Coke.'"[9]

For activists like Anne Moody who had known extreme hunger, the abundant food on display in these restaurants also served as a potent symbol of racial difference. When she was a child, Moody's family suffered from such dire food shortages that her mother would sometimes sneak into her landlord's cornfield and feed ears of corn intended for cattle to her children.[10] Having sufficient food was not something Moody had ever been able to take for granted. In contrast, the white hecklers at the 1963 Jackson sit-in were so confident in their ability to access food whenever they wanted it that instead of preserving it they weaponized it, using it to assault rather than to feed bodies. The contrast in attitudes and experiences was stark.

When civil rights activist Fannie Lou Hamer was a child, she first became aware of racism when she realized, "White people have clothes, they can have food to eat, and we work all the time, and we don't have anything."[11] One of the markers of being white, she realized, was having sufficient food, even enough to waste. Student Nonviolent Coordinating Committee (SNCC) member Betty Garmon remembered finally coming to the realization that "if you don't have a quarter to buy a hamburger, what good is the lunch counter?"[12] So although dignity and human rights were certainly at stake, the material food served at those lunch counters was not something that everyone could take for granted.

Although a sizable number of black southerners suffered from food insecurity, many were willing to share what little they had. Throughout the 1960s, many civil rights workers relocated temporarily to the region to participate in the fight against segregation and to agitate for voting rights. They were continually touched by the generosity of the people they met. Historian Charles Payne argues that the vital contributions of the African Americans who provided food and shelter to civil rights activists has been "largely overlooked" in accounts of the movement, yet the community organizing work performed by SNCC and other groups could not have been successful without the support of local people.[13]

Feeding civil rights workers was not only an act of generosity and sacrifice, it could be dangerous. Hostile whites resented the presence of those they labeled "outside agitators" in their region, and they sought to terrorize or punish the African Americans who supported their efforts. For example, in 1964, the proprietor of a black-run hotel in Philadelphia, Mississippi, reluctantly stopped feeding visiting activists after local whites threatened her physical safety and told her that they would bomb the hotel if she did not stop.[14] Although her decision to prioritize her safety and livelihood was understandable, others continued to feed and lodge civil rights workers regardless of the consequences. Prior to the civil rights movement, C. O. and Minnie Lou Chinn of Madison, Mississippi, were successful businesspeople who owned a farm and a café and made extra money selling bootlegged whiskey. They actively supported the civil rights initiatives and helped shelter and feed the out-of-town organizers. However, the Chinns suffered ceaseless white retaliation for supporting the movement, and they eventually lost nearly all of their property. C. O. was jailed frequently on trumped-up charges, and the family went from being one of the most prosperous in the town to becoming nearly destitute. At one point, Minnie Lou desperately confessed to a civil rights worker that she "ran out of food three days ago."[15]

Countless others, whose names have been lost to history, offered assistance when it was most needed. Late one night, the notorious Alabama sheriff Bull Connor released a group of arrested civil rights protestors, ominously depositing them on the side of a country road. Although they were happy to be out of jail, they were understandably afraid that they would meet an even worse fate after Connor left them alone in the dark, unsheltered and unprotected. Panicked, the young people took the risk of knocking on the door of the first ramshackle shack they stumbled upon, asking themselves, "One of ours, or God help us, poor whites?" Their relief was enormous when an elderly African American man answered their calls. Although he was too afraid to turn on the light and spoke only in whispers, he took them in. The next morning he bought food and fed them breakfast. The man was so terrified of local white people that he went to three different stores to purchase supplies so that he would not attract suspicion by buying unusually large quantities of food.[16] Like this brave Alabamaian, countless others managed to overcome their fear and to overlook the limitations of their own resources to help.

One Delta family that consisted of two parents, ten children, and a grandmother fed and shared their two-bedroom home with two civil rights workers, generously giving the visitors their own private room.[17] Mama Dolly Raines hosted two SNCC workers for an entire summer at her rural

Georgia home, feeding them vegetables from her garden and teaching them how to kill and butcher the chickens she raised.[18] Fellow Georgians Lucius and Emma Kate Holloway, the parents of four children, managed to scrape together the resources to feed and house a steady stream of civil rights workers who "would sleep on the floor, the sofa chairs, anywhere they could find a spot in the house."[19] Despite being in poor health, Dora White cooked breakfast for as many as fourteen student volunteers on any given morning before they went out to canvas for voters. Although having high blood pressure and "sweating in the kitchen" as she tried to summon the strength to continue, she cooked delicious "sauces and gourmet foods" until her body gave out.[20]

Local people not only housed and fed workers involved in voter registration drives and demonstrations in their region, they also cooked for imprisoned activists, who were often inadequately fed by local jailers. When Pine Bluff, Arkansas, resident Helen Hughes Jackson found out that the police would not provide food for the young people arrested during civil rights protests in that city, she asked for permission to feed them herself. Local authorities allowed her to bring in one meal a day as long as she wrapped individual portions separately and delivered them to the jail by promptly 11:30 a.m. Jackson agreed to the conditions, convinced local churches to donate food, and enlisted volunteers to prepare it. In appreciation of her efforts, those who were arrested joked that they felt so well cared for they almost did not want to be released.[21]

When local jailors did provide food, it was often inedible. While locked up in Newton, Georgia, Annette Jones White was served peas, raw onions, and rock-hard cornbread for dinner and a "breakfast of grits topped with grease and generous portions of pork belly complete with nipples." She found the food so appalling that she opted not to eat for several days.[22] After their release from incarceration, activists who refused to eat, whether due to the poor quality of the food or out of protest, could expect to be well fed by movement sympathizers. After a group of Freedom Riders were released from the notorious Parchman Penitentiary, many were hosted at an elaborate supper in Jackson. Local "church ladies" prepared "fried chicken, coleslaw, potato salad . . . [and] peach ice cream!" Carol Silver remarked that the decadent feast was "the Fourth of July ten times over."[23] Stokely Carmichael was similarly grateful to see "welcome tables heaped with food, delicious, clean, southern cooking, skillfully prepared and lovingly presented" after being released from jail, where he had participated in a week-long hunger strike to protest his incarceration.[24]

Potluck dinners like those Silver and Carmichael enjoyed where everyone contributed what they could became an important and dependable source of sustenance for many. SNCC activist Courtland Cox remembered that throughout the week, he often relied on generous, but sometimes still meager, donations from those who "didn't have a lot." To make up for any dietary shortfalls, he recalled, "On Sundays at church, we were able to load up, you know get the cake and the pie and the potato salad . . . a lot of fried chicken."[25] Many small business owners helped too. Miss Quin, the owner of a café in Mississippi, told her staff that when civil rights workers came by "you feed 'em whether they got money or not."[26] The owner of Nastie Sallie's, a small restaurant in Albany, Georgia, would sell activists enough food to feed four or five people for $2. Janie Culbreth Rambeau later remembered the restaurant's delicious shrimp and chicken boxes, sausage sandwiches, and overflowing ice cream cones, recalling that the proprietor sold enormous portions of affordable food to civil rights workers because "she was such a strong supporter of the movement."[27]

During the Montgomery Bus Boycott, Georgia Gilmore and a group of local women organized "the Club from Nowhere" and sold baked goods to raise money to pay for the transportation costs of black workers who had pledged not to ride on the discriminatory bus system. Eager to support the movement, but fearful of white reprisals, group members kept their identities hidden from the establishment, pretending that the goodies they made and the funds they raised came from "nowhere."[28] Before the boycott, Gilmore, a talented cook, worked at the National Lunch Company in downtown Montgomery. Afterward, she not only cooked to raise money to support the effort, she seized upon the opportunity to go into business for herself. Using money that Martin Luther King Jr. lent her, she expanded her kitchen and bought larger cooking vessels so that she could open a home restaurant that would provide food at low prices to the black community. According to John T. Edge, her kitchen became a kind of "clubhouse" where King, who loved her stuffed pork chops, could not only fortify his body but also conduct important meetings.[29] Gilmore's son, Mark Gilmore, remembered watching King and Lyndon Baines Johnson discussing the movement while eating deviled eggs at his mother's table. Johnson was likely not the only politician of national stature to eat Gilmore's food. Edge speculates, "Robert F. Kennedy may have joined King for strategy sessions fueled by pork chops, collard greens, and 7UP cake. Aboard Air Force One, John F. Kennedy likely ate her fried chicken and peach cobbler."[30]

Informal dining spaces like Gilmore's home became vital meeting places because segregation, whether by law, custom, or both, prevented white and black people from eating together publicly in most restaurants. Interracial meals often had to be held in secret or at black-owned restaurants that defiantly welcomed white customers. In Atlanta, activists, white and black, often gathered at Paschal's Restaurant. Founded by brothers James and Robert

Paschal in 1947, the restaurant immediately became the preeminent place where black professionals celebrated special occasions and well-off young people went on dates.[31] Buoyed by their initial success, the brothers opened an affiliated cocktail lounge and hotel, which became, according to the Reverend Jesse Jackson, "the finest hotel for blacks in the country." Paschal's was, he recalls, "the place to go."[32] After King left Montgomery for Atlanta, the Paschal brothers set aside meeting space where civil rights activists could eat, strategize, and recover from the labors. James remembered that for many the restaurant became "their first or second home." Civil rights workers, including the sporadically paid members of SNCC, who could not afford to pay for their fried chicken, collard greens, macaroni and cheese, and peach cobbler, could expect to dine for free.[33]

The food sharing that enabled civil rights activists to continue their work was also at the heart of cross-cultural exchanges as black, working-class southerners interacted, often for the first time, with the middle-class northerners, many of them white, who came South to support the cause of civil rights. Exchanging food was a powerful and sometimes unsettling experience. When southern African Americans ate alongside the white volunteers they hosted, they were breaking a deeply entrenched southern taboo against interracial dining. Black Mississippian Unita Blackwell remembered:

> Cooking . . . some pinto beans . . . that's all we had and . . . everybody just got around the pot . . . and that was an experience . . . just to see white people . . . coming around the pot and getting a bowl and . . . then sitting around talking, and sitting on the floor, sitting anywhere, cause you know, wasn't any great dining room tables and stuff that we had been used to working in the white people houses. . . . But this, you was sitting in the floor and they was talking and you know, we was sitting there laughing and . . . I guess they became very real and very human . . . we each to one another.[34]

Although eating together often helped break down boundaries, such newfound intimacies could lead to complicated dynamics. Laura Foner, a white volunteer from New York, spent almost a year living and working in Gould, Arkansas. She felt incredibly lucky to have the chance to live in the "comfortable home" of Carrie Dilworth, a legendary local activist, who became her "mentor, protector, and friend." However, she had a more fraught relationship with Bob Cableton, a black Mississippian with whom she shared meals. Although the pair worked well together and spent hours talking about politics and analyzing Malcolm X's speeches, there was an ever-present tension between them. Foner recalled that, "Despite mutual respect, his feelings toward me had a love/hate quality. . . . And my feelings were probably love/fear."[35]

African American Annette Jones White remembered hosting northern, white, middle-class volunteers in her home and cooking her favorite foods for them. "Everything I liked I fixed for them." However, she was fully aware of the racial and class dynamics, which made it hard to feel at ease during those "sticky times." She prepared fried green tomatoes for a young white man who did not bother to learn the name of the dish. Years later, she winced when she remembered the "ominous" and hard-to-decipher tone in his voice as he asked, "Are you going to fix some more of *them*?"[36] Fred Winn, the son of a San Francisco lawyer who spent the summer of 1964 in Mississippi, could only bring himself to take a small taste of the pigs' ears and pigs' feet he was offered. Although he never embraced those foods, he eventually learned to enjoy eating okra. However, he initially described eating the unfamiliar vegetable as akin to consuming "sandpaper slugs." It seems unlikely that the twenty-year-old volunteer, however well intentioned, could have hidden his disdain for their food culture from his hosts, who may have felt spurned for their acts of generosity in feeding him.[37]

Other northern visitors had a more positive initial impression of the regional food culture. One white volunteer wrote a letter to his family back home gushing about the "unbelievable" food he had eaten, which included biscuits, eggs, rice, cornbread, and sausage for breakfast and "so much dinner that no three people could eat it."[38] When black and white civil rights supporters ate together, not only were they defying local segregation customs, they were also transferring culinary knowledge, which the visitors carried with them after they left the region. Arlene Wilgoren, a white Brandeis University graduate who volunteered with SNCC in Arkansas for more than a year, remembered sampling foods that would have been entirely foreign in her "homogenous Jewish" community in Boston.[39] Although Wilgoren did not follow kosher rules, the transition of moving from a community where pork was a taboo product to one where it was a dietary staple must have been startling. Determined to adapt and to respect her hosts, she ate what was offered. She tried "greens and other vegetables cooked with fatback, which I tolerated but really did not like, sweet potato pie, which I love to this day, and chitterlings, which I tried only once." Although she had mixed emotions about the new foods she sampled, she found common ground with southern drinking culture. She loved evenings spent socializing at the local Elks Club "where you are allowed to bring your own liquor and buy 'setups'—mixers, lemon, lime or whatever else . . . We ate, drank, and danced until the wee hours."[40]

Northern African Americans living in the South for the first time often had to learn a new set of culinary lessons too. Harlem-born Peggy Trotter Dammond Preacely regarded spending time in the rural South as an opportunity to connect with her ancestors. For example, she volunteered to chop cotton so that she could experience some of the physical sensations of agricultural work. However, she too struggled to adjust to the foodways of rural Georgia. One day her host, Mama Dolly, surprised her with a hot breakfast of biscuits, meat, and gravy. Preacely licked her plate clean and complimented her host on the meal. Well aware that some of her food habits appeared peculiar to the city girl, Mama Dolly relished mischievously telling her startled guest, "Y'all were eating fried, smothered squirrel!"[41]

Supporters of the movement who generously fed others not only made themselves vulnerable to the judgment of northern guests who were used to eating different food, they sometimes saw their own food security comprised as a result of their support for the movement. Ironically, although one of the goals of the civil rights movement was to improve the living conditions of impoverished African Americans, in the short term their efforts sometimes made food shortages even worse. For example, officials in Leflore County targeted the food supply of an entire community. In 1962 they cut off the distribution of federal surplus food commodities in order to punish supporters of SNCC's voter registration drive in Mississippi. More than twenty thousand needy black families who had depended upon surplus foods to help them survive between cotton harvests were suddenly without sufficient food.[42]

In response to the crisis, organizers sent out desperate messages to supporters throughout the country who began collecting food donations. Comedian and activist Dick Gregory chartered a plane and sent fourteen thousand pounds of food to the state.[43] When Michigan State student Ivanhoe Donaldson got word about the food scarcity, he and his roommate held a food drive and drove a truck full of medical supplies and food to the Delta.[44] The northern group Friends of SNCC shipped tons of food and clothing and raised money to feed hungry Mississippians by hosting a benefit concert headlined by Harry Belafonte.[45] SNCC used these donations to set up their "own welfare system" that operated outside the confines of the formal state.[46]

Although the food flowed in, there was never enough to meet the overwhelming need in the community.[47] SNCC field director Bob Moses estimated that over the course of one month the organization was only able to provide food and clothing for about one thousand of the twenty-two thousand who needed the help.[48] Interestingly, he noted that the surplus commodities crisis radicalized many who participated in the civil rights struggle precisely because the food supply had been shut off. Moses observed, "For the first time they were seeing the connection between political participation and the food on their table."[49] Now that there were fewer reasons to stay in the good graces of white officials who had once dispensed commodity foods, many began to agitate for greater social change.[50] For example, the Meeks, the parents of eleven children, who had "no money, no food, no clothes, and no wood to keep warm by" decided that they had nothing to lose by attempting to register to vote. They and many like them clung to the hope that if they were successful, they could vote for officials who would change the policies that kept them impoverished.[51] By the fall of 1963, hundreds of hungry black residents of Leflore County were attempting to register to vote.[52] Furthermore, not only did black Mississippians try to use the political system to increase their access to food, they also developed new strategies of community activism designed to circumvent the existing social and political system that had made food scarce.

Because local officials had the power to decide how meager federal commodity provisions such as lard, flour, butter, and beans were allocated, this nutritional safety net had always been less than reliable.[53] However, as imperfect as the system was, many fared better under it than they would after the passage of the Food Stamps Act of 1964, which set up a system where impoverished participants could purchase coupons that they could then use to buy food at reduced prices.[54] For cash-strapped African Americans living in counties that decided to participate in the new program, the transition was devastating. Congress of Racial Equality staff member John Zippert explained:

> Tenant farmers would not want to switch from the commodity program because they had no money to pay the purchase requirement. They would have to borrow money and pay interest on it in . . . [to] the landlord or . . . the storekeeper, who took over the stamps as collateral. Either option meant that food stamp recipients would pay a premium for a government benefit to which they were entitled by law. Second, when food stamp recipients went to the store to make purchases, they were often overcharged on food costs in what was, in many cases, a captive consumer market.[55]

The poorest black Mississippians who could not afford to buy food stamps suffered from malnutrition and even starvation. At a 1967 Senate Subcommittee on Employment, Manpower, and Poverty hearing held at the Heidelberg Hotel in Jackson, Mississippi, civil rights activist Unita Blackwell told Senator Robert F. Kennedy that those who had lost access to surplus food had no other options but to "starve." She estimated that 95 percent of the children in her area did not have enough to eat.[56] NAACP lawyer Marian Wright echoed Blackwell's outrage and despair and challenged Kennedy to go beyond hearing about hunger. She asked him to travel around the state to witness its effects firsthand. Kennedy responded to her suggestion, took a tour of the state, and was appalled to discover "children with distended stomachs and with sores on their lips from malnutrition." He met a two-year-old boy who lived with his mother and five siblings in a dilapidated shack. They were barely surviving on rice and biscuits made from the family's dwindling supply of commodity flour. The youngest child was in such a weakened state that he could not interact with Kennedy, who desperately tried to engage him. Instead the child stared at the floor, "as if in a trance." Returning to Washington, DC, the senator begged his colleagues to act quickly to address this crisis. Although some shared his concerns, his appeal fell on the deaf ears of many, including B. Everett Jordon of North Carolina, who implausibly insisted that the bloated stomachs of the children Kennedy met might have been caused by overeating and not by a lack of food.[57]

Well aware of the widespread indifference to their suffering, African American Mississippians banded together to search for their own solutions to the crisis. In doing so, they drew upon the same strategy that had enabled many to survive the Great Depression: they formed cooperatives. SNCC member Worth Long recalled that organizers sometimes explained the model of the cooperative in terms of a familiar ritual among black southerners, the church potluck supper where "everybody brought in some food and put it down on the table. . . . It was a sharing."[58] Using that kind of collaborative thinking, a group of African American okra farmers formed the West Batesville Farmers' Cooperative in 1965, banding together to buy seed wholesale and to sell their crops. During their first year in business they learned some harsh lessons about how the system of marketing okra worked. Because they did not have contracts set up with wholesalers or frozen food companies, they had difficulty selling their crops for a consistent and reasonable price. Yet the members still found the experience empowering. They urged others to follow their example, saying, "You ain't going to make a whole lot of money when you start, but you'll have SOMETHING OF YOUR OWN."[59] SNCC member Mary E. Valera helped cooperative members tell their story in the form of a booklet titled, "Something of Our Own," which was widely read and circulated. For example, legendary organizer Stokely Carmichael asked the organization to send one thousand copies to the Alabama community where he worked because the people there craved instructions about how to establish cooperative enterprises.[60]

Fannie Lou Hamer, who learned her skills as a community organizer while working with SNCC, hoped to alleviate hunger by founding the cooperative Freedom Farm, which included a Pig Bank. Hamer urged black Mississippians to join the initiative, saying, "The time has come when we are going to get what we need ourselves."[61] The farm grew to almost seven hundred acres planted with both cash crops, such as cotton or soybeans, which could be sold to keep the farm in operation, and food crops like greens, beans, and sweet potatoes that members of the cooperative could eat. Hamer used fifty donated sows to start a Pig Bank. Families would care for a pregnant sow, return two of the offspring to the bank, and could keep the rest for their own use as food.[62] At least 865 families received pigs through the Pig Bank, and hundreds of families benefited from the food grown at Freedom Farm, which stayed in operation until 1977.[63]

Hamer's dream of black food sufficiency was widespread throughout the nation, not just in the rural South. Elijah Muhammad, who founded the African American religious group the Nation of Islam in 1934, believed, like Hamer, in the power of economic cooperation. He instructed his followers to "pool your resources, physically as well as financially, " and told them, "if one brother has a bowl of soup you have half that soup."[64] He was dedicated to the idea of using the collective power of the organization to produce food by and for their community. By the mid-1960s, the organization owned thousands of acres of farmland in Michigan, Alabama, and Georgia where they grew crops and raised animals for food. They hoped to control every aspect of the food chain. The NOI had their own slaughterhouse and dairy processing facility as well as their own trucks and planes to take the foods they produced to market. They owned supermarkets where consumers could buy these goods and restaurants where they could eat meals made from NOI produced food.[65] These businesses gave members of the community the opportunity to patronize black-owned establishments as well as the chance to socialize in pleasant, well-appointed, black-dominated spaces.

At the same time that the poor Mississippians Hamer worked with were struggling to find enough food to eat, another segment of the black community was dining far more luxuriously. A reporter for the *Wall Street Journal* who visited a Muslim-owned establishment favorably reported that Harlem's Temple Number Seven Restaurant, which had a dozen seats at the counter and ten tables that could seat four people each, was "spotless" and decorated with wax flowers and a portrait of the organization's founder.[66] A columnist for the *Chicago Defender* lavished even more praise on the Salaam restaurant in Chicago, calling it a "paradise" decorated with "magnificently hung drapes . . . chandeliers . . . [and] plush wall-to-wall carpeting."[67] In St. Louis a whole row of NOI-owned businesses soon sprang up, many of which sold food. In Washington, DC, the Shabazz restaurant not only served meals, it also boasted an affiliated health food store and a fish market.[68]

On the West Coast, the Black Panther Party was also engaged in the project of finding ways to feed the black community; however, their efforts were not aimed at establishing black businesses or cooperatives but in directly distributing food to the needy. Party leader Huey Newton argued that before people could be meaningfully engaged in political activities, they had to have their basic needs met. He called the organization's food charity work "survival pending revolution," arguing that these initiatives were designed to help community members sustain themselves as they evolved politically and became strong enough to challenge the entire social structure.[69] The BPP distributed free groceries, which included items like canned fruits and vegetables, potatoes, rice, bread, cereal, milk, chicken, and eggs to "Black and other poor people."[70] Their most well-known and ambitious food distribution program, the Free Breakfast Program, was aimed primarily at schoolchildren.

The BPP solicited donations of food, supplies, and space from local stores and organizations and would publicly shame anyone who would not contribute to their efforts to fight childhood hunger. Members of the group were responsible for cooking the food, transporting the children to the meal, and teaching them lessons about black history and politics while they ate.[71] The BPP claimed to have fed twenty thousand schoolchildren breakfasts including items such as eggs, grits, bacon, toast, home fries, fruit, and hot cakes during the 1968 to 1969 school year alone.[72] Although ideally they hoped to serve these meals in spaces such as churches or community centers with commercial cooking facilities, the BPP demonstrated a great deal of flexibility and imagination in finding ways to make sure one of their signature programs could continue.[73] In Los Angeles, party members who could not find more suitable facilities often resorted to serving breakfast to groups of children in private homes, including "homes of junkies, drug dealers, regular public assistance recipients, gamblers and gang bangers."[74]

These initiatives, while innovative, were insufficient to solve the enormous problem of hunger, but they were indicative of the spirit of the era when many black Americans resolved not only to produce their own food but also to define the terms of the national conversation about black food habits. Although having enough to eat was the primary concern for the most vulnerable members of the black community, many who were more well off shifted their focus and began thinking about food not only as a material substance but also as a symbolic medium. In the process they created the concept of "soul food."

According to historian William L. Vandeburg, the word *soul* emerged out of "black America's need for individual and group self-definition." The modifier, which was applied not only to food but also to things like music, clothing, hairstyles, and even to entire individuals ("soul" brothers or "soul" sisters), symbolized "a type of primal and spiritual energy and passionate joy available only to members of the exclusive confraternity."[75] Jessica Harris explains that it was in this context that the act of eating a "slave diet of hog and hominy became a political statement."[76] Psyche Williams-Forson further elucidates, arguing that "soul food" became representative of "shared oppressions but also . . . shared resistance to life's inequalities."[77] When eating southern regional foods together, members of the black community were performing a group identification that was rooted in a deep sense of a shared history. They were also celebrating the survival of the black community, which thrived in spite of being the victim of slavery and Jim Crow. Eating food associated with the plantation South became a significant way to demonstrate pride in a shared culture and in joint accomplishments.

Although the food served on the soul food table originated in the South, the concept did not. In that region people generally did not think of their daily fare as anything remarkable or of eating what they had always eaten as constituting a political act. For example, Hortense Spillers grew up in Memphis enjoying foods such as buffalo fish, chicken, collards seasoned with vinegar, black-eyed peas, and peach cobbler, dishes she loved and associated not only with gastronomic delight but also with her familial heritage, yet she never thought of them as racially specific "soul food." It was only after she was became an adult, traveled, and sampled a wide range of other foods that she "needed to identify [her] own neighborhood of cuisine."[78] What she later learned to recognize as the "culinary poetics" of a distinctively black style of cooking and eating was only visible to her from a distance and in contrast to her exposure to other cuisines.[79]

The concept of soul food first emerged in regions outside of the South where the foodways of African American migrants and their descendants stood out as distinctive. In the South, black and white southerners ate similar things. Alton Hornsby Jr., who grew up in Atlanta in the 1940s and 1950s, later recalled, "I don't know any of those so-called soul food items that southern Euro-Americans particularly did not eat."[80] Historian Frederick Douglass Opie agrees, noting that "the differences in eating habits are greater between northerners and southerners of any race than between white and black southerners."[81] Intriguingly, many black Americans living in the North while maintaining cultural ties to the South had the unique experience of straddling both of the culinary worlds Opie identifies. In the mid-twentieth century, the vast majority of Americans with direct knowledge about southern food culture who resided in northern or western cities were of African descent. In these contexts, their food culture was noticeably different. Because southern food predominated in most black neighborhoods but not in white ones, to many it soon appeared to be a racial rather than a regional style of eating.[82]

Although the plantation origins of soul food are clear, the northern counterpart was not identical to its southern cousin. Camille Bégin explains that "the reconstruction of the taste of southern foods as 'black foods'" that took place in the North represented a melding of the food habits of "southern rural migrants . . . an estranged white world and an earlier black urban culture."[83] This hybrid cuisine drew upon southern traditions, northern ingredients, and a host of new culinary ideas. Edna Lewis, one of the most influential African American cooks of the twentieth century, was emphatic about what she saw as the differences between southern food and soul food. Although she spent much of her career as a chef and author living in New York City, Lewis had grown up in Virginia eating what she deliberately labeled "southern" food. She did not embrace the transplanted version, famously labeling soul food as "hard times in Harlem—not true southern food."[84] Lewis claimed that while southern food was fresh and seasonal, soul food was greasy and consisted of many processed ingredients.[85]

In contrast, Amiri Baraka, a fellow New Yorker, celebrated the "good grease" that "came north when the people did" in his famous 1962 essay, "Soul Food." He praised a wide variety of foods including hog maw, chitterlings, sweet potato pie, Hoppin' John, fried fish, hushpuppies, black-eyed peas, collard greens, and barbecue as being both delicious and the "characteristic food" of black people.[86] Numerous African American political and cultural figures joined Baraka in his culinary reeducation project. Throughout the 1960s articles in black newspapers explained the concept of "soul food" to the uninitiated. Black restaurant owners began touting their wares under the new label of "soul food." Cookbook authors busied themselves trying to transform a living tradition into a set of printed instructions.[87]

The growing popularity of the concept of "soul food" coincided with rising disappointment about the results of the civil rights movement. The Civil Rights Act of 1964 outlawed discrimination in places of public accommodation, at long last handing a definitive victory to the thousands who had participated in sit-ins throughout the South and nation. Gaining the right to be served on equal terms was an important moral victory, but it was also, in some ways, a hollow one. Some southern restaurants resisted the court order by transforming themselves into private "clubs" where all the members were white. Others begrudgingly served black customers while making it clear that they were unwelcome.[88] Some resisted the law in more dramatic fashion. Lester Maddox, the owner of the Pickrick restaurant in Atlanta, greeted three African American theology students who attempted to enter his restaurant with a gun. White diners, determined to bar their entry at any cost, followed him outside carrying ax handles. The outraged Maddox, whose defense of segregation helped propel him into the Georgia's governor's mansion in 1966, ultimately opted to close his restaurant rather than to integrate.[89]

In light of this hostility, many activists found that they had no desire to patronize the white businesses they fought to desegregate. Furthermore, many regarded the food for sale at white restaurants as different and inferior to what they were accustomed to eating. SNCC members Courtland Cox and Stokely Carmichael visited a desegregated white-owned establishment only to encounter "absolutely the worst food we ever had." Cox recalled, only partially in jest, his disgust at discovering, "After all that effort, what we had was bad food."[90]

Prior to the passage of the Civil Rights Act of 1964, Carmichael responded to the criticism of a white woman who asked him why he persisted in going where he was not wanted. He explained that his demand for desegregation was about defending his right to move freely. It was not about a desire for specific foods, and it certainly did not come from a longing to be in the company of white people. He promised her, "Once we establish that principle, I guarantee you'll never see my face in this place again."[91] Many shared Carmichael's sentiments; however, others eagerly seized upon the opportunity to gain access to a much wider variety of consumer spaces. In fact, one of the painful and unintended consequences of desegregation was that it often hurt black businesses that no longer served a captive community without other options.

Patricia J. Armstrong, a participant in the Nashville sit-ins, mourned the fact that "after civil rights . . . [black owned] restaurants up and down Jefferson Street closed." David Swett, the owner of Swett's, a soul food restaurant founded in Nashville in 1954 and still in operation, agrees, saying, "Integration hurt African American businesses. People abandoned the businesses they had been going to, and when they got going they never looked back."[92] Despite the odds against it, Swett's survived when other businesses closed. More than half a century after desegregation, customers can still enjoy filling meals of meat loaf, turkey and dressing, candied yams, turnip greens, and pinto beans at Swett's Restaurant. Today, places like this have become far more rare than they were in the middle of the twentieth century while remaining just as culturally significant.

Sylvia Wood, a South Carolina native who moved to New York after World War II, opened Sylvia's Restaurant in Harlem in 1962. She began a long tenure of feeding the modified southern food that she had recently learned to refer to as "soul food" to a large cross section of the black community, to New Yorkers of other backgrounds, and, eventually, also to tourists hungry for the tastes of African American food culture that some were beginning to see as endangered.[93] Sylvia, who styled herself the "Queen of Soul," served a menu large enough to appeal to nearly any appetite, demonstrating the large range of traditional African American cooking. The restaurant is still open as of 2018, outlasting its founder's death in 2012. New York congressman Charles Rangel described the restaurant as an important social space, claiming, "From the beginning Sylvia's has always provided an opportunity for people to get together and be free to talk about how to be free."[94] The endurance of institutions like Sylvia's testifies to the significance of black community spaces and the enduring appeal of the concept of "soul food."

Many African American born before the 1960s learned, during the course of that decade, to think about food as a distinctive black cultural production and as a potential source of race pride, rather than taking it for granted as "just

Figure 6.1. African American–owned restaurant in Memphis, 1937. Photo by Dorothea Lange, Library of Congress, LC-DIG-ds-01454.

food." However, anyone born during or after that pivotal period came into a world where the concept of soul was the predominant—though never the only—way of describing black food traditions. To this group, soul food was a birthright, not a concept that had to be learned. According to Frederick Douglass Opie, a food historian and heir to the tradition, soul food was and still is:

> The product of a cultural mixture of various African tribes and kingdoms. Soul is the style of rural folk culture. Soul is black spirituality and experiential wisdom. And soul is putting a premium on suffering, endurance, and surviving with dignity. Soul food is African American, but it was influenced by other cultures. It is the intellectual invention and property of African Americans. Soul food is a fabulous-tasting dish made from simple, inexpensive ingredients. Soul food is enjoyed by black folk, whom it reminds of their southern roots.[95]

Fans of soul food who did not know how to cook but who wanted to enjoy this "fabulous-tasting" cuisine outside of a restaurant setting could, beginning in the late 1960s, turn to a proliferating number of cookbooks for a tutorial. Ruth L. Gaskin's *A Good Heart and a Light Hand*, a "collection of traditional Negro recipes," signifies the advent of a new culinary era. Gaskin revels in the pleasures of home cooking, saying, "There is a good feeling being around your own table eating in your own home." She confesses to eating lunches out, enjoying a restaurant meal on a special date, grabbing some Chinese takeout now and again, and admits that if she lived in one of the "larger northern cities" where "Soul Food Restaurants are starting to be popular" she might be tempted to try one. However, being "kind of spoiled," she confessed that she preferred home cooking and enjoyed eating a wide variety of foods including homemade sausage, fried chicken, and barbecued oysters in domestic privacy alongside selected family and friends.[96]

Gaskin identifies "six basic ingredients of traditional Negro food," including molasses, corn, greens, seafood, pork, and chicken.[97] In keeping with the spirit of the era, she playfully chides her mother for having forsaken the core principles of black cooking by forming a "Luncheon Club." Members of the group dressed up in their best clothes and took turns hosting meals taken "out of the Thursday food page in the newspaper." According to Gaskins, in deviating from "traditional foods" in favor of meals like "creamed chicken in patty shells," the members were guilty of "playing White." Fortunately, from Gaskins's perspective, the Luncheon Club quickly dissolved, and its members returned wholeheartedly to the soul food tradition.[98]

Gaskin's tutorial was soon followed by other texts designed simultaneously to document, create, and teach a tradition. Inez Yeargan Kaiser, who held a master's degree in home economics, wrote her 1968 *Soul Food Cookery* in order to offer instructions about how to make "stick to the ribs" dishes infused with soul, which she defined as "the seat of feelings and sentiment." "Soul food," she explained, consisted of "well-seasoned savory dishes that are difficult to eat without delight, enjoyment, and satisfaction" or to finish without having a "feeling of fullness."[99] In 1969 alone, three cookbooks (by Hattie Rhineheart Griffin, Jim Harwood and Ed Callahan, and Bob Jeffries) simply titled *Soul Food Cook Book* appeared. Armed with these texts, home cooks had access to instructions for preparing dishes ranging from gumbo to watermelon pickles. "Soul food," Jeffries argued, utilized whatever was available, including "fresh-caught fish, rabbit, possum, truck garden vegetables, easy-growing yams, sweet potatoes and corn."[100]

Increasingly, many proponents of soul food began to create an even more expansive definition of the term, moving from the concept of a cuisine rooted primarily in the plantation South to a more diasporic conception of both blackness and black cooking. Civil rights activists saw linkages between the domestic struggle for freedom and anticolonial movements on the continent of Africa. Many traveled there to help make these connections concrete, and in the process sampled some of the tastes of the continent. This awareness inspired many to embark on new explorations of the cultural connections between African-descended people throughout the globe, including in the realm of food. This orientation is captured in the title of Helen Mendes's 1971 *The African Heritage Cookbook*. A native of New York City, Mendes had exposure to a wide range of cooking styles and loved preparing dishes from French, Italian, and Spanish traditions. Although her mother from was South Carolina and cooked some southern dishes, she did not teach Mendes to cherish these traditions or how to prepare any of them herself. This changed beginning on the pivotal evening when Mendes prepared an elaborate French meal for a friend who complimented her on the food and then asked if she knew how to cook chitterlings, hog maws, or crackling bread. Mendes was ashamed to confess that she had never even tried chitterlings and had not tasted the other foods he mentioned since her childhood. She recalled, "For some time afterward I thought about this with increasing discomfort, and I resolved to learn to cook the traditional foods of my own people."[101]

Although motivated by passion, her approach to learning how to prepare soul food was a highly intellectual one. She embarked on the project of not only collecting African American recipes but also of tracing their origins back to West African food traditions. *The African Heritage Cookbook* includes a lengthy discussion about the West African origins of soul food alongside more than two hundred recipes of familiar soul food items such as neck bone stew and collard greens. Mendes urged her readers to draw not only historical but also political conclusions from her cooking instructions. Soul food, she argued, "unifies" African Americans with "their contemporary Black brothers and sisters around the world."[102] Her new knowledge and perspective had taught her to be "proud of the distinguished contributions my people have made to Brazilian, Haitian, West Indian, Creole, and Southern cooking."[103]

The growing interest in the African origins of southern food was visible in contemporary print culture and made material in the menus served at a wide variety of black cultural events. Increasingly, many were interested in tasting the historical antecedents of soul food.[104] Sometimes "African" dishes were described with some degree of geographical specificity. For example, in 1972, readers of the *Oakland Post* were treated to a recipe for beef "Ghana Stew" seasoned with nutmeg and served with cornmeal dumplings.[105] In 1976, *Ebony* magazine published a variety of recipes collected from the wives of diplomats from various African nations. Among other dishes, the article included instructions for how to make ginger-flavored fish from Ghana,

American Liberian pound cake, and vegetable soup from Cameroon. When trying to differentiate food on the distant continent from that eaten at home, the columnist explained, "Although some African and American recipes are similar, many African dishes are presented with more flair."[106] "Flair" proved to be hard to define, and for those who could not, for example, differentiate between a pound cake recipe from Liberia and one from Alabama, sometimes it appeared that what made food "African" was primarily the label.

In urban areas, participants in a wide variety of community events in the 1970s including Malcolm X Day celebrations and other cultural events could almost invariably expect to be served "African" food, though what precisely that meant was not always clear or consistent.[107] In 1969, caterer Sam Jordan treated a group of black journalists to a feast that would have sounded familiar to many familiar with southern food culture. They ate spare ribs, sweet potato casserole, potato salad, and "African" chicken, corn, and okra salad. Although the food was so fantastic that for those in attendance, "diets and weight watching were thrown to the wind," the reporter reviewing the feast did not specify what made some items on the menu specifically "African" beyond a "special seasoning" used on the okra.[108]

A 1969 food column in the *Sacramento Observer* is, in many ways, indicative of the spirit of the times. The columnist carefully describes several Fante traditions of preparing African yams before giving American readers a more familiar recipe for sweet potato casserole covered with miniature marshmallows. Apparently the writer presumed that her readers would be interested in learning about West African food traditions but potentially unwilling to try unfamiliar recipes at home or were unable to acquire African ingredients.[109] Although many were trained to look for the African antecedents in their diets, fewer changed what they ate to more closely resemble the original. The practice of eating "African" food sometimes, though certainly not always, represented a change in consciousness more than a shift in food practices.

Although a newfound appreciation for the soul food aesthetic, however it was defined, was palpable, it was not universal. Not all black eaters saw these foods as a source of pride or as a useful tool for constructing a shared sense of cultural belonging. In fact, some saw soul food as harmful, arguing that "slave food" was something that should be shunned, not celebrated. Clovis Semmes has demonstrated that an outspoken segment of the black community believed that the "culture (diet and lifestyle) of African-Americans had to change before their condition and status in America could change."[110] While soul food proponents regarded the cuisine as a source of cultural pride and a symbol of survival, which could be traced to West African roots, soul food detractors regarded it as an unhealthful way of eating that had been deliberately imposed by the slave master. Rather than embracing soul food, they advocated for a self-conscious dietary reordering in favor of the consumption of foods that they considered healthier, both physiologically and psychologically.

The most well-known critic of soul food in the 1960s and 1970s was Elijah Muhammad. He warned NOI members that "America continues to give her so-called Negroes the same bad food and drink that her (America's) fathers did in the days of servitude slavery."[111] It was up to the enlightened members of the race to escape from these unhealthy culinary habits. With this in mind, Muhammad banned a number of items associated with the soul food diet, including cornbread, sweet potatoes, black-eyed peas, and collard greens.[112] Among all of the NOI culinary taboos—and there were many—the prohibition against eating pork, "the filthiest and foulest animal human beings could have resorted to for food," was the strongest.[113] Spiritually astute and health-conscious members of the community were not only to stop eating pork and other foods closely associated with the plantation South, they were also instructed to avoid eating highly processed, excessively sweetened foods or those containing artificial colors or flavors.[114]

Muhammad warned that ignoring his advice could be deadly, instructing his followers, "Do not seek to 'gobble' down all the refined sugars and sweets . . . less you find yourself put in a refined 'box' that carries the dead."[115] Instead he promoted what he called "simple" foods, telling his followers they should eat only one time per day. According to Muhammad, an ideal meal consisted of lightly seasoned (in deliberate contrast to the flavorful soul food tradition) navy beans, a dish that Muhammad regarded as so pleasing and nourishing that it could be eaten every day of the week.[116]

The ideal NOI meal contained very little, if any, meat, fresh vegetables, whole grains, and pies made from Muhammad's beloved navy bean. Soon "bean pies" made from navy beans seasoned with nutmeg and cinnamon became an iconic NOI dessert, serving as a deliberate replacement for the southern sweet potato pie. Group members sold bean pies on street corners as well as in NOI-owned restaurants and grocery stores to raise money for the organization.[117] The menu of the Shabazz Restaurant in Washington, DC, gives insights into preferred NOI dining habits. Patrons might, for example, choose to dine on fish loaf, brown rice, whole wheat rolls, and "carrot fluff" made from mashed carrots blended with eggs and seasoned in much the same way as the ubiquitous bean pie.[118]

The NOI did not prohibit meat eating, but it was discouraged. "Meat," Muhammad warned, was "never intended for man to eat."[119] Many politically conscious African Americans outside of the NOI agreed, and in the early 1970s, vegetarianism became increasingly common in the black community. In Chicago, supporters of the Afro-Arts theater in hosted classes instructing those who attended on the benefits of giving up meat. Phil Cochran, the founder of the group, wanted to "prove to people that [vegetarian] food could taste just as succulent as that trash they was eatin'."[120] In that same city, the Institute for Positive Education, a cultural organization and community meeting space run by the poet Haki Madhubuti, endorsed a similar lifestyle. Madhubuti argued that vegetarianism was the most healthful way of life and that members of the black nation who refused to take care of their health by following such a diet were counterrevolutionaries unwilling to devote themselves and their bodies to the cause of liberation.[121] The Institute helped spread their message through a variety of public lectures about the relationship between food and health as well as by publishing the uncompromising *Commonsense Approach to Eating: The Need to Become a Vegetarian* by Johari A. Amini in 1972. Cultural nationalist groups on the East Coast, such as the Committee to Unify Newark and the East, agreed with these core dietary principles. Dedicated members ate a mostly vegetarian diet (although consuming fish was tolerated), which consisted of unprocessed foods, including fresh fruits and vegetables and whole grains. Eating these anointed, "healthy" foods was considered a race conscious obligation because, "when we are weak, the nation shares our weakness."[122]

The most well-known, politically conscious adherent of a vegetarian diet was the comedian and civil rights activist Dick Gregory. Gregory was actively involved in the civil rights movement and participated in marches, sit-ins, and voter registration drives, spending time in jail for his actions. It was as a result of his civil rights experiences that he decided to give up eating meat. In 1964, he was at a civil rights march in Alabama with his wife, Lillian, who was pregnant with twins. During the chaos of the demonstration, a white sheriff kicked her. Although appalled and outraged that a sheriff who was almost six-and-a-half feet all would kick a pregnant woman, Gregory maintained the discipline required of those who adhered to the principles of nonviolent protest and did not retaliate. That experience served as an epiphany as he realized that "if I would not hit a man who kicked my pregnant wife, then I could no longer participate in the destruction of any animal that has never harmed me."[123] He began to believe that the culture of violence surrounding white supremacy was linked to violence against animals. As someone who had been a victim of white violence, he was not willing to mete out violence against defenseless creatures. He learned to compare the mistreatment of even animals that were not used as food to slavery, noting that many are "shackled and chained like our ancestors, and they represent the domination and oppression we suffered for hundreds of years."[124]

Although he first gave up meat in protest against the culture of violence as manifested in animal suffering, like many of his fellow vegetarians,

Gregory also experienced a variety of health benefits from his new lifestyle, beginning when his lifelong sinus problems cleared up.[125] Determined to learn more about the healing properties of food, Gregory subjected himself to the tutelage of African American nutritionist and naturopath Alvenia Fulton, who helped guide him on his transition toward giving up all animal products (including eggs and cheese) and abandoning processed foods in favor of a raw diet of foods cooked only by "Mother Nature."[126]

Although politically active and culturally conscious African Americans disagreed about what precisely the ideal diet was, they agreed on the core concept that food choices were significant. Participants in the sit-ins demanded their right to eat iconic American foods on equal terms with their fellow citizens. Antipoverty activists in Mississippi and elsewhere were often preoccupied with the pressing concern of making sure people had enough to eat, making questions of what people ate secondary. Proponents of soul food used plantation foodways as a symbol of race pride and resiliency, while those who emphasized the African origins of that style of eating hoped to broaden the historical and cultural context of black foodways. Finally, those who advocated for "natural" or vegetarian diets were less concerned with heritage than with contemporary ideas about health, believing that a new historical moment called for a new set of food habits. Together their experiences are a testament to the diversity of African American food expression and to the core significance of food in shaping differing concepts of black identity throughout US history.

Epilogue

$\mathcal{T}$he most famous African American chef of the early twenty-first century learned how to cook from his Swedish grandmother. Marcus Samuelsson was born in Ethiopia in 1971 and orphaned when his birth mother died from tuberculosis when he was only a toddler. A Swedish couple adopted both him and his biological sister when he was three years old. Despite suffering such a profound and early loss, he managed to adapt to his new family and surroundings and had a happy childhood in Europe. His boyhood was colored by two overwhelming passions: soccer and a growing interest in learning how to cook. A driven and ambitious child, Samuelsson dreamed of a career as a professional athlete. However, he was crushed when, at the age of sixteen, he was cut from his soccer team by a coach who told him that although he had talent he had the wrong body type. That disappointment, though demoralizing, was not debilitating. After it became clear that he would not have a career in soccer, he had the self-awareness to find ways to nurture his other powerful interest.

Samuelsson's decision to become a culinary professional was not inspired by the example of his busy, homemaker mother, an indifferent cook who thought more about convenience than craft when getting food onto the table. The family dinner routine was cyclical and monotonous. Monday almost always meant meatballs, ligonberries, mashed potatoes, and gravy. Thursdays were reserved for split pea soup. Tuesday, fish night, was Samuelsson's favorite. Even though she saw preparing food as a duty and not a pleasure, his mother effortlessly modeled some of the skills that Samuelsson would later need in his profession. The young boy was amazed to watch her effortlessly scale, gut, fillet, and prepare fresh herring each week.

Occasionally Samuelsson's mother deviated from her set script. Sometimes she made cabbage rolls filled with pork. This, her most painstaking dish, was the one her son adored and remembered fondly. Other times she would make recipes taken from the pages of magazines marketed to busy middle-class housewives. She added a few dishes to her repertoire that alluded to international cooking styles and different taste sensibilities, hoping to transport imaginatively her family beyond the tastes of her native cuisine. However, these recipes called for convenience foods and were built upon a distorted understanding of the culinary conversations they claimed to reference. Although her efforts to expand the horizons of her children may have made some inroads into the imagination of her son who later developed a famously cosmopolitan cooking style, the meals themselves were lackluster. Samuelsson suspected that this food was something "not even a prisoner would tolerate." His mother made pasta sauce from "tinny tomato sauce and mushy peas" and pork roasts "from imagined Polynesian shores" garnished with pineapple rings and whipped cream.[1] Although meals like these sustained his body throughout his childhood, they did not inspire him. It was Samuelsson's adored Swedish "Mormor," his maternal grandmother, who taught him to love spending time in the kitchen.[2]

On Saturday, the family ate at Mormor's table. Samuelsson adored going to her house where "the yeasty aroma of freshly baked bread or the tang of drying rose hips hit you as soon as you walked in."[3] Although she spent most of her life living in poverty, she had learned to work with quality ingredients as a servant in well-to-do Swedish homes and had spent years patiently teaching herself to make "restaurant-worthy meals."[4] After retirement, Mormor treated her small home like "her own little food factory." She had a large garden and made everything from scratch. Her pantry overflowed with homemade jam and pickled fish and vegetables. She plucked chickens and butchered large cuts of meat. She taught her grandson how to make a roast chicken seasoned with cardamom, ginger, coriander, and stuffed with rosemary, apples, onions, and garlic. This meal made such a lasting impression on the young boy that as a professional chef his roasted chicken still played "homage to hers."[5]

The training that began at Mormor's knee led Samuelsson to culinary school, to prestigious apprenticeships in European restaurants, and eventually to a position as the executive chef at Aquavit, a Scandinavian restaurant in New York City. At the astonishingly young age of twenty-three, he received a three-star rating from the *New York Times*, and a culinary star was born.[6] Restaurant critic Ruth Reichl praised Samuelsson's "delicate and beautiful food," noting that he had mastered the art of "walking a tightrope between Swedish tradition and modern taste." She loved the tomato soup, the Swedish take on bouillabaisse, the roasted venison served with a twist of phyllo dough and cinnamon-flavored apples and potatoes, and the lamb chops accompanied by dried cherries. The lobster salad made with melon, fromage blanc, and mint was, Reichl raved, "maddeningly delicious."[7]

This was just the beginning of a long line of accolades and professional successes. In 1999 he received the Rising Star Chef Award from the James Beard Foundation, the first of several awards from the organization. In 2009 he had the honor of being the chef for the Obama administration's first state dinner. He has served as a host or a guest on a wide variety of television shows, and he won the competition *Top Chef Masters* in 2010. Samuelsson has also written several cookbooks and a memoir and sits at the helm of an empire consisting of eleven restaurants.[8] His ascendency has been remarkable. It is also, as Jessica Harris argues, "representative of the new and increasing diversity of those labeled 'African American.'" After all, Samuelsson, the country's best-known chef of African descent, has "no personal link to the history of African American enslavement in the country or the diet it spawned."[9] When describing his complex identity, Samuelsson has claimed to have "three personalities." He said, "If I don't open my mouth, I'm 100 percent Ethiopian. As soon as I open my mouth, I'm Swedish. And I live in America."[10]

Although he is not a descendent of the slaves who subsisted on the plantation staples of pork and corn, Samuelsson quickly learned to appreciate the value—both in aesthetic and in political terms—of African American cooking traditions. Like Helen Mendes before him, Samuelsson set out to give himself a culinary reeducation. In 2000, at the invitation of *Gourmet* magazine editor Ruth Reichl and journalist Lolis Eric Elie, Samuelsson returned to Ethiopia for the first time since the age of three. Disappointingly, though unsurprisingly, the sights and the smells of the country did not trigger any early, suppressed memories. The trip was, he recalled, "less a reunion than a whirlwind romance." Fall in love he did, beginning with his exposure to a ubiquitous spice blend called *berbere*. He was mesmerized by the complex blend of chili pepper, black pepper, salt, cardamom, ginger, nutmeg, cloves, cumin, coriander, allspice, fenugreek, *ajowan* seed, garlic, and cinnamon. The flavor was, he observed, "both masculine and feminine, shouting for attention and whispering at me to come closer . . . bright and crisp . . . earthy and slow."[11] That first taste was also transformational.

When he returned from Ethiopia, Samuelsson was determined to infuse the flavors of his original home into his cooking. He was also inspired to learn more about the food traditions elsewhere on the vast continent of Africa. This undertaking required several return trips and resulted in the publication of his 2006 cookbook *The Soul of a New Cuisine: A Discovery of the Foods and*

Flavors of Africa. Samuelsson tutored readers about how to make dishes such as trout served with spinach, which was inspired by Tanzanian cuisine, and fried fish served in baguettes that paid homage to a dish he had enjoyed in Zambia.[12] During his time in New York, he had become familiar with many dishes from the soul food table. This exposure to some of the foods of the African diaspora influenced his impressions of African foods. When he sampled Ghanaian cuisine he thought about Hoppin' John, the southern rice and black-eyed peas dish. However, in Ghana he ate black-eyed peas prepared with a different set of flavors. He urged his readers to go beyond their familiar palate of seasonings and to try black-eyed peas flavored with coconut milk, berbere, turmeric, Scotch bonnet peppers, tomatoes, onions, garlic, scallions, and a spiced butter.[13]

In 2008, he helped translate his love for the new foods he had discovered into brick and mortar in the form of Merkato 55, a short-lived pan-African restaurant named after an enormous market in Addis Ababa. The menu at Merkato 55 was inspired by *The Soul of a New Cuisine*.[14] Frank Bruni of the *New York Times* praised the restaurant's rendition of Ethiopian chicken *doro wat*, delicious chickpea dumplings that reminded him of "gnocchi that have undergone a spicy re-education," and the benne bread. However, among other things, Bruni complained that corn pap tasted like "wet salt" and mourned the fact that the shrimp fritters tasted nothing like shrimp. Although Bruni had faith that the restaurant could survive these growing pains and that these dishes could be perfected, the investors and the dining public were impatient.[15] Samuelsson sadly walked away after only six months resolved that he "would find a way to write [his] love letter to Africa another time."[16]

His next culinary venture, the Red Rooster, became a version of that love letter. The Harlem venue, which he opened in 2010, is planted a block away from Sylvia's legendary soul food restaurant and named after a legendary Harlem Renaissance nightspot. The restaurant was conceptualized as a tribute to the foods of the African diaspora as enjoyed in Harlem by the descendants of southern slaves and by immigrants from Africa and the Caribbean, and so much more. Samuelsson put the dishes of his childhood like his grandmother's meatballs alongside fried chicken on the menu, which also made self-conscious nods toward the foodways of other Harlem residents, including Latinos, Jewish people, and those with Italian roots. "Every ethnicity," Samuelsson claims, "has soul food."[17] Every menu decision was designed to tell a story and to place the African American food traditions of Harlem inside a vast and evolving international food story. For example, Red Rooster cornbread is served with honey butter as a nod to soul food as well as with a spicy tomato jam in homage to flavors drawn more directly from the African continent.[18]

The menu is as diverse as the man who created it and as complex as the neighborhood it resides in. But at its core, the Red Rooster is an homage to African America and to Samuelsson's evolving identity as a black New Yorker. Samuelsson is aware of the cultural importance of African American food traditions as well as of the historical significance of Harlem to the black community. He insists that the majority of the Red Rooster staff be comprised of people who live in the neighborhood.[19] When Samuelsson first met the legendary black New Orleans chef Leah Chase, he felt an immediate connection, confident that Chase knew he "wasn't just a European-raised/African-born chef with a big profile and a head full of highfalutin ideas." He warmly recalled, "Leah Chase saw me eat and knew that I was a brown-skinned boy who loved good food and also knew better than to waste any of it."[20] Samuelsson's expansive idea of what it means to be a "brown-skinned boy" who loves good food has been inspiring to many. Culinary historian and cultural critic Michael Twitty has applauded the fact that, in his estimation, "Marcus has given global provenance to our culinary culture by virtue of the fact that he is a global person. . . . I think [his] greatest accomplishment is bonding Africans with African Americans."[21]

Unsurprisingly, given his high profile, Samuelsson has also received criticism for his work and for the concept of Red Rooster. In 2012, chef and author Eddie Huang wrote a derogatory review of both Samuelsson's memoir *Yes, Chef* and of the Red Rooster in the *New York Observer*. Huang charged Samuelsson with condescending to Harlemites with a misguided attempt to "elevate" (Huang's description) soul food. Huang complained that most Harlem residents cannot afford to pay $28 for platters of Red Rooster fried chicken, further speculating that even those who could would find the atmosphere of the high-end restaurant unappealing. He argued that Samuelsson, an "eager culture vulture and self-proclaimed global flavor chaser is missing the point. What he doesn't realize about Harlem, soul food and perhaps himself is that they are all good enough already." In creating Red Rooster, Huang claimed that Samuelsson has done "a great injustice to a neighborhood, a culture and a history that has already seen its share of struggles."[22]

In a rejoinder to Huang's rebuke, writer Lolis Eric Elie charged Huang with being guilty himself of misunderstanding the residents of the neighborhood he sought to defend from a supposed outsider. Elie described Harlem as being comprised of people from varied backgrounds, a range of incomes, and diverse tastes. Furthermore, Elie bristled at Huang's implication that traditional soul food is the default cuisine of all black people who, in Huang's description, seem incapable of appreciating a fine dining experience or enjoying the cosmopolitan melding of flavors Samuelsson has become famous for. Elie sarcastically thanked Huang for his review, saying, "I suppose we people of color should be glad that we have Eddie Huang to fight for our right to restaurants that don't make no never mind about wine lists and white table cloths and international influences."[23]

The passions unleashed by Marcus Samuelsson's vision have been echoed in a variety of contemporary discussions about the significance of foodways in African American culture. Huang and Elie are hardly alone in their desire to delve into issues related to questions about what constitutes black cuisine and who has the right to market and sell this food. In the twenty-first century, intellectual debates about the meaning of African American foodways have become a larger part of the public discourse than ever before. A number of black food critics have highlighted the fact that chefs and food writers who are not members of the black community frequently profit from black culinary knowledge without adequately acknowledging their cultural and intellectual debt.

In a widely circulated open letter to white celebrity cook Paula Deen, Michael Twitty compellingly raised these issues in a way that highlights the complex origins of southern cuisine. Writing to Deen as a "a fellow Southerner, a cousin," he claimed an affinity based upon the fact that "sweet tea runs in our blood, in fact *is* our blood." Acknowledging that their "ancestors co-created the food and hospitality and manners" of the region, he criticized Deen for not adequately acknowledging that shared history. Elsewhere, Twitty has observed that the "wondrous thing" of southern food came at a "great cost," a cost that should be acknowledged.[24] With that in mind, he urged Deen not to forget "that the Southern food you have been crowned the queen of was made into an art largely in the hands of enslaved cooks."[25]

The experiences of Dora Charles, an African American woman who was the head cook at Deen's Lady & Sons' restaurant for more than twenty years, adds a specific human form to Twitty's critique. Charles revealed that although Deen called her a "soul sister" and promised to share the profits if the restaurant became successful, Deen also used racial epithets, asked black employees to wear degrading antebellum costumes, and never paid Charles more than minimum wage even after she became an internationally famous celebrity.[26] The uneven power differential between Charles and Deen made headlines because of the fame of the accused, but the dynamic was all-too-familiar to generations of African American cooks, most of whom never had a public platform from which to expose their abuse. Charles, however, managed to break the cycle, at least in her own life, when she not only publicly commented upon her relationship with her well-known employer but also when she found a way to put her own voice at the center of the southern food narrative instead. No longer obliged to stand in the shadow of a white woman who took most of the credit and all of the profit for shared culinary creations,

Charles wrote her own cookbook, *A Real Southern Cook: In Her Savannah Kitchen*. Her recipes for dishes such as "Cheesy Meatloaf with Mushroom Sauce," "Chicken Brunswick Stew," and "Eggs Baked in Tomato Sauce" are contextualized with stories of her family. Charles sees herself as being only the latest member of a "long line of good cooks," including her great grandmother who was enslaved.[27]

The themes explored by Twitty in his letter to Paula Deen have emerged and reemerged in other contexts. In 2016, in a shared column in the *Oxford American*, Nigerian-born chef Tunde Wey and the white founder of the Southern Foodways Alliance, John T. Edge, who has become the nation's best-known spokesperson on issues related to southern food culture, had an open conversation about thorny issues about the marketing and proprietorship of southern culinary knowledge. Wey asked Edge to interrogate the white privilege that "permits a humble, folksy, and honest white boy to diligently study the canon of appropriated black food, then receive extensive celebration in magazines, newspapers, and television programming for reviving the fortunes of Southern cuisine" while black voices are often left out of the discussion. Wey challenged Edge:

> John T., you have endorsed and celebrated the appropriation of black Southern food without consequence, and the consequences have compounded with interest. You have to return what you took to the place where it was, to the people to whom it belongs. And, after this principal has been repaid, the interest is due. You have to strip yourself of the marginal benefits of this appropriation willingly, with grace, or unwillingly by force and with shame. You're a graceful man, John T. So what will you willingly give up to ensure the Southern food narrative services properly and fully the contributions of black Southerners?[28]

Wey has worked to make the point about racial inequalities not just in the realm of southern food culture but in the entire structure of US wealth distribution. In 2018, at Saartj, a pop-up restaurant in New Orleans, Wey asked people of color to pay $12 for meals such as jollof rice, while white customers were charged $30 in acknowledgment of the fact that the median income of white residents of New Orleans is 2.5 times greater than that of their black neighbors.[29] Although these interventions alone cannot shift centuries-old power dynamics where most of the profits from southern cooking traditions have landed in white hands, they have inspired dialogue and soul searching in some quarters. For example, Wey was surprised that the majority of white customers actually paid the $30 he requested for their meal.[30] His challenge made an impression on Edge too. Like Twitty in his letter to Deen, Edge has argued that southern cooking is a syncretic, hybrid tradition. Given this fact, he honestly told Wey that he could not "walk away from writing about black life" because to do so would mean he could not write about himself or about his region where "black and white culture are enmeshed and codependent." However, Edge told Wey that he would promise to "aim to listen more and speak less . . . to cede what is not mine and try to understand the difference."[31]

For many members of the black culinary intelligentsia, the issue of who profits from southern food is only one among other pressing concerns about how the national dialogue about American food culture is framed. Many have argued that the food media often caricatures African American foodways as one-dimensional and that many make assumptions about the food identities of people of color without allowing food creators speak for themselves. In an article specifically addressed to the food media titled, "Rules of Engagement," Twitty urges outsiders exploring the food culture of a different group to do so without bringing stereotyped preconceptions into the conversation. He instructs, "Until you know how a chef self-identifies or locates their identity, assume nothing, except that they embody a place in American culture and its inherent diversity. . . . Interview them as people not as archetypes."[32]

African American vegan chef Bryant Terry melded the concerns about who profits from black culture and about simplistic depictions of a multifaceted culture in his critique of the "Thug Kitchen" website and cookbooks created by Michelle Davis and Matt Holloway, two white Californians, who use profanity-laden prose to encourage their readers to cook plant-based foods.[33] Initially their publications were printed anonymously, allowing readers to make their own inferences about the racial, ethnic, and gendered identity of the creators. After a 2014 article in *Epicurious* revealed that the authors are white, many were outraged, offended, or disappointed by the revelation.[34] Summarizing the responses of many, Terry accused Davis and Holloway of "masking in African-American street vernacular for their own amusement and profit."[35] Although the Thug Kitchen creators did not overtly racialize their fictional "thug" persona, many have argued that their inference was clear. John McWhorter, who teaches linguistics at Columbia University, has argued that "*thug* today is a nominally polite way of using the N-word. . . . When somebody talks about thugs ruining a place, it is almost impossible today that they are referring to somebody with blond hair."[36] Terry and other critics of Davis and Holloway claimed that the duo knowingly coopted a distinctive element of urban black culture and a black persona to market and sell their recipes.

Terry was angered not only by their unacknowledged borrowing from black culture but also by what he saw as the inaccurate historical assumptions embedded in their "thug" portrayal. Terry argued that the rhetorical device of the "thug" is designed to be comedic, in part, because urban African American food culture suffers from the "stigma and stereotype of being based in fatty pork-based dishes and butter-heavy comfort foods." In contrast to this myth, Terry pointed out that "that kind of meat-heavy, indulgent decadence was scarce for millions struggling under the oppression of segregation before the industrialization of our food system." Instead, Terry, pointed out, "When we peel away the negative stereotypes and reductive portrayals of African-American food, we see a diverse and complex culinary tradition with nutrient-rich foods like collards, mustards, turnips, butter beans, black-eyed peas, green beans, sugar snap peas and the like at the cuisine's core."[37] He observed that despite the significance of vegetables in the soul food diet and in the West African diets that predated it, in the US national imagination, eating a plant-based diet is often associated with whiteness.

Terry has not been alone in his quest to complicate the national perception about black food traditions and contemporary eating habits. In the twenty-first century there has been an upsurge of interest among many in the black community in adopting a plant-based, vegan diet. Despite this trend, Gloria Oladipo has observed that in American culture, "the most prominent visualization [of a vegan] is a preppy, skinny white girl preaching about the need for a raw, organic, all-natural, gluten-free, juice pressed diet." She argues that this idea does real harm, claiming, "Having this narrative centered in the vegan movement keeps people of color out and acts as a convenient erasure of vegans of color all together."[38] Author Aph Po agrees with this perception and has also worked to "dismantle the stereotype that veganism was a 'white person's' thing" by profiling vegans of color, both historical figures like Dick Gregory and Coretta Scott King, and living people like Venus Williams and Cory Booker on her websites "100 Black Vegans" and "Black Vegans Rock."[39] Collectively these voices have made significant inroads into national conversations about black food habits and alternative dietary practices in general.

African Americans who identify as vegans have become such a large part of the national conversation about food, health, and ethics that media outlets produced outside of the black community have noticed.[40] Most influentially, in 2017, Kim Severson profiled a number of African American food writers, chefs, and activists about their reasons for choosing this lifestyle in a *New York Times* article titled "Black Vegans Step Out for Their Health and Other Causes." This widely circulated article promises to play an important role in highlighting black culinary diversity to the public at large.[41]

Much of this vibrant culinary conversation was inspired by Amie Breeze Harper's influential 2009 anthology, *The Sistah Vegan Project: Black Female Vegans Speak on Food, Identity, Health, and Society*, which includes contributions from a number of African American, vegan women who describe their experiences and food philosophies.[42] The anthology was inspired by Harper's desire to connect with other vegans of color and her curiosity about how they would respond to a controversial PETA campaign that compared human slavery to the mistreatment of animals. With that as a starting place, she asked her contributors to reflect about how their experiences with racism impacted the way they thought about issues like food, health, the environment, and the treatment of animals. Personally, Harper was drawn to veganism due both to health concerns and to a growing realization that the oppression of nonhuman animals was linked to the same system that justified the torture, enslavement, and subjugation of human beings. This is how she briefly explains what she sees as the relationship between history, racism, the mistreatment of animals, and health:

> Black women were used as wet nurses for slave masters' children. Their wombs were used to produce more slaves whether they wanted to or not. This is frighteningly similar to the suffering chickens and cows go through. They are exploited to the point where we use their reproductive cycles to feed us. This scary parallel goes even deeper. As women continue eating these eggs and flesh products, so high in hormones and other unhealthy substances, it makes estrogen levels in their bodies even higher. Our reproductive systems suffer because of the exploitation of the reproductive systems of chickens and cows.[43]

Given this horrific history and its ongoing legacy, Harper views antiracism and veganism as intertwined practices. Harper and many other vegans of color have expressed frustration at the fact that white-dominated vegan groups often seem unwelcoming and insensitive to nonwhite people, not only because, as Oladipo points out, in the national imagination "healthy" eaters are often depicted as being white, but because many white vegans are unwilling to acknowledge the relationship between white supremacy and the food system. They argue that white supremacists conspired to deprive people of color access to adequate food choices historically and continue to do so in the present day. Articulating a point of view that shares much in common with the radical black vegetarians who gave up meat eating in the 1960s and 1970s, Zachary Toliver argues, "Foods like chitlins (pig intestines) and pigs' feet—these are not our true heritage, and they should not represent blackness. Our ancestors *had* to consume these disgusting body parts to survive slavery, but there's zero excuse to do so in the 21st century."[44]

For African Americans who make the decision to eat a plant-based diet, which Bryant Terry argues is actually more similar to the foods eaten by many of their ancestors, the condescension and misunderstanding that they confront from white vegans is sometimes only one part of the struggle in their attempt to construct an affirming vegan, black identity. Heir to the creation of the idea of meat and carbohydrate heavy "soul food" as *the* black way of eating, some have grappled with the identity-shaping implications of making different dining decisions. Some wonder what those who subscribe to the idea of soul food as a unifying, singular cuisine are implying about those who make different culinary decisions. In response to the conflation of meat-heavy soul food and blackness, Toliver quips, "Just because you now know *seven new ways to eat kale*, that doesn't make you any more or less black—to the world or to yourself—than before acquiring said kale knowledge." To explain this, he points to ways that black vegans can enjoy the soul food aesthetic while not eating animal products. He humorously claims, for example, that black vegans remain "just as nervous about whether or not [their] white friends properly seasoned the food" as carnivorous members of the community.[45]

Harper too turns to the vehicle of humor to write about how her decision to give up the "gospel bird" "shocked all my card carrying 'I'm a bonafide black person' friends." She has worked to cultivate a different culinary vision of blackness that does not involve the doomed cycle of "bragging about how many deep fried dead animals they overdosed on at a family bbq, and then excuse themselves to go take their high blood pressure medicine and insulin for their diabetes." Although there is an element of earnest critique in her description of the traditional soul food diet, her caricature of an out-of-control black carnivore in need of salvation from "a white girl from the mid-west who is on a 'mission' to bring them 'good' food for her college internship" is also written as a tongue-in-cheek acknowledgment of the distorted prism through which many outside the community view black food habits.[46]

In the twenty-first century, African American food traditions are vibrant and diverse. The soul food tradition that emerged from the plantation South is still alive and celebrated, but it coexists alongside the culinary diversity represented by Marcus Samuelsson's international culinary medleys and in the company of culinary criticism generated by a new generation of food activists seeking ways to protect black bodies from the ravages of a food supply tainted by a history of white supremacy. Jessica Harris points out that even those who identify closely with the concept of soul food often only eat the "traditional southern diet" during celebrations, "on Sundays, on holidays, and at family reunions."[47]

Barack and Michelle Obama, the most closely watched African American taste-setters of the twenty-first century, represent the intersecting power of the southern, black culinary tradition with the ever-expanding food options of a cosmopolitan nation. During his days living in Chicago, the future president fondly remembered eating "fried chicken, catfish, Hoppin' John, collard greens, meatloaf, corn bread and other soul-food standards" at MacArthur's. Eating these foods was clearly an act that not only satisfied his appetite but also symbolized his identification and cultural affinity with black Americans.[48] Later, while living in the White House, the first family continually made headlines for their dining choices as they ate their way across the city, the nation, and the world, choosing restaurants that served many types of cuisine. Their sense of culinary adventure was so well known that the food journalism of the Obama era is replete with advice about "How to Eat Like the Obamas." The *DC Metro* provided tips to anyone who wanted to take a culinary tour of the city inspired by the appetites of the "First Eater, Chowhound-in-Chief, Executive Dining Officer," who ate everywhere from the African American–owned iconic U Street restaurant Ben's Chili Bowl, to the high-end French restaurant Citronelle.[49] Despite the obvious diversity of their tastes, racist denigrators seemed never to tire of creating Photoshopped images of the president and first lady gorging on watermelon and fried chicken, symbols used to denote blackness and essential difference.[50] These tropes demonstrate not only the sheer folly of the idea that Obama's election signified the advent of a postracial society but also the fact that centuries after the beginning of African slavery in the Americas, African American food traditions are still devalued, oversimplified, and misunderstood by many.

Yet for many who have, like Michelle Obama, learned to ignore racist criticisms and to "surround yourself with people who uplift you, who hold you up," the future seems promising.[51] Jessica Harris, one of the most influential and prolific chroniclers of black food traditions, is optimistic, saying, "We've journeyed far, and the rest is attainable in the bountiful world of American food." Harris anticipates continuing national conversations about the role that African-descended people played in creating American food traditions and ongoing chances to enjoy and celebrate what she calls the African American "long love affair with food."[52] Today, varied African American food traditions are practiced, celebrated, analyzed, and promoted by a prolific and robust community of black food practitioners, intelligentsia, and activists who range from the celebrity chef Marcus Samuelsson to the intrepid culinary historian Michael Twitty to the activist and theorist Amie Breeze Harper. Although their experiences, their food stories, and their histories are intertwined, they are not identical. Together these stories remind us that the history of black food expression is rich, diverse, and complex. It is not, and never has been, a single story.

Notes

INTRODUCTION

1. Michael W. Twitty, *The Cooking Gene: A Journey through African American Culinary History in the Old South* (New York: Amistad, 2017), 25–26.

2. Twitty, *The Cooking Gene*, 34–35.

3 Twitty, *The Cooking Gene*, 33–35.

4. Twitty, *The Cooking Gene*, 37–38.

5. Michael W. Twitty, "The Southern Discomfort Tour," The Cooking Gene Blog, https://thecookinggene.com/the-southern-discomfort-tour/, accessed July 26, 2018; Michael W. Twitty, "Why I'm Going to Pick Cotton for 8 Hours Tomorrow . . . and Yes its 2012," October 23, 2012, Afroculinaria Blog, https://afroculinaria .com/2012/10/23/why-im-going-to-pick-cotton-for-8-hours-tomorrow-and-yes -its-2012/, accessed July 26, 2018.

6. Twitty, *The Cooking Gene*, 40.

7. Twitty, *The Cooking Gene*, 70–71.

8. Twitty, *The Cooking Gene*, 70.

9. Manuel Roig-Franzia, "Tracing His Urge to Cook through Slavery and the South," *Washington Post*, August 18, 2017, https://www.washingtonpost.com/outlook/ tracing-his-urge-to-cook-through-slavery-and-the-south/2017/08/18/1aeaa6de-6e19- 11e7-96ab-5f38140b38cc_story.html?utm_term=.b184a01eff64, accessed July 26, 2018.

10. Twitty, *The Cooking Gene*, 73.

11. Roig-Franzia, "Tracing His Urge."

12. Julia Bainbridge, "Michael W. Twitty: 'I Want Southern Food to Be the Basis of a New Discussion on Shared Southern Identity,'" *Atlanta Magazine*, September 18, 2017, http://www.atlantamagazine.com/dining-news/michael-w-twitty-want-southern -food-basis-new-discussion-shared-southern-identity/, accessed July 26, 2018.

13. Chimamanda Ngozi Adichie, "The Danger of a Single Story," TEDGlobal, July 2009, https://www.ted.com/talks/chimamanda_adichie_the_danger_of_a_single_ story, accessed July 26, 2018.

14. Adrian Miller, *Soul Food: The Surprising Story of an American Cuisine, One Plate at a Time* (Chapel Hill: University of North Carolina Press, 2017), 11.

15. Paul Gilroy, *The Black Atlantic: Modernity and Double Consciousness* (Cambridge: Harvard University Press, 1993), 19.

16. For a wonderful discussion about the symbolic significance of Africa throughout African American history, see Robin D. G. Kelley, *Freedom Dreams: The Black Radical Imagination* (Boston: Beacon Books, 2003), 13–35.

17. Salman Rushdie, *Imaginary Homelands: Essays and Criticism, 1981–1991* (London: Granta Books, 1991), 11.

18. Rushdie, *Imaginary Homelands*, 12.

19. Jessica Harris, *High on the Hog: A Culinary Journey from Africa to America* (New York: Bloomsbury, 2011), 245.

20. James C. McMann, *Stirring the Pot: A History of African Cuisine* (Athens: Ohio University Press, 2009), 7.

21. Freda De Knight, *A Date with a Dish: A Cook Book of American Negro Recipes* (New York: Hermitage Press, 1948), xiv.

22. Gilroy, *The Black Atlantic*, 34.

23. Twitty, *The Cooking Gene*, 14.

24. Frederick Douglass Opie, *Hog and Hominy: Soul Food from Africa to America* (New York: Columbia University Press, 2008), xi, xii.

25. See for example, August Meier, "Whither the Black Perspective in Afro-American Historiography?" *Journal of American History* 70, no. 1 (June 1983): 101–5.

26. John Blassingame, *The Slave Community: Plantation Life in the Antebellum South* (New York: Oxford University Press, 1972), 105.

CHAPTER 1

1. Quoted in J. D. La Fleur, *Fusion Foodways of Africa's Gold Coast in the Atlantic Era* (Leiden: Brill, 2012), 1. For more information about this and other contemporary proverbs, see Alice Bellagamba, Sandra E. Greene, and Martin A. Klein, *African Voices on Slavery and the Slave Trade, Volume 2* (Cambridge: Cambridge University Press, 2016), 64–67; R. Sutterland Rattray, *Ashanti Proverbs: The Primitive Ethics of a Savage People* (Oxford: Clarendon Press, 1916); and J. G. Christaller, *Three Thousand Six Hundred Ghanaian Proverbs*, trans. by Kofi Ron Lange (Lewiston, NY: Edwin Mellon Press, 1990), 150.

2. Thomas Edward Bowdich, *Mission from Cape Coast Castle to Ashantee* (London: Griffin and Faran, 1873), 267, 272.

3. Bowdich, *Mission from Cape Coast Castle to Ashantee*, 17, 27, 33.

4. Bowdich, *Mission from Cape Coast Castle to Ashantee*, 319; Stephanie E. Smallwood, *Saltwater Slavery: A Middle Passage from Africa to American Diaspora* (Cambridge: Harvard University Press, 2007), 44.

5. Bowdich, *Mission from Cape Coast Castle to Ashantee*, 267.

6. The scholarly discussion about African cultural continuities and the process of creolization is rich. To begin an exploration of these dynamics, see Gwendolyn Midlo

Hall, *Slavery and African Ethnicities in the Americas: Restoring the Links* (Chapel Hill: University of North Carolina Press, 2007); Michael Gomez, *Exchanging Our Country Marks: The Transformation of African Identities in the Colonial and Antebellum South* (Chapel Hill: University of North Carolina Press, 1998); and Sidney W. Mintz and Richard Price, *The Birth of African-American Culture: An Anthropological Perspective* (Boston: Beacon Press, 1992).

7. Hall, *Slavery and African Ethnicities*, 165.

8. James C. McMann, *Stirring the Pot: A History of African Cuisine* (Athens: Ohio University Press, 2009), 109.

9. Jessica Harris, *High on the Hog: A Culinary Journey from Africa to America* (New York: Bloomsbury, 2011), 11.

10. Frederick Douglass Opie, *Hog and Hominy: Soul Food from Africa to America* (New York: Columbia University Press, 2008), 6.

11. McCann, *Stirring the Pot*, 136.

12. McCann, *Stirring the Pot*, 42, 111, 117, 120; Opie, *Hog and Hominy*, 8–9, 12.

13. McCann, *Stirring the Pot*, 60, 109–10; Harris, *High on the Hog*, 244; Opie, *Hog and Hominy*, 9, 14; La Fleur, *Fusion Foodways*, 69, 72, 162–63.

14. Gregory Maddox, *Sub-Saharan Africa: An Environmental History* (Santa Barbara, CA: ABC-CLIO, 2006), 56; La Fleur, *Fusion Foodways*, 68–69.

15. McCann, *Stirring the Pot*, 23.

16. McCann, *Stirring the Pot*, 24–25; Stanley Alpern, "Exotic Plants of Western Africa: Where They Came from and When," *History in Africa* 35 (2008): 63–102.

17. McCann, *Stirring the Pot*, 38–40.

18. Alfred W. Crosby, *The Columbian Exchange: Biological and Cultural Consequences of 1492* (Westport, CT: Greenwood, 1972).

19. La Fleur, *Fusion Foodways*, 14.

20. Philip D. Curtin, *The Atlantic Slave Trade: A Census* (Madison: University of Wisconsin Press, 1969), 270; James Rawley and Stephen D. Behrendt, *The Transatlantic Slave Trade: A History* (Lincoln: University of Nebraska Press, 2005), 365; Stanley B. Alpern, "The European Introduction of Crops into West Africa in Precolonial Times," *History in Africa* 19 (1992): 13–43.

21. James McMann, *Maize and Grace: Africa's Encounter with a New World Crop, 1500–2000* (Cambridge: Harvard University Press, 2005), 23–24, 28; Judith A. Carney and Richard Nicholas Rosomoff, *In the Shadow of Slavery: Africa's Botanical Legacy in the Atlantic World* (Berkeley: University of California Press, 2009), 55–56.

22. La Fleur, *Fusion Foodways*, 156.

23. McMann, *Stirring the Pot*, 51–55; Mark H. Zanger, "Cassava," in *The Oxford Companion to American Food and Drink*, ed. Andrew F. Smith (New York: Oxford University Press, 2007), 96–97.

24. McMann, *Stirring the Pot*, 60; Fran Osseo-Asare, *Food Culture in Sub-Saharan Africa* (Westport, CT: Greenwood Press, 2005), 13–14.

25. McMann, *Stirring the Pot*, 131–33; Alpern, "The European Introduction of Crops," 26; Andrew F. Smith, "Peanuts," in *The Oxford Companion to American Food and Drink*, 440–41.

26. Harris, *High on the Hog*, 18; Carney and Rosomoff, *In the Shadow of Slavery*, 141–42.

27. Joseph Hawkins, *A History of a Voyage to the Coast of Africa and Travels into the Interior* (Philadelphia, 1797), 10.

28. Hawkins, *A History of a Voyage*, 10–11.

29. Ira Berlin has made a useful distinction between "slave societies," structured around the system of slavery, and "societies with slaves," where slavery is less integral to the social and economic framework. See, for example, *Many Thousands Gone: The First Two Centuries of Slavery in North America* (Cambridge: Harvard University Press, 1998).

30. Hawkins, *A History of a Voyage*, 10.

31. J. D. Fage has expressed skepticism at the veracity of Hawkins's reports of his African travels. J. D. Fage, "Hawkins' Hoax? A Sequel to 'Drake's Fake,'" *History in Africa* 18 (1991): 83–91.

32. McCann, *Stirring the Pot*, 3.

33. McCann, *Stirring the Pot*, 12.

34. Hawkins, *A History of a Voyage*, 126.

35. "Palm Oil," in *The Oxford Companion to Food and Drink*, eds. Alan Davidson and Tom Jaine (Oxford: Oxford University Press, 2006), 571–72.

36. Hawkins, *A History of a Voyage*, 127.

37. Hawkins, *A History of a Voyage*, 130–31.

38. Leo Waibel, "The Political Significance of Tropical Vegetable Fats for the Industrial Countries of Europe," *Annals of the Association of American Geographers* 33, no. 2 (June 1943): 118–28; David Northrup, "The Compatibility of the Slave and Palm Oil Trades in the Bight of Biafra," *Journal of African History* 17, no. 3 (1976): 353–64.

39. G. Ugo Nwokeji, *The Slave Trade and Culture in the Bight of Biafra* (Cambridge: Cambridge University Press, 2010), 3.

40. Albert Van Dantzig and Willem Bosman, "Willem Bosman's 'New and Accurate Description of the Coast of Guinea': How Accurate Is It?" *History in Africa* 1 (1974): 101–8.

41. Willem Bosman, *A New and Accurate Description of the Coast of Guinea* (London: J. Knapton, 1705), 299.

42. Bosman, *A New and Accurate Description*, 393.

43. Bosman, *A New and Accurate Description*, 392–93.

44. Bosman, *A New and Accurate Description*, 125.

45. Bosman, *A New and Accurate Description*, 124.

46. Bosman, *A New and Accurate Description*, 124.

47. "Estimates," Voyages: The Transatlantic Slave Trade Database, http://www.slavevoyages.org/assessment/estimates, accessed May 25, 2017.

48. Gerhard Seibart, "Sao Tome and Principe: The First Plantation Economy in the Tropics," in *Commercial Agriculture: The Slave Trade and Slavery in Atlantic Africa*, eds. Robin Law, Suzanne Schwarz, and Silke Strickrodt (Woodbridge, Suffolk: James Currey, 2013), 60.

49. Linda M. Heywood and John K. Thornton, *Central Africans, Atlantic Creoles, and the Foundations of the Americas* (Cambridge: Cambridge University Press, 2007), 216.

50. Carney and Rosomoff, *In the Shadow of Slavery*, 47.

51. Heywood and Thornton, *Central Africans, Atlantic Creoles*, 216.

52. Carney and Rosomoff, *In the Shadow of Slavery*, 47; Seibart, "Sao Tome and Principe," 57.

53. Heywood and Thornton, *Central Africans, Atlantic Creoles*, 216.

54. La Fleur, *Fusion Foodways*, 116–21.

55. Smallwood, *Saltwater Slavery*, 43.

56. La Fleur, *Fusion Foodways*, 92.

57. John Gerarde, *The Herball or Generall Historie of Plantes* (London: John Norton, 1597), 76–77.

58. Carney and Rosomoff, *In the Shadow of Slavery*, 55.

59. Smallwood, *Saltwater Slavery*, 44.

60. Heywood and Thornton, *Central Africans, Atlantic Creoles*, 215.

61. La Fleur, *Fusion Foodways*, 92.

62. Olaudah Equiano, *The Interesting Narrative of the Life of Olaudah Equiano or Gustavus Vassa, the African* (London, 1790), 16–17.

63. Equiano, *The Interesting Narrative*, 38, 50.

64. Equiano, *The Interesting Narrative*, 56.

65. Equiano, *The Interesting Narrative*, 50.

66. Johannes Postma, *The Dutch in the Atlantic Slave Trade, 1600–1815* (Cambridge: Cambridge University Press, 1990), 165.

67. William Snelgrave, *A New Account of Some Parts of Guinea, and the Slave Trade* (London, 1734), 162–91.

68. Bosman, *A New and Accurate Description*, 265.

69. Carney and Rosomoff, *In the Shadow of Slavery*, 68.

70. Carney and Rosomoff, *In the Shadow of Slavery*, 67.

71. John Thornton, *Africa and Africans in the Making of the Atlantic World, 1400–1800, Second Edition* (Cambridge: Cambridge University Press, 1998), 155–56.

72. Thornton, *Africa and Africans*, 156.

73. Carney and Rosomoff, *In the Shadow of Slavery*, 67; Marcus Rediker, *The Slave Ship: A Human History* (New York: Penguin, 2007), 237.

74. Harris, *High on the Hog*, 32.

75. Sowande M. Mustakeem, *Slavery at Sea: Terror, Sex, and Sickness in the Middle Passage* (Urbana, IL: University of Illinois Press, 2016), 65–66.

76. Mustakeem, *Slavery at Sea*, 68–69.

77. Carney and Rosomoff, *In the Shadow of Slavery*, 73–77.

78. Harris, *High on the Hog*, 32; Rediker, *The Slave Ship*, 237.

79. Osseo-Asare, *Food Culture in Sub-Saharan Africa*, 14.

80. Quoted in Bertie R. Mandelblatt, "'Beans from *Rochel* and Manioc from *Prince's Island*': West Africa, French Atlantic Commodity Circuits, and the Provisioning of the French Middle Passage," *History of European Ideas* 34, no. 4 (2008): 411.

81. Jennifer Jensen Wallach, *How America Eats: A Social History of US Food and Culture* (Lanham, MD: Rowman & Littlefield, 2013), 11–13; for more information about early modern ideas about malleable bodies, see Trudy Eden, *The Early American Table: Food and Society in the New World* (DeKalb: Northern Illinois University Press, 2008); Ken Albala, *Eating Right in the Renaissance* (Berkeley: University of California Press,

2002); Rebecca Earle, *The Body of the Conquistador: Food, Race and the Colonial Experience in Spanish America, 1492–1700* (Cambridge: Cambridge University Press, 2012).

82. For more about food and race-making projects, see Jennifer Jensen Wallach, "Food and Race," in *The Routledge History of American Foodways*, eds. Michael D. Wise and Jennifer Jensen Wallach (London: Routledge, 2016): 293–310.

83. Rediker, *The Slave Ship*, 237.

84. Jean Barbot, *A Description of the Coasts of North and South-Guinea* (London, 1702), 465.

85. Quoted in Mustakeem, *Slavery at Sea*, 69.

86. Mustakeem, *Slavery at Sea*, 70–71.

87. Rediker, *The Slave Ship*, 285.

88. Michael W. Twitty, *The Cooking Gene: A Journey through African American Culinary History in the Old South* (New York: Amistad, 2017), 208.

89. Kenneth F. Kiple and Brian T. Higgins, "Mortality Caused by Dehydration during the Middle Passage," *Social Science History* 13, no. 4 (January 1989): 420–37.

90. Jean Barbot, *A Description of Guinea* (1684), in *Documents Illustrative of the History of the Slave Trade to America, 1441–1700*, ed. Elizabeth Donnan (Washington, DC, 1965), 282–300.

91. Eric Robert Taylor, *If We Must Die: Shipboard Insurrections in the Era of the Transatlantic Slave Trade* (Baton Rouge: Louisiana State University Press, 2009), 32–33; Ramesh Mallipeddi, "'A Fixed Melancholy': Migration, Memory, and the Middle Passage," *Eighteenth Century* 55, no. 2 (2014): 235–53.

92. Rediker, *The Slave Ship*, 17–19.

93. Alexander Falconbridge, *An Account of the Slave Trade on the Coast of Africa* (London, 1788), 23.

94. John Woodall, *The Surgions Mate: The First Compendium on Naval Medicine, Surgery and Drug Therapy, 1617*, edited and annotated by Irmgard Muller (Basel, Switzerland: Birkhauser, 2016), 43.

95. Map 9: Volume and direction of the trans-Atlantic slave trade from all African to all American Regions, Voyages: The Transatlantic Slave Trade Database, http://www.slavevoyages.org/assessment/intro-maps, accessed May 25, 2017.

96. Smallwood, *Saltwater Slavery*, 159.

CHAPTER 2

1. The Works Progress Administration Library of Congress Project, *Slave Narratives: A Folk History of Slavery in the United States with Interviews from Former Slaves, Volume II*, Arkansas Narratives Part 5 (Library of Congress: Washington, DC, 1941), 338. The full text is available here: https://memory.loc.gov/mss/mesn/025/025.pdf.

2. Marcie Cohen Ferris, *The Edible South: The Power of Food and the Making of an American Region* (Chapel Hill: University of North Carolina Press, 2016), 13.

3. Andrew F. Smith, *Peanuts: The Illustrious History of the Goober Pea* (Urbana: University of Illinois Press, 2007), 8.

4. Judith A. Carney and Richard Nicholas Rosomoff, *In the Shadow of Slavery: Africa's Botanical Legacy in the Atlantic World* (Berkeley: University of California Press, 2009), 22.

5. Carney and Rosomoff, *In the Shadow of Slavery*, 7, 65–66; Carney and Rosomoff argue that African biological products are often overlooked in discussions of the Columbian Exchange and other trade networks. However, they argue that more than one hundred species of great importance to the global food supply originated in Africa. These include sorghum, watermelon, coffee, okra, black-eyed peas, and kola nuts.

6. Jessica Harris, *High on the Hog: A Culinary Journey from Africa to America* (New York: Bloomsbury, 2011), 16. Historian Philip Morgan has discovered references to enslaved people eating yams in eighteenth-century Carolina. Whether these observers were referring to attempts to cultivate true African yams in Carolina or using the term *yam* to refer to another tuber is unknown. See Philip Morgan, *Slave Counterpoint: Black Culture in the Eighteenth Century Chesapeake and Lowcountry* (Chapel Hill: University of North Carolina Press, 1998), 141.

7. Carney and Rosomoff, *In the Shadow of Slavery*, 113; Joseph E. Holloway, "Africanisms in African American Names in the United States," in *Africanisms in American Culture*, ed. Joseph E. Holloway (Bloomington: Indiana University Press, 2005), 104; Robert L. Hall, "Food Crops, Medicinal Plants, and the Atlantic Slave Trade," in *African American Foodways: Explorations of History and Culture*, ed. Anne L. Bower (Urbana: University of Illinois Press, 2007), 20–21.

8. Mary Tolford Wilson, "Peaceful Integration: The Owner's Adoption of his Slaves' Food," *Journal of Negro History* 4, no. 2 (1964): 116.

9. Carney and Rosomoff, *In the Shadow of Slavery*, 148–50.

10. This generalization, like most, may not have always held. Depending upon when and where they were captured, some Africans may have had a great deal of familiarity with some European and American ingredients.

11. David Eltis, Philip Morgan, and David Richardson, "Agency and Diaspora in Atlantic History: Reassessing the African Contribution to Rice Cultivation in the Americas," *American Historical Review* 112, no. 5 (December 2007): 1332.

12. Theresa Singleton, "The Archeology of Slave Life," in *Images of the Recent Past: Readings in Historical Archaeology*, edited by Charles E. Orser Jr. (Walnut Creek, CA: Altamira, 1996), 142.

13. James McWilliams, *A Revolution in Eating: How the Quest for Food Shaped America* (New York: Columbia University Press, 2005), 134–37; R. Douglas Hurt, *American Agriculture: A Brief History* (West Layfayette, IN: Purdue University Press, 2002), 48–49; Peter H. Wood, *Black Majority: Negroes in Colonial South Carolina* (New York: Alfred A. Knopf, 1974), 28–32.

14. Christopher Cumo, *The Ongoing Columbian Exchange: Stories of Biological and Economic Transfer in World History* (Santa Barbara, CA: ABC-CLIO, 2015), 91.

15. McWilliams, *A Revolution in Eating*, 136.

16. McWilliams, *A Revolution in Eating*, 136.

17. Wood, *Black Majority*, 36.

18. Daniel C. Littlefield, *Rice and Slaves: Ethnicity and the Slave Trade in Colonial South Carolina* (Urbana: University of Illinois Press, 1981), 81.

19. Judith A. Carney, *Black Rice: The African Origins of Rice Cultivation in the Americas* (Cambridge: Harvard University Press, 2001), 145–46.

20. Carney, *Black Rice*, 144–47; Carney and Rosomoff, *In the Shadow of Slavery*, 153.

21. Wood, *Black Majority*, 60.

22. See for example, Eltis, Morgan, and Richardson, "Agency and Diaspora in Atlantic History," 1329–58.

23. Wood, *Black Majority*, 61.

24. Carney and Rosomoff, *In the Shadow of Slavery*, 153; McWilliams, *A Revolution in Eating*, 157; Wood, *Black Majority*, 61.

25. Eugene Genovese, *Roll, Jordan, Roll: The World the Slaves Made* (New York: Vintage, 1976), 545.

26. Carney, *Black Rice*, 114–17; James C. McMann, *Stirring the Pot: A History of African Cuisine* (Athens: Ohio University Press, 2009), 38–40.

27. Carney and Rosomoff, *In the Shadow of Slavery*, 177–86.

28. Nancy Harmon Jenkins, "Cooks on the Map; This Month: Dr. Jessica B. Harris, Brooklyn; Tracking Cuisines with African Past," *New York Times*, February 28, 1990.

29. Karen Hess, *The Carolina Rice Kitchen: The African Connection* (Columbia, SC: University of South Carolina Press, 1998), 96.

30. Hess, *The Carolina Rice Kitchen*, 101; Ferris, *The Edible South*, 13; "Ham," in *The Oxford Companion to Food, Second Edition*, eds. Alan Davidson and Tom Jaine (Oxford: Oxford University Press, 2006), 368–69.

31. John Edward Phillips, "The African Heritage of White America," in *Africanisms in American Culture*, ed. Joseph E. Holloway, 378–79 (Bloomington: Indiana University Press, 2005); Frederick Douglass Opie, *Hog and Hominy: Soul Food from Africa to America* (New York: Columbia University Press, 2008), 29.

32. Carney and Rosomoff, *In the Shadow of Slavery*, 169; Carolyn Kolb and C. Paige Gutierrez, "Gumbo," in *The New Encyclopedia of Southern Culture, Volume 7, Foodways*, ed. John T. Edge (Chapel Hill: University of North Carolina Press, 2007), 177–79; Opie, *Hog and Hominy*, 29.

33. Harris, *High on the Hog*, 17.

34. Mary Randolph, *The Virginia Housewife; Or Methodical Cook* (Baltimore: John Plaskitt, 1836), 81.

35. Randolph, *The Virginia Housewife*, 17–18.

36. Hess, *The Carolina Rice Kitchen*, 94.

37. Jeffrey M. Pilcher, *Que Vivan Los Tamales!: Food and the Making of Mexican Identity* (Albuquerque: University of New Mexico Press, 1998).

38. Theda Purdue, *Cherokee Women: Gender and Culture Change, 1700–1835* (Lincoln: University of Nebraska Press, 1998), 20–21.

39. Thomas Astley, *A New General Collection of Voyages and Travels, Volume 2* (London: T. Astley, 1745), 638.

40. Robert A. Gilmer, "Native American Contributions to African American Foodways: Slavery, Colonialism, and Cuisine," in *Dethroning the Deceitful Pork Chop:*

Rethinking African American Foodways from Slavery to Obama, ed. Jennifer Jensen Wallach (Fayetteville: University of Arkansas Press, 2015), 20.

41. James C. McCann, *Stirring the Pot: A History of African Cuisine* (Athens: Ohio University Press, 2009), 50.

42. Calvin Trillin, "Tamales on the Delta," *The New Yorker*, January 6, 2014, http://www.newyorker.com/magazine/2014/01/06/tamales-on-the-delta; Amy C. Evans, "Introduction: Hot Tamales and the Mississippi Delta," Southern Foodways Alliance, http://www.southernfoodways.org/interview/hot-tamales-the-mississippi-delta/; Gilmer, "Native American Contributions to African American Foodways," 19–20.

43. Jessica B. Harris, "Three Is a Magic Number," *Southern Quarterly* 44, no. 2 (2007): 9–15.

44. Michael W. Twitty, *The Cooking Gene: A Journey through African American Culinary History in the Old South* (New York: Amistad, 2017), 180.

45. Darrin Nordahl, *Eating Appalachia: Rediscovering Regional American Flavors* (Chicago: Chicago Review Press, 2015), 118–19; Helen C. Rountree, *The Powhatan Indians of Virginia: Their Traditional Culture* (Norman: University of Oklahoma Press, 1989), 52–53; J. Michael Luster, "Persimmons," in *The New Encyclopedia of Southern Culture: Foodways*, 221. See also Rayna Green, "Mother Corn and Dixie Pig: Native Food in the Native South," in *The Larder: Food Studies Methods from the American South*, eds. John T. Edge, Elizabeth Engelhardt, and Ted Ownby (Athens: University of Georgia Press, 2013), 155–65.

46. McWilliams, *A Revolution in Eating*, 91–102; 137–55.

47. Jennifer Jensen Wallach, *How America Eats: A Social History of US Food and Culture* (Lanham, MD: Rowman & Littlefield, 2013), 13–14; Matt McMillen, "Beef," in *The New Encyclopedia of Southern Culture: Foodways*, 26–27; Charles Reagan Wilson, "Pork," in *The New Encyclopedia of Southern Culture: Foodways*, 88–92.

48. Opie, *Hog and Hominy*, 6.

49. Purdue, 25, 121–22; Opie, *Hog and Hominy*, 19–20.

50. Wallach, *How America Eats*, 13–14; Opie, *Hog and Hominy*, 19.

51. Charles Reagan Wilson, "Biscuits," in *The New Encyclopedia of Southern Culture: Foodways*, 122–25.

52. Robert L. Hall, "Africa and the American South: Culinary Connections," *Southern Quarterly* 44, no. 2 (Winter 2007): 19–52; Opie, *Hog and Hominy*, 18; Harris, *High on the Hog*, 71–72.

53. Carney and Rosomoff, *In the Shadow of Slavery*, 177–78: William C. Whit, "Soul Food as Cultural Creation," in *African American Foodways*, 48–49.

54. Gilmer, "Native American Contributions to African American Foodways," 17–30.

55. McWilliams, *A Revolution in Eating*, 38.

56. Genovese, *Roll, Jordan, Roll*, 544.

57. Charles Joyner, *Down by the Riverside: A South Carolina Slave Community* (Urbana: University of Illinois Press, 1984), 91.

58. For different antebellum theories about how to best feed enslaved people, see "Agricultural Department: Management of Negroes," *De Bow's Review* 10, no. 3 (March

1851): 325; "Negro Management upon Southern Estates," in *The Industrial Resources, Etc. of the Southern and Western States*, ed. James Dunwoody Brownson De Bow (New Orleans: Office of *De Bow's Review*, 1853), 331.

59. Genovese, *Roll, Jordan, Roll*, 544; Opie, *Hog and Hominy*, 33–35.

60. Anne Yentsch, "Excavating the South's African American Food History," in *African American Foodways*, 63.

61. Solomon Northup, *Twelve Years a Slave* (Auburn, NY: Derby and Miller, 1853), 214–15.

62. Frederick Douglass, *Narrative of the Life of Frederick Douglass, Written by Himself* (Boston: Anti-Slavery Office, 1845), 75.

63. Northup, *Twelve Years a Slave*, 215.

64. Douglass, *Narrative of the Life of Frederick Douglass*, 74.

65. Joyner, *Down by the Riverside*, 91.

66. Genovese, *Roll, Jordan, Roll*, 543.

67. Melville Herskovits, *The Myth of the Negro Past* (Boston: Beacon Press, 1990), 132–33.

68. Kelley Fanto Deetz, *Bound to the Fire: How Virginia's Enslaved Cooks Helped Invent American Cuisine* (Lexington, KY: University Press of Kentucky, 2017), 4.

69. Quoted in Genovese, *Roll, Jordan, Roll*, 541, 545.

70. Philip Morgan, *Slave Counterpoint: Black Culture in the Eighteenth Century Chesapeake and Lowcountry* (Chapel Hill: University of North Carolina Press, 1998), 134.

71. Ira Berlin, *Many Thousands Gone: The First Two Centuries of Slavery in North America* (Cambridge: Harvard University Press, 1998), 112–13; Morgan, *Slave Counterpoint*, 143.

72. Samuel H. Williamson and Louis P. Cain, "Measuring Slavery in 2016 Dollars," Measuringworth.com, https://www.measuringworth.com/slavery.php#foot2.

73. Roger L. Ranson, "The Economics of the Civil War," EH.net, http://eh.net/encyclopedia/the-economics-of-the-civil-war/; Ta-Nehesi Coates, "Slavery Made America: The Case for Reparations," *Atlantic Monthly*, June 24, 2014, https://www.theatlantic.com/business/archive/2014/06/slavery-made-america/373288/; David Brion Davis, "The Impact of British Abolitionism on American Sectionalism," in *In the Shadow of Freedom: The Politics of Slavery in the National Capitol*, eds. Paul Finkelman and Donald R. Kennon (Athens: Ohio State University Press, 2011), 21.

74. Paul A. David, Herbert G. Gutman, Richard Sutch, Peter Temin, and Gavin Wright, *Reckoning with Slavery: A Critical Study of the Quantitative History of American Negro Slavery* (New York: Oxford University Press, 1976), 354.

75. Douglass, *Narrative of the Life of Frederick Douglass*, 35.

76. Harriet Jacobs, *Incidents in the Life of a Slave Girl, Written by Herself* (Boston, 1861), 71–72.

77. Genovese, *Roll, Jordan, Roll*, 76–77.

78. Sam Bower Hilliard, *Hog Meat and Hoecake: Food Supply in the Old South, 1840–1860* (Athens: University of Georgia Press, 2014), 55–62; Herbert C. Covey and Dwight Eisnach, *What the Slaves Ate: Recollections of African American Foods and Foodways from the Slave Narratives* (Santa Barbara, CA: ABC CLIO, 2009), 21; Robert William Fogel and

Stanley Engerman, *Time on the Cross: The Economics of American Negro Slavery* (Boston: Little, Brown, and Company, 1974), 109–10; Ferris, *The Edible South*, 29–30.

79. "Agricultural Department: Management of Negroes," *De Bow's Review* 10 (1851), 325.

80. Covey and Eisnach, *What the Slaves Ate*, 20.

81. John Blassingame, *The Slave Community: Plantation Life in the Antebellum South* (New York: Oxford University Press, 1972), 158.

82. Richard H. Steckel, "A Peculiar Population: The Nutrition, Health, and Mortality of American Slaves from Childhood to Maturity," *Journal of Economic History* 46, no. 3 (September 1986): 721–41; Fogel and Engerman, *Time on the Cross*, 109–10; Covey and Eisnach, *What the Slaves Ate*, 26–30.

83. Richard H. Steckel, "Women, Work, and Health under Plantation Slavery," in *More Than Chattel: Black Women and Slavery in the Americas*, eds. David Barry Gasper and Darlene Clark Hine (Bloomington, IN: Indiana University Press, 1996), 51.

84. Steckel, "A Peculiar Population, 721.

85. Kenneth F. Kiple and Virginia H. Kiple, "Slave Child Mortality: Some Nutritional Answers to a Perennial Puzzle," *Journal of Social History* 10, no. 3 (Spring 1977): 284–309.

86. Booker T. Washington, "Chicken, Pigs, and People," *The Outlook* 68 (May 1901): 291.

87. Works Progress Administration, *Slave Narratives: A Folk History of Slavery in the United States with Interviews from Former Slaves, Volume II*, Arkansas Narratives Part 5 (Library of Congress: Washington, DC: 1941), 338. The full text is available here: https://memory.loc.gov/mss/mesn/025/025.pdf.

88. Douglass, *Narrative of the Life of Frederick Douglass*, 27.

89. Douglass, *Narrative of the Life of Frederick Douglass*, 48.

90. Works Progress Administration, *Slave Narratives, Volume II*, 130. The full text is available here: https://memory.loc.gov/mss/mesn/025/025.pdf.

91. Jacobs, *Incidents in the Life of a Slave Girl*, 22.

92. Charles Ball, *Slavery in the United States: A Narrative of the Life and Adventures of Charles Ball* (New York: John S. Taylor, 1837), 44.

93. Fogel and Engerman, *Time on the Cross*, 115.

94. Tyson Gibbs, Kathleen Cargill, Leslie Sue Lieberman, and Elizabeth Reitz, "Nutrition in a Slave Population: An Anthropological Examination," *Medical Anthropology* 4, no. 2 (1980): 262.

95. Richard Sutch, "The Care and Feeding of Slaves," in *Reckoning with Slavery: A Critical Study of the Quantitative History of American Negro Slavery*, eds. Paul A. David, Herbert G. Gutman, Richard Sutch, Peter Temin, and Gavin Wright (New York: Oxford University Press, 1976), 233–34.

96. Sutch, "The Care and Feeding of Slaves," 268–71.

97. Kenneth F. Kiple and Virgina Himmelsteib King, *Another Dimension of the Black Diaspora: Diet, Disease, and Racism* (Cambridge: Cambridge University Press, 1981).

98. Fogel and Engerman, *Time on the Cross*, 110–11.

99. Ball, *Slavery in the United States*, 188–202.

100. Ball, *Slavery in the United States*, 189.

101. Frederick Douglass, *The Life and Times of Frederick Douglass* (Boston: Du-Wolf & Fiske, 1892), 77–79.

102. Booker T. Washington, *Up from Slavery* (Garden City, NY: The Country Life Press, 1901), 4–5.

103. Jacobs, *Incidents in the Life of a Slave Girl*, 73–74.

104. Douglass, *Narrative of the Life of Frederick Douglass*, 15–16.

105. Kenneth Stampp, *The Peculiar Institution: Slavery in the Ante-Bellum South* (New York: Knopf, 1956), 79; John W. Blassingame, *The Slave Community: Plantation Life in the Antebellum South* (New York: Oxford University Press, 1972), 42, 92; Michael Twitty, "Gardens," in *World of the Slave: Encyclopedia of the Material Life of Slaves in the United States*, eds. Martha B. Katz-Hyman and Kym S. Rice (Santa Barbara, CA: Greenwood, 2011), 245–50.

106. Covey and Eisnach, *What the Slaves Ate*, 74.

107. Ball, *Slavery in the United States*, 166.

108. Covey and Eisnach, *What the Slaves Ate*, 74; Morgan, *Slave Counterpoint*, 140–42.

109. Morgan, *Slave Counterpoint*, 140; Covey and Eisnach, *What the Slaves Ate*, 226; Yentsch, "Excavating the South's African American Food History," 67.

110. Yentsch, "Excavating the South's African American Food History," 65–67; McWilliams, *A Revolution in Eating*, 160; Covey and Eisnach, *What the Slaves Ate*, 244–56.

111. Yentsch, "Excavating the South's African American Food History," 69.

112. Juliet E. K. Walker, *The History of Black Business in America: Capitalism, Race, Entrepreneurship* (New York: Macmillan Library Reference, 1998), 69.

113. Kathleen Hilliard, *Masters, Slaves, and Exchange: Power's Purchase in the Old South* (New York: Cambridge University Press, 2014), 24, 44.

114. Philip D. Morgan, "The Ownership of Property by Slaves in the Mid-Nineteenth-Century Low Country," *Journal of Southern History* 49, no. 3 (August 1983): 399–420.

115. Linda Civitello, *Cuisine and Culture: A History of Food and People, Second Edition* (Hoboken, NJ: John Wiley and Sons, 2008), 211.

116. Covey and Eisnach, *What the Slaves Ate*, 97–99; Morgan, *Slave Counterpoint*, 136–37.

117. Hilliard, *Masters, Slaves, and Exchange*, 92.

118. Psyche Williams-Forson, *Building Houses Out of Chicken Legs: Black Women, Food, and Power* (Chapel Hill: University of North Carolina Press, 2006), 197.

119. John Solomon Otto and Augustus Marion Burns III, "Black Folks and Poor Buckras: Archeological Evidence of Slave and Overseer Living Conditions on an Antebellum Plantation," *Journal of Black Studies* 14, no. 2 (December 1983): 185–200.

120. Christopher F. Fennell, "Early African America: Archeological Studies of Significance and Diversity," *Journal of Archeological Research* 19, no. 1 (March 2011): 1–49.

121. Douglass, *Narrative of the Life of Frederick Douglass*, 57.

122. Douglass, *Narrative of the Life of Frederick Douglass*, 82.

CHAPTER 3

1. The Works Progress Administration Library of Congress Project, *Slave Narratives: A Folk History of Slavery in the United States with Interviews from Former Slaves, Volume IX*, Mississippi Narratives (Library of Congress: Washington, DC: 1941), 4. The full text is available here: http://lcweb2.loc.gov/mss/mesn/090/090.pdf.

2. The Works Progress Administration Library of Congress Project, *Slave Narratives: A Folk History of Slavery in the United States with Interviews from Former Slaves, Volume II*, Arkansas Narratives Part 1 (Library of Congress: Washington, DC: 1941), 41. The full text is available here: https://memory.loc.gov/mss/mesn/021/021.pdf.

3. Works Progress Administration, *Slave Narratives*, Arkansas Narratives Part 1, 312.

4. Works Progress Administration, *Slave Narratives*, Arkansas Narratives Part 1, 118.

5. Vincent Harding, *There Is a River: The Black Struggle for Freedom in America* (New York: Houghton Mifflin, 1981), 219.

6. W. E. B. Du Bois, *Black Reconstruction in America, 1860–1880* (New York: Free Press, 1998), 64–74.

7. Jim Downs, *Sick from Freedom: African-American Illness and Suffering during the Civil War and Reconstruction* (New York: Oxford University Press, 2012), 47–48.

8. Affidavit of a Joseph Miller, 26 Nov. 1864, filed with H-8 1865, Registered Letters Received, series 3379, Tennessee Assistant Commissioner, Bureau of Refugees, Freedmen, & Abandoned Lands, Record Group 105, National Archives. Full text available from the Freedmen and Southern Society Project: http://www.freedmen.umd.edu/JMiller.html.

9. Downs, *Sick from Freedom*, 18–21.

10. Downs, *Sick from Freedom*, 31.

11. Booker T. Washington, *Up from Slavery* (Garden City, NY: The Country Life Press, 1901), 10.

12. Works Progress Administration, *Slave Narratives*, Mississippi, 3.

13. Works Progress Administration, *Slave Narratives*, Mississippi, 24.

14. Works Progress Administration, *Slave Narratives*, Mississippi, 38.

15. Washington, *Up from Slavery*, 15.

16. Quoted in Anne Yentsch, "Excavating the South's African American Food History," in *African American Foodways: Explorations of History and Culture*, ed. Anne L. Bower (Urbana: University of Illinois Press, 2007), 78.

17. Washington, *Up from Slavery*, 21–22.

18. Leon Litwack, *Been in the Storm So Long: The Aftermath of Slavery* (New York: Knopf, 1979), 329.

19. Eric Foner, *A Short History of Reconstruction, Updated Edition* (New York: Harper Perennial, 2015), 68.

20. Foner, *A Short History of Reconstruction*, 68.

21. Du Bois, *Black Reconstruction*, 225.

22. Foner, *A Short History of Reconstruction*, 69.

23. Quoted in Litwack, *Been in the Storm So Long*, 415.

24. Litwack, *Been in the Storm So Long*, 415.

25. The literature about southern agriculture, sharecropping, and debt peonage is extensive and includes Jeannie Whayne, *A New Plantation South: Land, Labor, and Federal Favor in Twentieth Century Arkansas* (Charlottesville: University of Virginia Press, 1996), 55; Pete Daniel, *The Shadow of Slavery: Peonage in the South, 1901–1969* (Urbana: University of Illinois Press, 1990); Donald H. Grubbs, *Cry from the Cotton: The Southern Tenant Farmer's Union and the New Deal* (Chapel Hill: University of North Carolina Press, 1971); Jack Temple Kirby, *Rural Worlds Lost: The American South, 1920–1960* (Baton Rouge, LA: Louisiana State University Press, 1986); Pete Daniel, *Breaking the Land: The Transformation of Cotton, Tobacco and Rice Cultures since 1880* (Urbana: University of Illinois Press, 1985); Gilbert C. Fite, *Cotton Fields No More* (Lexington: University of Kentucky Press, 1984); David Eugene Conrad, *The Forgotten Farmers: The Story of Sharecroppers in the New Deal* (Westport: Greenwood Publishers, 1965), 37–63.

26. Ereven J. Long, "The Agricultural Ladder: Its Adequacy as a Model for Farm Tenure Research," *Land Economics* 26, no. 3 (August 1950): 268–73.

27. Michael B. Dougan, *Arkansas Odyssey* (Little Rock: Rose Publishing, 1994), 425.

28. Hortense Powdermaker, *After Freedom: A Cultural Study of the Deep South* (New York: Viking Press, 1939), 99–101.

29. Yentsch, "Excavating the South's African American Food History," 78–80.

30. Sharon Ann Holt, *Making Freedom Pay: North Carolina Freedpeople Working for Themselves* (Athens: University of Georgia Press, 2000), 20; The Works Progress Administration Library of Congress Project, *Slave Narratives: A Folk History of Slavery in the United States with Interviews from Former Slaves, Volume XI, Part II*, North Carolina (Library of Congress: Washington, DC: 1941), 236–43. Full text available here: http://lcweb2.loc.gov/mss/mesn/112/112.pdf.

31. Ira Berlin, *The Making of African America: The Four Great Migrations* (New York: Penguin Books, 2010), 141.

32. Allison Davis, Burleigh B. Gardner, and Mary R. Gardner, *Deep South: A Social Anthropological Study of Caste and Class* (Columbia: University of South Carolina Press, 2009), 383–85; W. O. Atwater and Chas. D. Woods, *Dietary Studies with Reference to the Food of the Negro in Alabama, 1895 and 1896* (Washington, DC: Government Printing Office, 1897), 17.

33. Atwater and Woods, *Dietary Studies*, 18.

34. Kim Lacy Rogers, *Life and Death in the Delta: African American Narratives of Violence, Resilience, and Social Change* (London: Palgrave, 2006), 28.

35. Nate Shaw and Theodore Rosengarten, *All God's Dangers: The Life of Nate Shaw* (New York: Knopf, 1974), 31.

36. Shaw and Rosengarten, *All God's Dangers*, 372.

37. Marcie Cohen Ferris, *The Edible South: The Power of Food and the Making of an American Region* (Chapel Hill: University of North Carolina Press, 2016), 101; Charles S. Johnson, Edwin R. Embree, and W. W. Alexander, *The Collapse of Cotton Tenancy: Summary of Field Studies and Statistical Surveys, 1933–35* (Chapel Hill: University of North Carolina Press, 1935), 16; Powdermaker, *After Freedom*, 79; Yentsch,

"Excavating the South's African American Food History," 76; Alison Collis Greene, "'Human Beings Do Not Behave Like Test Tube Experiments': Dorothy Dickens and the Science of Home Economics in Mid-Twentieth Century Mississippi," *Journal of Mississippi History* 75, no. 1 (Spring 2013): 11–12.

38. Richard Wright, *12 Million Black Voices* (New York: Basic Books, 2002), 38–39.

39. Tom E. Terrill and Jerrold Hirsch, eds. *Such as Us: Southern Voices of the Thirties* (New York: W. W. Norton, 1979), 55.

40. Terrill and Hirsch, *Such as Us*, 90–91.

41. Davis, Gardner, and Gardner, *Deep South*, 285.

42. Johnson, Embree, and Alexander, *The Collapse of Cotton Tenancy*, 16.

43. Davis, Gardner, and Gardner, *Deep South*, 379.

44. Davis, Gardner, and Gardner, *Deep South*, 381–82.

45. Rogers, *Life and Death in the Delta*, 29.

46. Davis, Gardner, and Gardner, *Deep South*, 381.

47. Atwater and Woods, *Dietary Studies*, 19.

48. Ferris, *The Edible South*, 128–30; Johnson, Embree, and Alexander, *The Collapse of Cotton Tenancy*, 16–17; Jacqueline Jones, *Labor of Love, Labor of Sorrow: Black Women, Work, and the Family from Slavery to the Present* (New York: Basic Books, 2009), 84–85.

49. Atwater and Woods, *Dietary Studies*, 20.

50. The Works Progress Administration Library of Congress Project, *Slave Narratives: A Folk History of Slavery in the United States with Interviews from Former Slaves, Volume II*, Arkansas Narratives Part 5 (Library of Congress: Washington, DC: 1941), 3–4. The full text is available here: https://memory.loc.gov/mss/mesn/025/025.pdf.

51. Edward H. Beardsley, *A History of Neglect: Health Care for Blacks and Mill Workers in the Twentieth-Century South* (Knoxville: University of Tennessee Press, 1987), 54–58. Nicholas P. Hordeman, *Shucks, Shacks, and Hominy Blocks Corn as a Way of Life in Pioneer America* (Baton Rouge: Louisiana State University Press, 1981), 149–50. Ferris, *The Edible South*, 133–36.

52. Richard Wright, *Black Boy: A Record of Childhood and Youth* (New York: HarperPerennial, 2007), 102–3.

53. Psyche Williams-Forson, *Building Houses Out of Chicken Legs: Black Women, Food, and Power* (Chapel Hill: University of North Carolina Press, 2006), 13–26.

54. Juliet E. K. Walker, *The History of Black Business in America: Capitalism, Race, Entrepreneurship* (New York: Macmillan Library Reference, 1998), 135–36.

55. Walker, *The History of Black Business in America*, 135–36.

56. Walker, *The History of Black Business in America*, 136.

57. W. E. B. Du Bois, *The Philadelphia Negro* (New York: Shocken Books, 1967), 35; Janet Theophano, *Eat My Words: Reading Women's Lives through the Cookbooks They Wrote* (New York: St. Martin's, 2003), 56–57; William Frank Mitchell, *African American Food Culture* (Westport, CT: Greenwood Press, 2009), 15.

58. Du Bois, *The Philadelphia Negro*, 35; Juliet E. K. Walker, ed., *Encyclopedia of African American Business History* (Westport, CT: Greenwood Press, 1999), 130.

59. Walker, *The History of Black Business in America*, 177.

60. Williams-Forson, *Building Houses Out of Chicken Legs*, 31–33.

61. Malinda Russell, *Domestic Cook Book: Containing a Careful Selection of Useful Recipes for the Kitchen* (Ann Arbor, MI: William L. Clements Library, 2007), 5.

62. Bill Daley, "Pioneer Shared 'Old Southern Cooking,'" *Chicago Tribune*, June 19, 2013; Abby Fisher, *What Mrs. Fisher Knows about Old Southern Cooking, Soups, Pickles, Preserves, Etc.* (San Francisco: Women's Cooperative Printing Office, 1881), 50.

63. Walker, *The History of Black Business in America*, 160–61.

64. Mia Bay, *To Tell the Truth Freely: The Life of Ida B. Wells* (New York: Hill and Wang, 2009), 82–86.

65. W. E. B. Du Bois, ed. *The Negro in Business* (Atlanta, GA: Atlanta University, 1899), 12.

66. Walker, *The History of Black Business in America*, 162.

67. Angela Jill Cooley, *To Live and Dine in Dixie: The Evolution of Urban Food Culture in the Jim Crow South* (Athens, GA: University of Georgia Press, 2015), 23–24; Tera Hunter, *To 'Joy My Freedom: Southern Black Women's Lives and Labors after the Civil War* (Cambridge, MA: Harvard University Press, 1998), 26.

68. Rebecca Sharpless, *Cooking in Other Women's Kitchens: Domestic Workers in the South, 1865–1960* (Chapel Hill, NC: University of North Carolina Press, 2010), 5–8.

69. Sharpless, *Cooking in Other Women's Kitchens*, 179.

70. Elizabeth Ross Haynes, "Negroes in Domestic Service in the United States," *Journal of Negro History* 8, no. 4 (1923): 384–442.

71. Vanessa May, "'Obtaining a Decent Livelihood': Food Work, Race, and Gender in W. E. B. Du Bois's *The Philadelphia Negro*," *Labor: Studies in Working-Class History of the Americas* 12, no. 1–2 (2015): 123.

72. Sharpless, *Cooking in Other Women's Kitchens*, 110.

73. Sharpless, *Cooking in Other Women's Kitchens*, 14.

74. Davis, Gardner, and Gardner, *Deep South*, 443.

75. Sharpless, *Cooking in Other Women's Kitchens*, 7.

76. Sharpless, *Cooking in Other Women's Kitchens*, 23.

77. Davis, Gardner, and Gardner, *Deep South*, 82.

78. Neil R. McMillan, *Dark Journey: Black Mississippians in the Age of Jim Crow* (Urbana: University of Illinois Press, 1990), 23.

79. Angela Jill Cooley argues that discomfort about black servants did encourage some white southerners to briefly debate the benefits of trying to recruit and train white servants. See Cooley, *To Live and Dine in Dixie*, 26–27.

80. Sharpless, *Cooking in Other Women's Kitchens*, 185.

81. Powdermaker, *After Freedom*, 117.

82. Powdermaker, *After Freedom*, 118.

83. Sharpless, *Cooking in Other Women's Kitchens*, 77–78.

84. Sharpless, *Cooking in Other Women's Kitchens*, 74–77; Powdermaker, *After Freedom*, 119–20; Hunter, *To 'Joy My Freedom*, 60–61.

85. Quoted in Rogers, *Life and Death in the Delta*, 91–92.

86. Anne Moody, *Coming of Age in Mississippi: The Classic Autobiography of Growing Up Poor and Black in the Rural South* (New York: Dell, 1992), 29.

87. Martha McCulloch Williams, *Dishes and Beverages of the Old South* (New York: McBride Nast & Co., 1913), 15.

88. Micki McEyla, *Clinging to Mammy: The Faithful Slave in Twentieth-Century America* (Cambridge, MA: Harvard University Press, 2007), 82.

89. To read more about the idea of the innately talented black cook, see also Doris Witt, "The Intersections of Literary and Culinary Studies," in *African American Foodways: Explorations of History & Culture*, ed. Anne L. Bower (Urbana: University of Illinois Press, 2007), 107; and Helen Zoe Veit, *Modern Food, Moral Food: Self-Control, Science, and the Rise of Modern American Eating in the Early Twentieth Century* (Chapel Hill: University of North Carolina Press, 2013), 116–17.

90. Cooley, *To Live and Dine in Dixie*, 33–34.

91. Idella Parker with Mary Keating, *Idella: Marjorie Rawlings's "Perfect Maid"* (Gainsville, FL: University of Florida Press, 1992), 69. See also Rebecca Sharpless, "Neither Friends nor Peers: Idella Parker, Marjorie Kinnan Rawlings, and the Limits of Gender Solidarity at Cross Creek," *Journal of Southern History* 78, no. 2 (May 2012): 327–60.

92. Emma and William McKinney, *Aunt Caroline's Dixieland Recipes: A Rare Collection of Choice Southern Dishes* (Chicago: Laird & Lee, 1922); Jennifer Jensen Wallach, *How America Eats: A Social History of US Food and Culture* (Lanham, MD: Rowman & Littlefield, 2013), 186.

93. Wallach, *How America Eats*, 186.

94. Yentsch, "Excavating the South's African American Food History," 81.

95. Marcie Cohen Ferris, *Matzoh Ball Gumbo: Culinary Tales of the Jewish South* (Chapel Hill, NC: University of North Carolina Press, 2010), 31.

96. Ferris, *Matzoh Ball Gumbo*, 66–67.

97. For an overview of southern food habits, see Sam Bower Hilliard, *Hog Meat and Hoecake: Food Supply in the Old South, 1840–1860* (Athens: University of Georgia Press, 2014); and Ferris, *The Edible South*.

98. "Negroes and Their Food," Margaret Mead Papers, Manuscript Division, Library of Congress, Box 125, Folder 11.

99. Wright, *Black Boy*, 21–22.

100. Wright, *Black Boy*, 11, 22.

101. Wright, *Black Boy*, 16.

102. John Dollard, *Caste and Class in a Southern Town* (Madison, WI: University of Wisconsin Press, 1989), 147.

103. Sharpless, *Cooking in Other Women's Kitchens*, 138–41.

104. Powdermaker, *After Freedom*, 119.

105. Quoted in Leon Litwack, *Trouble in Mind: Black Southerners in the Age of Jim Crow* (New York: Vintage, 1999), 171.

106. Hunter, *To 'Joy My Freedom*, 27.

107. Cooley, *To Live and Dine in Dixie*, 23–24; Hunter, *To 'Joy My Freedom*, 28.

108. Sharpless, *Cooking in Other Women's Kitchens*, 151–52.

109. Dollard, *Caste and Class in a Southern Town*, 302.

110. Litwack, *Trouble in Mind*, 171.

111. Powdermaker, *After Freedom*, 119.

112. Litwack, *Trouble in Mind*, 168.

113. Quoted in Litwack, *Trouble in Mind*, 172.

114. Moody, *Coming of Age in Mississippi*, 123.

115. Jessica Harris, *Iron Pots & Wooden Spoons: Africa's Gifts to New World Cooking* (New York: Simon & Schuster, 1999), xxiv.

116. Jessica Harris, *High on the Hog: A Culinary Journey from Africa to America* (New York: Bloomsbury, 2011), 1–2.

CHAPTER 4

1. Charlotte Hawkins Brown, *The Correct Thing to Do, to Say, to Wear* (New York: G. K. Hall, 1995), 47, 54–57.

2. Psyche Williams-Forson, *Building Houses Out of Chicken Legs: Black Women, Food, and Power* (Chapel Hill: University of North Carolina Press, 2006), 93–95.

3. For a more extensive discussion of the food of racial uplift, see Jennifer Jensen Wallach, *Every Nation Has Its Dish: Black Bodies and Black Food in Twentieth-Century America* (Chapel Hill: University of North Carolina Press, 2019).

4. David C. Barnett, "Radio Show Chronicled Blacks' Harsh Realities," NPR, "All Things Considered," March 3, 2008, https://www.npr.org/templates/story/story .php?storyId=87780799, accessed July 27, 2008; Charlotte Hawkins Brown, "The Negro and Social Graces," The Charlotte Hawkins Brown Museum, http://www .nchistoricsites.org/chb/chb-radio.htm, accessed July 27, 2018.

5. Brown, "The Negro and Social Graces."

6. Brown, *The Correct Thing*, 47.

7. Brown, *The Correct Thing*, 48–49.

8. Brown, *The Correct Thing*, 47.

9. Alice Dunbar-Nelson, *Give Us Each Day: The Diary of Alice Dunbar-Nelson*, ed. Gloria T. Hull (New York: W. W. Norton, 1984), 87, 132, 162; Mary Church Terrell, *A Colored Woman in a White World* (New York: G. K. Hall & Co., 1996), 122–24; Margaret Murray Washington, "We Must Have a Cleaner Social Morality," in *Lift Every Voice: African American Oratory, 1787–1900*, eds. Philip S. Foner and Robert J. Branham (Tuscaloosa, AL: University of Alabama Press, 1997), 867–68.

10. Psyche Williams-Forson, "Chickens and Chains: Using African American Foodways to Understand Black Identities," in *African American Foodways: Explorations of History and Culture*, ed. Ann L. Bower (Urbana: University of Illinois Press, 2007), 127–28.

11. James M. Dormon, "Shaping the Popular Image of Post-Reconstruction American Blacks: The 'Coon Song' Phenomenon of the Gilded Age," *American Quarterly* 40 (1988): 450–71; Jennifer Jensen Wallach, *How America Eats: A Social History of U.S. Food and Culture* (Lanham: Rowman & Littlefield, 2013), 190.

12. Dorman, "Shaping the Popular Image," 453. Both the Jazz Archives at Tulane University and the Archives of the Smithsonian National Museum of American History have extensive collections of sheet music, including numerous "coon songs."

13. Jennifer Jensen Wallach, "Food and Race," in *The Routledge History of American Foodways*, eds. Michael D. Wise and Jennifer Jensen Wallach (New York: Routledge, 2016), 293–310.

14. "A Sunday Evening Talk," October 6, 1907, BTWP, Volume 9, 368; Wallach, *Every Nation Has Its Dish*, 49–70.

15. "To Warren Logan," November 23, 1899, *The Booker T. Washington Papers*, Volume 5, 270; Washington to Mr. Saffold, September 14, 1898, BTWP-TA, Box 001.002, Folder 1898.

16. Axioms from Dr. George M. Beard's "Sexual Neurasthenia," in *Pacific Medical and Surgical Journal*, ed. William S. Whitwell (San Francisco: W. S. Duncombe Publishers, 1885), 204; Charlotte Biltekoff, *Eating Right in America: The Cultural Politics of Food and Health* (Durham: Duke University Press, 2013), 24. See also Harvey Levenstein, "The New England Kitchen and the Failure to Reform Working-Class Eating Habits," in *Revolution at the Table: The Transformation of the American Diet* (Berkeley: University of California Press, 2003), 44–59; Laura Shapiro, *Perfection Salad: Women and Cooking at the Turn of the Century* (Berkeley: University of California Press, 2009), 139–54; Wallach, *How America Eats*, 12–14; Clarissa Dickson Wright, *A History of English Food* (London: Random House UK, 2011); and Colin Spencer, *British Food: An Extraordinary Thousand Years of History* (New York: Columbia University Press, 2002).

17. "A Sunday Evening Talk," December 10, 1911, *The Booker T. Washington Papers*, Volume 11, eds. Louis R. Harlan and Raymond W. Smock (Urbana: University of Illinois Press, 1981), 409.

18. Roger Horowitz, *Putting Meat on the American Table* (Baltimore: Johns Hopkins University Press, 2006), 13.

19. Wallach, *How America Eats*, 13; Charles Reagan Wilson, "Cornbread," in *The New Encyclopedia of Southern Culture: Foodways*, 152–54.

20. Wilson, "Cornbread," 152–54.

21. Elizabeth S. D. Engelhardt, *A Mess of Greens: Southern Gender and Southern Food* (Athens, GA: University of Georgia Press, 2011), 52.

22. Aaron Bobrow-Strain, *White Bread: A Social History of the Store-Bought Loaf* (Boston: Beacon Press, 2013), 14.

23. W. E. B. Du Bois, "Food," *Crisis*, August 1918, 165.

24. Du Bois, "Food."

25. Frederick L. Hoffman, *The Race Traits and Tendencies of the American Negro* (New York: Macmillan, 1896).

26. For a more extended discussion of the intertwined intellectual histories of ideas about food and ideas about race, which this section is derived from, see Wallach, "Food and Race."

27. Julien Joseph-Vivrey, *A Natural History of the Negro Race*, trans. J. H. Guenebault (Charleston, SC: D. J. Dowling, 1837), 25–26.

28. Arthur de Gobineau, *The Inequality of Human Races*, trans. Adrian Collins (London: Heinemann, 1915), 205.

29. Wallach, *Every Nation Has Its Dish*, 81, 86.

30. W. E. B. Du Bois, letter to the editor of the *Philadelphia Record*, W. E. B. Du Bois Papers, mums312-b004-i340, Special Collections and University Archives,

University of Massachusetts, W. E. B. Du Bois Library, http://credo.library.umass
.edu/view/full/mums312-b004-i340; Review of *Race Traits and Tendencies of the
American Negro* by Frederick L. Hoffman, *Annals of the American Academy of Political
and Social Science* 9 (January 1897): 127–33.

31. W. E. B. Du Bois, ed., *The Health and Physique of the Negro America* (Atlanta:
Atlanta University Press, 1906), 52.

32. Brown, *The Correct Thing*, 81.

33. M. M. Manring, *A Slave in a Box: The Strange Career of Aunt Jemima* (Charlottesville: University of Virginia Press, 1997), 140; Wallach, *How America Eats*, 189.

34. Rebecca Sharpless, *Cooking in Other Women's Kitchens* (Chapel Hill: University
of North Carolina Press, 2010), xv.

35. Jim Heimann, ed., *Menu Design in America* (Berlin: Taschen, 2011), 126–27,
140–41.

36. Daley's menu, 1936, New York Public Library Buttolph Menu Collection.

37. Tony Horwitz, "The Mammy Washington Almost Had," *The Atlantic*,
May 31, 2013, https://www.theatlantic.com/national/archive/2013/05/the-mammy-
washington-almost-had/276431/, accessed July 27, 2018; Micki McElya, *Clinging
to Mammy: The Faithful Slave in Twentieth-Century America* (Cambridge: Harvard
University Press, 2007), 116–59.

38. "Mammy's Cupboard," https://www.roadsideamerica.com/story/3344, accessed July 27, 2018.

39. Heimman, *Menu Design in America*, 183.

40. Mary Church Terrell, "The Black Mammy Monument (1923)," in *From
Megaphones to Microphones: Speeches of American Women, 1920–1960*, eds. Sandra J.
Sarkela, Susan Mallon Ross, and Margaret A. Lowe (Westport, CT: Praeger, 2003),
15.

41. Miriam J. Petty, *Stealing the Show: African American Performers and Audiences in
1930s Hollywood* (Berkeley: University of California Press, 2016), 42.

42. Wallach, *Every Nation Has Its Dish*, 23–25.

43. Terrell, *A Colored Woman in a White World*, 122–23.

44. Terrell, *A Colored Woman in a White World*, 122–23.

45. Mary Church Terrell, "The Woman's World," *The Colored American*, March 17,
1900, 6.

46. T. Thomas Fortune, "The Present Relations of Labor and Capitol (1896),"
in *Lift Every Voice: African American Oratory, 1787–1900*, eds. Philip S. Foner and
Robert J. Branham (Tuscaloosa, AL: University of Alabama Press, 1997), 649.

47. Wallach, *Every Nation Has Its Dish*, 43–44; 49–70; 114–15.

48. Jennifer Ritterhouse, *Growing Up Jim Crow: How Black and White Southern
Children Learned Race* (Chapel Hill: University of North Carolina Press, 2006), 86.

49. Mia Bay, "Traveling Black/Buying Black: Retail and Roadside Accommodations during the Segregation Era," in *Race and Retail: Consumption Across the Color
Line*, edited by Mia Bay and Ann Fabian (New Brunswick, NJ: Rutgers University
Press, 2015), 17.

50. Bay, "Traveling Black/Buying Black," 19–20.

51. Isabel Wilkerson, *The Warmth of Other Sons: The Epic Story of America's Great Migration* (New York: Vintage, 2011), 197.

52. Bay, "Traveling Black/Buying Black," 15.

53. Psyche Williams-Forson, *Building Houses Out of Chicken Legs: Black Women, Food, and Power* (Chapel Hill: University of North Carolina Press, 2006), 125.

54. Frederick Douglass Opie, *Hog and Hominy: Soul Food from Africa to America* (New York: Columbia University Press, 2008), 57.

55. Williams-Forson, *Building Houses*, 116.

56. Howell Raine, *My Soul Is Rested: Movement Days in the Deep South Remembered* (New York: Penguin, 1983), 135.

57. Bay, "Traveling Black/Buying Black," 16.

58. Bay, "Traveling Black/Buying Black," 23.

59. John Howard Griffin, *Black Like Me* (New York: Signet, 1976), 97.

60. Griffin, *Black Like Me*, 97.

61. Bay, "Traveling Black/Buying Black," 24.

62. Jacinda Townsend, "How the *Green Book* Helped African-American Tourists Navigate a Segregated Nation," *Smithsonian Magazine*, April 2016, https://www.smithsonianmag.com/smithsonian-institution/history-green-book-african-american-travelers-180958506/, accessed July 27, 2018; New York Public Library, "Navigating the *Green Book*," http://publicdomain.nypl.org/greenbook-map/, accessed July 27, 2018; Victor Green, *The Negro Traveler's Green Book* (Spring 1956), http://library.sc.edu/digital/collections/greenbookmap.html, accessed July 27, 2018.

63. Chris Jackson, "Reverse Migration," *The Atlantic*, January 10, 2011, https://www.theatlantic.com/national/archive/2011/01/reverse-migration/69233/, accessed July 27, 2011.

64. US Census Bureau, "The Great Migration, 1910–1970, https://www.census.gov/dataviz/visualizations/020/, accessed July 27, 2018.

65. Richard Wright, *12 Million Black Voices* (New York: Basic Books, 2002), 104.

66. Wright, *12 Million Black Voices*, 114.

67. Chicago Commission on Race Relations, *The Negro in Chicago: A Study of Race Relations and a Race Riot* (Chicago: University of Chicago Press, 1922), 162–65.

68. Chicago Commission on Race Relations, *The Negro in Chicago*, 170–72.

69. Wilkerson, *The Warmth of Other Sons*, 339.

70. Wilkerson, *The Warmth of Other Sons*, 356–57.

71. Tracy Poe, "The Origins of Soul Food in Black Urban Identity: Chicago, 1915–1947," *American Studies International* (February 1999), 18.

72. Janice Tuck Lively, "Lillian Harris Dean," *Encyclopedia of the Harlem Renaissance*, eds. Cary D. Wintz and Paul Finkelman (New York: Routledge, 2004), 298–99; Paul Devlin, "Lillian Harris Dean," *Harlem Renaissance Lives*, eds. Henry Louis Gates and Evelyn Brooks Higginbotham (New York: Oxford University Press, 2009), 149–50; Jessica Harris, *High on the Hog: A Culinary Journey from Africa to America* (New York: Bloomsbury, 2011), 177–78.

73. Ralph Ellison, *Invisible Man* (New York: Vintage Books, 1995), 264.

74. "The Store . . . " *Chicago Defender*, July 4, 1914; "Pig Ankle Joints," *Chicago Defender*, May 29, 1915, 4; Harris, *High on the Hog*, 175–76.

75. Harris, *High on the Hog*, 183–84, and Wilkerson, *The Warmth of Other Sons*, 277–78.

76. Wilkerson, *The Warmth of Other Sons*, 236.

77. Poe, "The Origins of Soul Food," 8; Camille Bégin, *Taste of the Nation: The New Deal Search for America's Food* (Urbana: University of Illinois Press, 2016), 89–90.

78. "Chance to Prolong Life—Be Modest in All Things," *Chicago Defender*, November 12, 1915, 5; A. Wilberforce Williams, "Obesity," *Chicago Defender*, October 11, 1924, 12; "Loud Talking in the Pekin," *Chicago Defender*, April 23, 1910, 1.

79. Poe, "The Origins of Soul Food," 8.

80. Quoted in John R. Grossman, *Land of Hope: Chicago, Black Southerners, and the Great Migration* (Chicago: University of Chicago Press, 1989), 131.

81. St. Clair Drake and Horace Cayton, *Black Metropolis: A Study of Negro Life in a Northern City* (Chicago: University of Chicago Press, 1993), 547–48.

82. Robert T. Dirks and Nancy Duran, "African American Dietary Patterns at the Beginning of the 20th Century," *Journal of Nutrition* 31, no. 7 (July 2001): 1881–89.

83. Hasia Diner, *Hungering for America: Italian, Irish, and Jewish Foodways in the Age of Migration* (Cambridge: Harvard University Press, 2003).

84. Opie, *Hog and Hominy*, 62–63.

85. Andrew Coe, *Chop Suey: A Cultural History of Chinese Food in the United States* (Oxford: Oxford University Press, 2009), 169.

86. Dunbar-Nelson, *Give Us Each Day*, 191.

87. Grossman, *Land of Hope*, 264.

88. Paul Freedmen, *Ten Restaurants That Changed America* (New York: Liverwright Publishing, 2016), 279.

CHAPTER 5

1. "Divine Plays Host at Super-Banquet; 24-Hour Feast Began Saturday Midnight, with 200 Items on Menu Tempting 'Angels,'" *New York Times*, September 25, 1939, 18.

2. Kwame Anthony Appiah and Henry Louis Gates Jr., eds., *Africana: The Encyclopedia of the African and African American Experience* (New York: Oxford University Press, 2005), 97.

3. Robert Weisbrot, *Father Divine and the Struggle for Racial Equality* (Urbana: University of Illinois Press, 1983), 9.

4. Jill Watts, *God, Harlem U.S.A.* (Berkeley: University of California Press, 1995), 4–5.

5. Weisbrot, *Father Divine and the Struggle for Racial Equality*, 85–86.

6. Watts, *God, Harlem U.S.A.*, 44.

7. Watts, *God, Harlem U.S.A.*, xii, 90.

8. Weisbrot, *Father Divine and the Struggle for Racial Equality*, 80.

9. Weisbrot, *Father Divine and the Struggle for Racial Equality*, 80.

10. Jessica Harris, *High on the Hog: A Culinary Journey from Africa to America* (New York: Bloomsbury, 2011), 188.

11. "Divine Plays Host at Super-Banquet," 18.

12. "Divine Plays Host at Super-Banquet," 18.

13. "Chanting Throng Parades in Harlem, 'Father' Divine in Airplane, Soars over Followers as They Sing His Praises," *New York Times*, April 2, 1934, 3.

14. Maggi M. Morehouse, *Fighting in the Jim Crow Army: Black Men and Women Remember World War II* (Lanham, MD: Rowman & Littlefield, 2000), 25.

15. Jane Ziegelman and Andrew Coe, *A Square Meal: A Culinary History of the Great Depression* (New York: Harper, 2016), 61.

16. Ziegelman and Coe, *A Square Meal*, 63.

17. National Public Radio, "Creamed, Canned, and Frozen: How the Great Depression Revamped US Diets," August 15, 2016, https://www.npr.org/sections/thesalt/2016/08/15/489991111/creamed-canned-and-frozen-how-the-great-depression-changed-u-s-diets, accessed June 19, 2018.

18. Janet Poppendieck, *Breadlines Knee-Deep in Wheat: Food Assistance in the Great Depression* (Berkeley, CA: University of California Press, 2014), 239.

19. Ziegelman and Coe, *A Square Meal*, 74; Megan J. Elias, *Food in the United States, 1809–1945* (Santa Barbara, CA: ABC CLIO, 2009), 133.

20. Elias, *Food in the United States*, 26.

21. Megan Elias, "Summoning the Food Ghosts: Food History as Public History," *Public Historian* 34, no. 2 (Spring 2012): 13–29.

22. Frederick Douglas Opie, *Hog and Hominy: Soul Food from Africa to America* (New York: Columbia University Press, 2008), 93–94.

23. Watts, *God, Harlem U.S.A.*, 82.

24. Weisbrot, *Father Divine and the Struggle for Racial Equality*, 70–71.

25. Leonard Norman Primiano, "'And as We Dine, We Sing and Praise God': Father and Mother Divine's Theologies of Food," in *Religion, Food, and Eating in North America*, eds. Benjamin Zeller, Marie Dallam, Reid Nelson, and Nora Rubel (New York: Columbia University Press, 2014), 47.

26. Weisbrot, *Father Divine and the Struggle for Racial Equality*, 122.

27. Watts, *God, Harlem U.S.A.*, 105; Sara Harris, *Father Divine: Holy Husband* (Garden City, NY: Doubleday & Company, 1953), 210–12.

28. Weisbrot, *Father Divine and the Struggle for Racial Equality*, 125–31.

29. Cheryl Lynn Greenberg, *To Ask for an Equal Chance: African Americans in the Great Depression* (Lanham, MD: Rowman & Littlefield, 2009), 21–41.

30. Richard Wright, *Black Boy: A Record of Childhood and Youth* (New York: HarperPerennial, 2007), 300–1.

31. Watts, *God, Harlem U.S.A.*, 119; Jerry W. Ward and Robert J. Butler, eds., *The Richard Wright Encyclopedia* (Westport, CT: Greenwood, 2008), 89; Bruce Allen Dick, "A Forgotten Chapter: Richard Wright, Playwrights, and the Modern Theater," in *Richard Wright in a Post-Racial Imaginary*, eds. William E. Dow, Alice Mikal Craven, and Yoko Nakammu (New York: Bloomsbury, 2014), 192; Toru Kiuchi and Yoshinobu Hakutani, *Richard Wright: A Documented Chronology, 1908–1960* (Jefferson, NC: McFarland, 2014), 118.

32. Quoted in Watts, *God, Harlem U.S.A.*, 49.

33. Watts, *God, Harlem U.S.A.*, xi, xii, 88.

34. Harris, *High on the Hog*, 210–12.

35. Greenberg, *To Ask for an Equal Chance*, 49.

36. Greenberg, *To Ask for an Equal Chance*, 57–58.

37. Greenberg, *To Ask for an Equal Chance*, 63.

38. Benjamin Kahan, "The Other Harlem Renaissance: Father Divine, Celibate Economics, and the Making of Black Sexuality," *Arizona Quarterly: A Journal of American Literature, Culture, and Theory* 65, no. 4 (Winter 2009): 49.

39. Michael B. Dougan, *Arkansas Odyssey* (Little Rock, AR: Rose Publishing Company, 1994), 438.

40. Greenberg, *To Ask for an Equal Chance*, 43–64.

41. Richard Rothstein, *The Color of Law: A Forgotten History of How Our Government Segregated America* (New York: Liveright, 2017), 156.

42. Rothstein, *The Color of Law*, 19.

43. "Convert Pays Relief," *New York Times*, August 14, 1938, 3.

44. "Father Divine Group Buys 'Krum Elbow,' Estate Facing Roosevelt's on the Hudson," *New York Times*, July 29, 1938, 1.

45. Kahan, "The Other Harlem Renaissance," 9–50.

46. Robert A. Hill, "Marcus Garvey: 'The Negro Moses,'" Africana Age, Schomburg Center for Research in Black Culture, http://exhibitions.nypl.org/africanaage/essay-garvey.html, accessed June 20, 2018.

47. "'Black House' for Capitol: Negroes to Erect Residence Near White House for Leader," *New York Times*, August 18, 1920.

48. Robin D. G. Kelley, *Race Rebels: Culture, Politics, and the Black Working Class* (New York: Free Press, 1996), 25.

49. Colin Grant, *Negro with a Hat: The Rise and Fall of Marcus Garvey* (New York: Oxford University Press, 2008), 217–33; E. David Cronon, *Black Moses: The Story of Marcus Garvey* (Madison: University of Wisconsin Press, 1955), 80–84.

50. Marcus Garvey, "Lesson 15: Personality," in *Marcus Garvey Life and Lessons: A Centennial Companion to the Marcus Garvey and Universal Improvement Association Papers*, eds. Robert A. Hill and Barbara Bair (Berkeley, CA: University of California Press, 1987), 283.

51. Tony Martin, *Race First: The Ideological and Organizational Struggles of Marcus Garvey and the Universal Negro Improvement Association* (Dover, MA: Majority Press, 1976), 34.

52. Grant, *Negro with a Hat*, 34.

53. Hill, "Marcus Garvey."

54. Marcus Garvey, "Articles by Marcus Garvey," in *Life and Lessons*, 93.

55. Judith Stein, *The World of Marcus Garvey: Race and Class in Modern Society* (Baton Rouge, LA: Louisiana State University Press, 1986), 275.

56. Grant, *Negro with a Hat*, 453.

57. Watts, *God, Harlem U.S.A.*, 116.

58. Cronon, *Black Moses*, 163.

59. Weisbrot, *Father Divine and the Struggle for Racial Equality*, 190–96.

60. Weisbrot, *Father Divine and the Struggle for Racial Equality*, 192.

61. Wallach, *Every Nation Has Its Dish*, 139–44.

62. George Schuyler, "An Appeal to Young Negroes," Ella Baker Papers, Schomburg Center for Research in Black Culture, Box 2, Folder 2; Barbara Ransby, *Ella Baker and the Black Freedom Movement: A Radical Democratic Vision* (Chapel Hill: University of North Carolina Press, 2005), 82–85; Jessica Gordon, *Collective Courage: A History of African American Cooperative Economic Thought and Practice* (University Park, PA: Pennsylvania State University Press, 2014), 113; Jeffrey Ferguson, *The Sage of Sugar Hill: George S. Schuyler and the Harlem Renaissance* (New Haven: Yale University Press, 2005), 122.

63. W. E. B. Du Bois, *Economic Co-Operation among Negro Americans* (Atlanta: Atlanta University Press, 1907).

64. Jessica Gordon Nembhard, *Collective Courage: A History of African American Cooperative Economic Thought and Practice* (University Park: The Pennsylvania State University Press, 2014), 104–5.

65. W. E. B. Du Bois, "Segregation," *Crisis*, January 1934, 20.

66. Cronon, *Black Moses*, 190.

67. "Four Million Dozens of Eggs," *Philadelphia Tribune*, June 4, 1936, 4; "Race Owns Stores," *Chicago Defender*, July 13, 1935, 3; "First Chain Store Unit Organized," *Atlanta Daily World*, March 9, 1934, 1; Clarence Jackson Jr., "Consumers' Cooperative Store Opens," *Philadelphia Tribune*, October 31, 1935, 1; "Capital Launches First Consumers' Cooperative Group," *Baltimore Afro-American*, December 5, 1936, 8; "The Richmond Cooperative," *New Journal and Guide*, October 29, 1938, 8.

68. Nembhard, 135–36.

69. "Dunbar Co-Op Sells 100,000 Quarts of Milk," *Atlanta Daily World*, June 26, 1937, 8; Nembhard, *Collective Courage*, 133; "Harlem's Own Cooperative, Inc.," Ella Baker Papers, Box 2, Folder 6.

70. Lizabeth Cohen, *Making a New Deal: Industrial Workers in Chicago, 1919–1939* (Cambridge: Cambridge University Press, 1990), 152.

71. Frederick Douglass Opie, *Southern Food and Civil Rights: Feeding the Revolution* (Charleston, SC: American Palate, 2017), 9–10.

72. Opie, *Southern Food*, 23.

73. Opie, *Southern Food*, 27–28.

74. Nelson Lichtenstein, "Labor and the Working Class in World War II," in "World War II and the American Home Front," National Parks Service, https://www.nps.gov/nhl/learn/themes/wwiihomefront.pdf, 95, accessed June 20, 2018.

75. William M. Tuttle Jr., "The American Family on the Home Front," in "World War II and the American Home Front," 53.

76. John W. Jeffries, "Mobilization and Its Impact," in "World War II and the American Home Front," 40.

77. Rebecca Sharpless, *Cooking in Other Women's Kitchens: Domestic Workers in the South, 1865–1960* (Chapel Hill: University of North Carolina Press, 2010), 178.

78. Jacqueline Jones, *Labor of Love, Labor of Sorrow: Black Women, Work, and the Family from Slavery to the Present* (New York: Basic Books, 1985), 201.

79. George E. Demar, "Negro Women Are American Workers, Too," *Opportunity*, April 1943, reprinted in *Bitter Fruit: African American Women in World War II*, ed. Maureen Honey (Columbia, MO: University of Missouri Press, 1999), 104.

80. Maureen Honey, *Bitter Fruit: African American Women in World War II* (Columbia, MO: University of Missouri Press, 1999), 8.

81. Harris, *High on the Hog*, 191.

82. Amy Bentley, *Eating for Victory: Food Rationing and the Politics of Domesticity* (Urbana: University of Illinois Press, 1998), 48.

83. Sharpless, *Cooking in Other Women's Kitchens*, 179.

84. Judy Barrett Litoff and David C. Smith, "To the Rescue of the Crops: The Women's Land Army during World War II," *Prologue* 25, no. 4 (Winter 1993), http://www.archives.gov/publications/prologue/1993/winter/landarmy.html, accessed June 20, 2018.

85. Litoff and Smith, "To the Rescue of the Crops."

86. Litoff and Smith, "To the Rescue of the Crops."

87. Cecilia Gowdy-Wygant, *Cultivating Victory: The Women's Land Army and the Victory Garden Movement* (Pittsburgh: University of Pittsburgh Press, 2013), 120–24; Stephanie A. Carpenter, *On the Farm Front: The Womens' Land Army in World War II* (DeKalb, IL: University of Northern Illinois Press, 2003), 90: Litoff and Smith, "To the Rescue of the Crops."

88. African-American Women's Land Army tobacco farm worker Mrs. Sam Crawford working the field, Maryland, United States, 8 October 1943, Photo from the National Archives, World War II Database, https://ww2db.com/image .php?image_id=6059, accessed June 20, 2018.

89. Gowdy-Wygant, *Cultivating Victory*, 125–26; Carpenter, *On the Farm Front*, 137–45; Judith Barrett Litoff, "Southern Women in a World War," in *Remaking Dixie: The Impact of World War II on the American South*, ed. Neil R. McMillan (Jackson, MS: University Press of Mississippi, 1997), 62.

90. Stephanie A. Carpenter, "At the Agricultural Front: The Women's Land Army during World War II," PhD Dissertation, Iowa State University, 1997, 274–76.

91. "Women Enrolled in New Land Army," *New York Times*, May 26, 1943.

92. Bentley, *Eating for Victory*, 117–18.

93. Richard Sterner, *The Negro's Share: A Study of Income, Consumption, Housing, and Public Assistance* (New York: Harper & Brother's, 1943), 103.

94. Christopher Paul Moore, *Fighting for America: Black Soldiers—the Unsung Heroes of World War II* (New York: One World Ballentine Books, 2005), 164.

95. "Enroll Today in the Yard Victory Garden Contest," *Detroit Tribune*, March 20, 1943, 5.

96. See for example, "How to Plant Your Victory Garden," *Detroit Tribune*, April 17, 1943, 5.

97. Bentley, *Eating for Victory*, 124.

98. Bentley, *Eating for Victory*, 137–40.

99. Jeffries, "Mobilization and Its Impact," https://www.nps.gov/nhl/learn/ themes/wwiihomefront.pdf, 22.

100. Bentley, *Eating for Victory*, 81.

101. Morehouse, *Fighting in the Jim Crow Army*, 102.

102. Quoted in Bentley, *Eating for Victory*, 83; Roland Fallin, "Is There Democracy?" *Baltimore African American*, October 14, 1944.

103. Bureau of Naval Personnel, Historical Section, *The Negro in the Navy* (Washington, DC, 1947), https://www.history.navy.mil/research/library/online-reading -room/title-list-alphabetically/n/negro-navy-1947-adminhist84.html, accessed on June 20, 2018.

104. Richard E. Miller, *The Messmen Chronicles: African Americans in the U.S. Navy, 1932–1943* (Annapolis, MD: Naval Institute Press, 2004), 211.

105. Miller, *The Messman Chronicles*, 93–94.

106. Miller, *The Messman Chronicles*, 156.

107. Miller, *The Messman Chronicles*, 94.

108. Miller, *The Messman Chronicles*, 249.

109. Miller, *The Messman Chronicles*, 250.

110. Harvard Sitkoff, "African Americans and Other Minorities on the Home Front," in "World War II and the American Home Front," 115.

111. Morehouse, *Fighting in the Jim Crow Army*, 4.

112. Morehouse, *Fighting in the Jim Crow Army*, 123.

113. Editor's Note, *The Crisis*, March 1945, reprinted in Honey, *Bitter Fruit*, 141.

114. Muriel Ruhn, "My Most Humiliating Jim Crow Experience," *Negro Digest*, September 1945, reprinted in Honey, *Bitter Fruit*, 337–38.

115. Patrick S. Washburn, "The Pittsburgh *Courier*'s Double V Campaign in 1942," *American Journalism* 3, no. 2 (2013): 73–86.

116. Pauli Murray, "A Blueprint for First Class Citizenship," *The Crisis*, November 1944, reprinted in Hone, *Bitter Fruit*, 277.

CHAPTER 6

1. Marcie Cohen Ferris, *The Edible South: The Power of Food and the Making of an American Region* (Chapel Hill: University of North Carolina Press, 2016), 251–55.

2. Ferris, *The Edible South*, 255.

3. Erica Buist, "That's Me in That Picture," *The Guardian*, March 27, 2015, https:// www.theguardian.com/artanddesign/2015/mar/27/hunter-gray-1963-jackson-missis- sippi-sit-in, accessed on July 9, 2018; Southern Foodways Alliance, "Counter Histories," https://www.southernfoodways.org/film/counter-histories-jackson/, accessed July 9, 2018; Trip Burns, "Real Violence 50 Years Ago at Woolworths," *Jackson Free Press*, May 23, 2013, http://www.jacksonfreepress.com/news/2013/may/23/real-violence- 50-years-ago-woolworth/, accessed July 9, 2018; Anne Moody, *Coming of Age in Mis- sissippi: The Classic Autobiography of Growing Up Poor and Black in the Rural South* (New York: Dell, 1992), 289–93; Ed King and Trent Watts, *Ed King's Mississippi: Behind the Scenes of Freedom Summer* (Jackson: University Press of Mississippi, 2014), 14.

4. Moody, *Coming of Age in Mississippi*, 292.

5. Moody, *Coming of Age in Mississippi*, 292.

6. Christopher W. Schmidt, *The Sit-Ins: Protest and Legal Change during the Civil Rights Era* (Chicago: University of Chicago Press, 2018), 14; for an excellent account of some the legal issues at stake, see also Angela Jill Cooley, *To Live and Dine in Dixie* (Athens: University of Georgia Press, 2015), 105–27.

7. Ella Baker, "Bigger Than a Hamburger," *The Southern Patriot*, May 1960, http://www.crmvet.org/docs/sncc2.htm, accessed July 9, 2018.

8. Jennifer Jensen Wallach, *Every Nation Has Its Dish: Black Bodies and Black Food in Twentieth-Century America* (Chapel Hill: University of North Carolina Press, 2019), 156–60.

9. Digital SNCC Gateway, "February 1960, Sit-Ins in Greensboro," https://snccdigital.org/events/sit-ins-greensboro/, accessed June 21, 2018.

10. Moody, *Coming of Age in Mississippi*, 13.

11. Quoted in Ted Ownby, *American Dreams in Mississippi: Consumers, Poverty, and Culture, 1830–1998* (Chapel Hill, NC: University of North Carolina Press, 1999), 151.

12. SNCC Digital Gateway, "Betty Garman (Robinson)," https://snccdigital.org/people/betty-garman-robinson/, accessed June 21, 2018.

13. Charles Payne, *I've Got the Light of Freedom: The Organizing Tradition and the Mississippi Freedom Struggle* (Berkeley, CA: University of California Press, 2007), 130.

14. Doug McAdam, *Freedom Summer* (New York: Oxford University Press, 1990), 279.

15. Moody, *Coming of Age in Mississippi*, 354; Charles E. Cobb Jr., "Guns and the Southern Freedom Struggle: What's Missing When We Teach about Nonviolence," *Huffington Post*, September 23, 2014, https://www.huffingtonpost.com/the-zinn-education-project/guns-and-the-southern-fre_b_5868338.html, accessed July 9, 2018; Becca Walton, "C. O. Chinn," *The Mississippi Encyclopedia*, eds. Ted Ownby, Charles Reagan Wilson, Ann J. Abadie, Odie Lindsey, and James G. Thomas (Jackson, MS: The University Press of Mississippi, 2017), 208.

16. Stokely Carmichael with Ekwueme Michael Thelwell, *Ready for Revolution: The Life and Struggles of Stokely Carmichael (Kwame Ture)* (New York: Scribners, 2005), 189.

17. Elizabeth Martinez, *Letters from Mississippi: Reports from Civil Rights Volunteers and Freedom School Poetry of the 1964 Freedom Summer* (Brookline, MA: Zephyr Press, 2007), 48–49.

18. SNCC Digital Gateway, "Voter Registration Expands in Southwest Georgia," https://snccdigital.org/events/voter-registration-expands-southwest-georgia/, accessed July 9, 2018.

19. SNCC Digital Gateway, "Lucius and Emma Kate Holloway," https://snccdigital.org/people/lucius-sr-emma-kate-holloway, accessed July 9, 2018.

20. SNCC Digital Gateway, "Strong People," https://snccdigital.org/wp-content/uploads/2017/12/SWGA_Transcript03.pdf, accessed July 9, 2018.

21. Holly Y. McGee, "It Was the Wrong Time, and They Just Weren't Ready," in *Arsnick: The Student Nonviolent Coordinating Committee in Arkansas*, eds. Jennifer

Jensen Wallach and John A. Kirk (Fayetteville, AR: University of Arkansas Press, 2011), 52.

22. Annette Jones White, "Finding Form for the Expression of My Discontent," in *Hands on the Freedom Plow: Personal Accounts by Women in SNCC*, eds. Faith S. Holsaert, Martha Prescod, Norman Noonan, Judy Richardson, Betty Garman Robinson, Jean Smith Young, and Dorothy M. Zellner (Urbana: University of Illinois Press, 2010), 112–13.

23. Quoted in Ferris, *The Edible South*, 259.

24. Carmichael, *Ready for Revolution*, 211.

25. SNCC Digital Gateway, "The Black Panther: Going into Lowndes County," https://snccdigital.org/wp-content/uploads/2017/12/Lowndes_Transcript02.pdf, accessed July 9, 2018.

26. Payne, *I've Got the Light of Freedom*, 155.

27. Janie Culbreth Rambeau, "Ripe for the Picking," in *Hands on the Freedom Plow*, 95–96.

28. Frederick Douglass Opie, *Southern Food and Civil Rights: Feeding the Revolution* (Charleston, SC: American Palate, 2017), 60–64; John T. Edge, *The Potlikker Papers: A Food History of the Modern South* (New York: Penguin Press, 2017), 22–24.

29. Edge, *The Potlikker Papers*, 23.

30. Edge, *The Potlikker Papers*, 24.

31. Opie, *Southern Food*, 100.

32. Quoted in Dave Hoekstra, *The People's Place: Soul Food Restaurants and Reminiscences from the Civil Rights Era to Today* (Chicago: Chicago Review Press, 2015), 88.

33. Opie, *Southern Food*, 99–106; Robbi Brown, "Remembering a Soul Food Legend Who Nurtured Civil Rights Leaders," *New York Times*, December 5, 2008, https://www.nytimes.com/2008/12/06/us/06paschal.html?_r=0, accessed July 9, 2018.

34. *Eyes on the Prize* interview with Unita Blackwell, May 7, 1986, http://digital.wustl.edu/e/eop/eopweb/bla0015.0999.011unitablackwell.html, accessed July 9, 2018.

35. Laura Foner, "Arkansas SNCC Memories," in *Arsnick*, 151.

36. SNCC Digital Gateway, "Strong People: Call to Justice," https://snccdigital.org/wp-content/uploads/2017/12/SWGA_Transcript02.pdf, 37, accessed July 9, 2018; Bruce Watson, *Freedom Summer: The Savage Season of 1964 That Made Mississippi Burn and Made America a Democracy* (New York: Penguin Books, 2011), 111–12.

37. Watson, 111.

38. Martinez, *Letters from Mississippi*, 48–49.

39. Arlene (Wilgoren) Dunn, "My Arkansas Journey," in *Arsncick*, 160.

40. Dunn, "My Arkansas Journey," 162.

41. Peggy Trotter Dammond Preacely, "It Was Simply in My Blood," in *Hands on the Freedom Plow*, 168.

42. SNCC Digital Gateway, "Leflore County Cuts Off Surplus Commodities," https://snccdigital.org/events/leflore-county-cuts-off-surplus-commodities/, accessed July 10, 2018.

43. Wesley Hogan, *Many Minds, One Heart: SNCC's Dream for a New America* (Chapel Hill: University of North Carolina Press, 2009), 87, 136; SNCC Digital Gateway, "Leflore County Cuts Off Surplus Commodities."

44. SNCC Digital Gateway, "Ivanhoe Donaldson," https://snccdigital.org/people/ivanhoe-donaldson/, accessed July 10, 2018.

45. SNCC Digital Gateway, "Friends of SNCC," https://snccdigital.org/inside-sncc/sncc-national-office/friends-of-sncc/, accessed July 10, 2018.

46. John Dittmer, *Local People: The Struggle for Civil Rights in Mississippi* (Urbana: University of Illinois Press, 1995), 144–47.

47. Payne, *I've Got the Light of Freedom*, 158–60.

48. Dittmer, *Local People*, 146.

49. SNCC Digital Gateway, "Sam Block," https://snccdigital.org/people/sam-block/.

50. Payne, *I've Got the Light of Freedom*, 158; Angela Jill Cooley, "Freedom's Farms: Activism and Sustenance in Rural Mississippi," in *Dethroning the Deceitful Pork Chop: Rethinking African American Foodways from Slavery to Obama*, ed. Jennifer Jensen Wallach (Fayetteville, AR: University of Arkansas Press, 2015), 206–7.

51. Payne, *I've Got the Light of Freedom*, 159.

52. Clayborne Carson, *In Struggle: SNCC and the Black Awakening of the 1960s* (Cambridge, MA: Harvard University Press, 1995), 80.

53. Beth Osborne Dapont and Shannon Lee Bade, "The Evolution, Cost, and Operation of the Private Food Assistance Network," Institute for Research on Poverty Discussion Paper No. 1211-00, https://www.irp.wisc.edu/publications/dps/pdfs/dp121100.pdf, 6, accessed July 10, 2018; Edge, *The Potlikker Papers*, 49.

54. Cooley, "Freedom's Farms," 208; Edge, *The Potlikker Papers*, 50.

55. Quoted in Dapont and Bade, "The Evolution, Cost, and Operation," 12.

56. Ellen B. Meacham, *Delta Epiphany: Robert F. Kennedy in Mississippi* (Jackson, MS: University Press of Mississippi, 2018), 79.

57. Edge, *The Potlikker Papers*, 50–53; Ferris, *The Edible South*, 289–90; Meacham, *Delta Epiphany*, 177–78.

58. SNCC Digital Gateway, "Roots of Organizing, Forms of Resistance," https://snccdigital.org/wp-content/uploads/2017/12/RootsOfOrganizing_Transcript03.pdf, accessed July 10, 2018.

59. SNCC Digital Gateway, Mary E. Valera, "Something of Our Own," https://snccdigital.org/wp-content/uploads/2016/09/Booklet_SomethingOfOurOwn_Pt1.optimized.pdf, accessed July 10, 2018.

60. Valera, "Something of Our Own"; SNCC Digital Gateway, "Learning from Our Experience, Maria Valera's Perspective, Part 3," https://snccdigital.org/our-voices/learning-from-experience/part-3/, accessed July 10, 2018; SNCC Digital Gateway, "Learning from Our Experience, Maria Valera's Perspective, Part 2," https://snccdigital.org/our-voices/learning-from-experience/part-2/, accessed July 10, 2019.

61. SNCC Digital Gateway, "Fannie Lou Hamer Founds Freedom Farm Cooperative," https://snccdigital.org/events/fannie-lou-hamer-founds-freedom-farm-cooperative/, accessed July 10, 2018.

62. Edge, *The Potlikker Papers*, 59–60; Ferris, *The Edible South*, 295–96; Cooley, "Freedom's Farms," 211–13.

63. Cooley, "Freedom's Farms," 212–13.

64. Elijah Muhammad, *Message to the Blackman in America* (Atlanta, GA: Messenger Elijah Muhammad Propagation Society, 1965), 174–75.

65. Opie, *Southern Food*, 151–53.

66. Quoted in Opie, *Southern Food*, 153.

67. Quoted in Edward E. Curtis IV, *Black Muslim Religion in the Nation of Islam, 1960–1975* (Chapel Hill: University of North Carolina Press, 2006), 103–4.

68. Curtis, *Black Muslim Religion*, 103.

69. David Hilliard, ed. *The Black Panther Party: Service to the People Programs* (Albuquerque, NM: University of New Mexico Press, 2008), 35.

70. Hilliard, *The Black Panther Party*, 35–36.

71. Joshua Bloom, and Waldo E. Martin Jr., *Black Against Empire: The History and Politics of the Black Panther Party* (Berkeley, CA: University of California Press, 2016), 184.

72. Hilliard, *The Black Panther Party*, 30; Bloom, *Black Against Empire*, 184.

73. Hilliard, *The Black Panther Party*, 31.

74. Bloom, *Black Against Empire*, 185.

75. William L. Van Deburg, *New Day in Babylon: The Black Power Movement and American Culture, 1965–1975* (Chicago: University of Chicago Press, 1992), 195.

76. Jessica Harris, *High on the Hog: A Culinary Journey from Africa to America* (New York: Bloomsbury, 2011), 208.

77. Psyche Williams-Forson, "Take the Chicken Out of the Box: Demystifying the Sameness of African American Culinary Heritage in the U.S.," in *Edible Identities: Food as Cultural Heritage*, eds. Rhonda L. Brulotte and Michael A. Di Giovine (New York: Routledge, 2016), 98.

78. Hortense Spillers, *Black, White, and in Color: Essays on American Literature and Culture* (Chicago: University of Chicago Press, 2003), 56.

79. Spillers, *Black, White, and in Color*, 47.

80. Quoted in Frederick Douglas Opie, *Hog and Hominy: Soul Food from Africa to America* (New York: Columbia University Press, 2008), 130.

81. Opie, *Hog and Hominy*, 130.

82. Paul Freedman, *Ten Restaurants That Changed America* (New York: Liverwright Publishing, 2016), 279.

83. Camille Bégin, *Taste of the Nation: The New Deal Search for America's Food* (Urbana: University of Illinois Press, 2016), 89–90.

84. Quoted in Denise Gee, "The Gospel of Great Southern Food," *Southern Living*, June 1996, 126–28.

85. Francis Lam, "Edna Lewis and the Black Roots of American Cooking," *New York Times*, October 28, 2015, https://www.nytimes.com/2015/11/01/magazine/edna-lewis-and-the-black-roots-of-american-cooking.html, accessed July 10, 2018.

86. LeRoi Jones (Amiri Baraka), *Home: Social Essays* (New York: Akashi Classics, 2009), 120–33.

87. Wallach, *Every Nation Has Its Dish*, 162–69.

88. Edge, *The Potlikker Papers*, 44–45.

89. Ferris, *The Edible South*, 271–73.

90. SNCC Digital Gateway, "The Black Panther from Protest to Power," https://snccdigital.org/wp-content/uploads/2017/12/Lowndes_Transcript01.pdf.

91. Carmichael, *Ready for Revolution*, 530.

92. Hoekstra, *The People's Place*, 117.

93. Freedman, *Ten Restaurants*, 251–87.

94. Quoted in Hoekstra, *The People's Place*, 165.

95. Opie, *Hog and Hominy*, xi, xii.

96. Ruth Gaskins, *A Good Heart and a Light Hand: Ruth L. Gaskins' Collection of Traditional Negro Recipes* (New York: Simon & Schuster, 1968), viii–ix; Toni Tipton-Martin, *The Jemima Code: Two Centuries of African American Cookbooks* (Austin: University of Texas Press, 2015), 86–87.

97. Gaskins, *A Good Heart and a Light Hand*, xiii.

98. Gaskins, *A Good Heart and a Light Hand*, xi–xii.

99. Inez Yeargen Kaiser, *Soul Food Cookery* (New York: Putnam, 1968), 1; Tipton-Martin, *The Jemima Code*, 88–89.

100. Tipton-Martin, *The Jemima Code*, 92–94.

101. Helen Mendes, *The African Heritage Cookbook* (New York: The Macmillan Company, 1971), 12–13.

102. Mendes, *The African Heritage Cookbook*, 85.

103. Mendes, *The African Heritage Cookbook*, 12.

104. Jennifer Jensen Wallach, "How to Eat to Live: Black Nationalism and the Post-1964 Culinary Turn," June 2, 2014, https://southernstudies.olemiss.edu/study-the-south/how-to-eat-to-live/; Harris, *High on the Hog*, 212–13.

105. Charles Aikens, "African Cookbook Tempts with Ghana Stew, Punch," *Oakland Post*, May 25, 1972, 9.

106. "African Foods," *Ebony*, August 1976, 139–42.

107. "Black Messages," *San Francisco Sun Reporter*, May 6, 1972, 37; "Dinner Is Tomorrow," *Oakland Post*, November 12, 1970, 10.

108. "The Skywriters Adventure in Gastronomy," *San Francisco Sun Reporter*, September 6, 1969, 14.

109. "Ham Plus Sweet Potatoes Can Be a Favorite on Easter," *Sacramento Observer*, April 3, 1969, 17.

110. Clovis Semmes, "The Role of African American Health Beliefs and Practices in Social Movements and Cultural Revitalization," *Minority Voices* 6 (1990): 47.

111. Elijah Muhammad, *How to Eat to Live, Book No. 2* (Phoenix, AZ: Secretarious MEMPS Publications, 1972), 107.

112. Elijah Muhammad, *How to Eat to Live, Book No. 1* (Phoenix, AZ: Secretarious MEMPS Publications, 1967), 4–5.

113. Muhammad, *How to Eat to Live, Book No. 2*, 119.

114. Opie, *Hog and Hominy*, 159; Semmes, The Role of African American Health Beliefs," 49.

115. Muhammad, *How to Eat to Live, Book No. 2*, 89.

116. Muhammad, *How to Eat to Live, Book No. 2*, 71.

117. Opie, *Hog and Hominy*, 160.

118. Curtis, *Black Muslim Religion*, 103.

119. Muhammad, *How to Eat to Live, Book No. 2*, 135.

120. Quoted in Semmes, The Role of African American Health Beliefs," 53.

121. Don. L. Lee (Haki Madhudbuti), *From Plan to Planet: Life Studies: The Need for Afrikan Minds and Institutions* (Detroit: Broadside Press, 1973), 87.

122. Wallach, "How to Eat to Live."

123. Dick Gregory and Shelia P. Moses, *Callus on My Soul: A Memoir* (Atlanta: Longstreet Press, 2000), 111.

124. Gregory, *Callus on My Soul*, 112.

125. Gregory, *Callous on My Soul*, 112.

126. Dick Gregory, *Dick Gregory's Natural Diet for Folks Who Eat: Cookin' with Mother Nature* (New York: Harper & Row, 1973), 14–15; Alvenia M. Fulton, *Vegetarianism: Fact or Myth? Eating to Live* (Chicago: B.C.A. Publishing, 1978).

EPILOGUE

1. Marcus Samuelsson with Veronica Chambers, *Yes, Chef: A Memoir* (New York: Random House, 2013), 16.

2. Samuelsson, *Yes, Chef*, 15–18.

3. Samuelsson, *Yes, Chef*, 19.

4. Samuelsson, *Yes, Chef*, 20.

5. Samuelsson, *Yes, Chef*, 19–25.

6. Marcus Samuelsson, "Timeline," Marcus Samuelsson website, http://marcussamuelsson.com/timeline/, accessed July 26, 2018.

7. Ruth Reichl, "Aquavit," *New York Times*, September 29, 1995, https://www.nytimes.com/1995/09/29/arts/restaurants-895595.html, accessed July 11, 2018.

8. Marcus Samuelsson, Marcus Samuelsson website, http://marcussamuelsson.com, accessed July 26, 2018; The History Makers, "Marcus Samuelsson," http://www.thehistorymakers.org/biography/marcus-samuelsson, accessed July 26, 2018.

9. Jessica Harris, *High on the Hog: A Culinary Journey from Africa to America* (New York: Bloomsbury, 2011), 241.

10. Quoted in Lolis Eric Elie, "The Soul of a New Cuisine," *Gourmet*, October 2000, http://www.gourmet.com.s3-website-us-east-1.amazonaws.com/magazine/2000s/2000/10/newcuisine.html, accessed July 12, 2018.

11. Samuelsson, *Yes, Chef*, 223.

12. Marcus Samuelsson, *The Soul of a New Cuisine: A Discovery of the Foods and Flavors of Africa* (New York: Houghton Mifflin, 2006), 173, 134.

13. Samuelsson, *The Soul of a New Cuisine*, 173.

14. Samuelsson, *Yes, Chef*, 261–69.

15. Frank Bruni, "A Taste of Africa (and Beyond)," *New York Times*, April 23, 2008, https://www.nytimes.com/2008/04/23/dining/23rest.html, accessed July 26, 2018.

16. Samuelsson, *Yes, Chef*, 269.

17. Glen Collins, "Marcus Samuelsson Opens in Harlem," *New York Times*, September 7, 2010, https://www.nytimes.com/2010/09/08/dining/08rooster.html, accessed July 12, 2018.

18. Samuelsson, *Yes, Chef*, 302.

19. Kathleen Squires, "Marcus Samuelsson on *Yes, Chef,* Red Rooster, and Eddie Huang," *Paper,* June 25, 2012, http://www.papermag.com/chef-marcus-samuelsson -on-yes-chef-red-rooster-and-eddie-huang-1426137230.html, accessed July 12, 2018.

20. Samuelsson, *Yes, Chef,* 58.

21. Michael Twitty, "Note on Marcus Samuelsson and the *New York Times* Freedom Garden Piece," Afroculanaria, June 25, 2012, https://afroculinaria.com/2012/06/25/ note-on-marcus-samuelson-and-the-new-york-times-piece/, accessed July 12, 2018.

22. Eddie Huang, "Marcus Samuelsson's Overcooked Memoir Makes His Pricey Harlem Discomfort Food Hard to Swallow," *New York Observer,* June 25, 2012, http://observer.com/2012/06/marcus-samuelssons-overcooked-memoir-prompts-a -new-look-at-his-pricey-harlem-discomfort-food/, accessed July 27, 2018.

23. Lolis Eric Elie, "On Marcus Samuelsson and Red Rooster: What It Means to Be a Harlem Restaurant," July 2, 2012, https://newyork.seriouseats.com/2012/07/mar cus-samuelsson-eddie-huang-yes-chef-red-rooster-harlem.html#comments-119569, accessed July 12, 2018.

24. Julia Bainbridge, "Michael W. Twitty: I Want Southern Food to Be the Basis of a New Discussion on Shared Southern Identity," *Atlanta Magazine,* September 18, 2017, http://www.atlantamagazine.com/dining-news/michael-w-twitty-want-south ern-food-basis-new-discussion-shared-southern-identity/, accessed July 26, 2018.

25. Michael Twitty, "An Open Letter to Paula Deen," Afroculinaria Blog, https:// afroculinaria.com/2013/06/25/an-open-letter-to-paula-deen/, accessed June 25, 2013.

26. Kim Severson, "Paula Deen's Cook Tells of Slights, Steeped in History," *New York Times,* July 24, 2013, https://www.nytimes.com/2013/07/25/us/paula-deens- soul-sister-portrays-an-unequal-bond.html, accessed July 27, 2018.

27. Kim Severson, "Dora Charles Moves on from Paula Deen, and Makes It All About the Seasoning," August 31, 2015, https://www.nytimes.com/2015/09/02/ dining/paula-deen-chef-dora-charles.html, accessed July 27, 2018; Dora Charles, *A Real Southern Cook: In Her Savannah Kitchen* (New York: Houghton Mifflin, 2015), 58.

28. John T. Edge and Tunde Wey, "Who Owns Southern Food?" *Oxford American,* June 3, 2016, https://www.oxfordamerican.org/magazine/item/870-who-owns -southern-food, accessed July 27, 2018.

29. Maura Judkis, "One Chef's Social Experiment: Charge Minorities $12, White People $30," *Washington Post,* March 2, 2018, https://www.washingtonpost .com/news/food/wp/2018/03/02/one-chefs-social-experiment-charge-minorities -12-white-people-30/?utm_term=.db55bb67dc6c, accessed July 27, 2018.

30. Judkis, "One Chef's Social Experiment."

31. Edge and Wey, "Who Owns Southern Food?"

32. Michael Twitty, "Rules of Engagement: Food Journalism in a Multicultural America," *Gravy* (Spring 2017), https://www.southernfoodways.org/rules-of-en gagement-food-journalism-in-a-multicultural-america/, accessed July 12, 2008.

33. Thug Kitchen, https://www.thugkitchen.com/, accessed July 27, 2018.

34. Matt Duckor, "Thug Life: A Behind-the-Scenes Look at the Master Minds of Thug Kitchen," Epicurious, September 29, 2014, https://www.epicurious.com/ archive/blogs/editor/2014/09/thug-kitchen-author-real-names-revealed.html, ac-

cessed July 27, 2018; Akeya Dickson, "Thug Kitchen: A Recipe in Black Face," The Root, September 20, 2014, https://www.theroot.com/thug-kitchen-a-recipe-in -blackface-1790877230, accessed July 27, 2018; Amie Breeze Harper, "On Ferguson, Thug Kitchen, and Trayvon Martin: Intersections of [Post]Racial Consciousness, Food Justice, and Hip Hop Vegan Ethics," October 9, 2014, The Sistah Vegan Project, http://www.sistahvegan.com/2014/10/09/on-ferguson-thug-kitchen-and -trayvon-martin-intersections-of-postrace-consciousness-food-justice-and-hip-hop -vegan-ethics/, accessed July 27, 2018.

35. Bryant Terry, "The Problem with 'Thug' Cuisine," CNN, October 10, 2014, https://www.cnn.com/2014/10/10/living/thug-kitchen-controversy-eatocracy/, accessed July 13, 2018.

36. Melissa Block interview with James McWhorter, *All Things Considered*, "The Racially Charged Meaning Behind the Word 'Thug,'" April 30, 2015, https://www .npr.org/2015/04/30/403362626/the-racially-charged-meaning-behind-the-word-thug, accessed July 13, 2018.

37. Terry, "The Problem with 'Thug' Cuisine," https://www.cnn.com/2014/10/10/ living/thug-kitchen-controversy-eatocracy/.

38. Gloria Oladipo, "Decolonizing Veganism to Make It More Accessible and Less Racist," *AfroPunk*, November 1, 2017, http://afropunk.com/2017/11/decoloniz ing-veganism-make-accessible-less-racist/, accessed July 13, 2018.

39. Aph Ko, Black Vegans Rock, http://www.blackvegansrock.com/, accessed July 27, 2018; Aph Ko, "#BlackVegansRock: 100 Black Vegans to Check Out," Striving with Systems Blog, September 11, 2015, https://strivingwithsystems.com/2015/06/11/ blackvegansrock-100-black-vegans-to-check-out/, accessed July 27, 2018.

40. Robin Scher, "Veganism Is Being Redefined in Black Communities," AlterNet, March 13, 2018, https://www.alternet.org/food/rise-black-vegans, accessed July 27, 2018.

41. Kim Severson, "Black Vegans Step Out for Their Health and Other Causes," *New York Times*, November 28, 2017, https://www.nytimes.com/2017/11/28/dining/ black-vegan-cooking.html, accessed July 27, 2018.

42. Amie Breeze Harper, *Sistah Vegan: Black Female Vegans Speak on Food, Identity, Health, and Society* (Herndon, VA: Lantern Books, 2009).

43. "Sistah Vegans: The Satya Interview with Amie Breeze Harper," *Satya* (March 2007), http://www.satyamag.com/mar07/harper.html, accessed July 27, 2018.

44. Zachary Toliver, "Here Are 11 Things You Can Expect to Happen If You're Vegan while Black," Peta.org, https://www.peta.org/living/food/black-vegans/, accessed July 27, 2018.

45. Toliver, "11 Things."

46. Amie Breeze Harper, "I'm Black and I Burn When It's 67 Degrees: Blackness Card Rejected," The Sistah Vegan Project, http://www.sistahvegan.com/2018/06/21/ im-black-and-i-burn-when-its-67-degrees-blackness-card-rejected/, accessed July 27, 2018.

47. Harris, *High on the Hog*, 226.

48. Barack Obama, *The Audacity of Hope: Thoughts on Reclaiming the American Dream* (New York: Broadway Books, 2007), 249.

49. Kristin Tice Studeman, "Eat Like the Obamas: The Best Restaurants They Dined at Over the Last 8 Years," *Vogue*, January 18, 2017, https://www.vogue.com/article/obama-family-favorite-restaurants, accessed July 27, 2018; Eater Staff, "Where to Eat Like Michelle Obama," DC Eater, December 12, 2016, https://dc.eater.com/maps/michelle-obama-restaurants-map-dc, accessed July 27, 2018; Jessica Sideman, "It's Michelle Obama's Birthday: Here Are All the DC Restaurants Where She's Celebrated," *Washingtonian*, January 17, 2018, https://www.washingtonian.com/2018/01/17/its-michelle-obamas-birthday-here-are-all-the-dc-restaurants-where-shes-celebrated/, accessed July 27, 2018; "Eat Like Michelle Obama," *Food and Wine*, https://www.foodandwine.com/slideshows/eat-michelle-obama, accessed July 27, 2018; Shabib, "The Obamas Eat Their Way through DC," *DC Metro*, May 18, 2017, http://www.dcmetroplus.com/dining-category/the-obamas-eat-their-way-through-dc/, accessed July 27, 2018.

50. Jesse Bering, "Culinary Racism: Trying to Explain the Obama Fried Chicken Incident and Others Like It," Slate.com, November 1, 2011, http://www.slate.com/articles/health_and_science/science/2011/11/obama_fried_chicken_incident_explaining_racist_food_stereotypes.html, accessed July 27, 2018; William R. Black, "How Watermelons Became a Racist Trope," *The Atlantic*, December 8, 2014, https://www.theatlantic.com/national/archive/2014/12/how-watermelons-became-a-racist-trope/383529/, accessed July 27, 2018; Kandie Isaac J. Bailey, "Confronting Racism in the Age of Obama," Neimanreports.org, June 10, 2015, http://niemanreports.org/articles/confronting-racism-in-the-age-of-obama/, accessed July 27, 2018.

51. Kandie Johnson, "Michelle Obama Speaks Candidly about Dealing with Haters," *Black Enterprise*, June 16, 2016, http://www.blackenterprise.com/michelle-obamas-advice-dealing-haters/, accessed July 27, 2018.

52. Harris, *High on the Hog*, 244.

Bibliography

ARCHIVAL COLLECTIONS

Amherst, MA
  Special Collections and University Archives
    W. E. B. Du Bois Papers, 1868–1963
New Orleans, LA
  Tulane University
    Hogan Jazz Archive
New York, NY
  New Public Library, Schomburg Center for Research in Black Culture
    Ella Baker Papers
Tuskegee, AL
  Tuskegee University Archives
    Booker T. Washington Papers
Washington, DC
  Library of Congress, Manuscript Division
    Margaret Mead Papers

PERIODICALS

Atlanta Daily World
Atlanta Magazine
Atlantic
Baltimore Afro-American
Black Enterprise
Chicago Defender
Chicago Tribune

The Crisis
DC Metro
De Bow's Review
Detroit Tribune
Ebony
Food and Wine
Jackson Free Press
New Journal and Guide
New Yorker
New York Times
Oakland Post
Pacific Medical and Surgical Journal
Paper Magazine
Philadelphia Tribune
Sacramento Observer
San Francisco Sun Reporter
Satya
Vogue
Washingtonian
Washington Post

BLOGS, WEBSITES, AND ONLINE PUBLICATIONS

A. Breeze Harper, sistahvegan.com
Alternet, alternet.org
Aph Ko, Black Vegans Rock, http://www.blackvegansrock.com/
Eater, Washington DC, dc.eater.com
Epicurious, epicurious.com
Marcus Samuelsson, marcussameulsson.com
Michael W. Twitty, afroculinaria.com
Michael W. Twitty, thecookinggene.com/blog/
National Public Radio, NPR.org
Naval History and Heritage Command, https://www.history.navy.mil/
New York Public Library, nypl.org
Nieman Reports, niemanreports.org
People for the Ethical Treatment of Animals, peta.org
Roadside America—Guide to Uniquely Odd Tourist Attractions, roadsideamerica
    .com
Slate, slate.com
SNCC Digital Gateway, snccdigital.org
Southern Foodways Alliance, southernfoodways.org
The Root, theroot.com
Thug Kitchen, thugkitchen.com

PRIMARY SOURCES

Adichie, Chimamanda Ngozi. "The Danger of a Single Story." TEDGlobal, July 2009. https://www.ted.com/talks/chimamanda_adichie_the_danger_of_a_single_story, accessed July 26, 2018.

Astley, Thomas. *A New General Collection of Voyages and Travels, Volume 2.* London: T. Astley, 1745.

Atwater, W. O., and Charles D. Woods. *Dietary Studies with Reference to the Food of the Negro in Alabama, 1895 and 1896.* Washington, DC: Government Printing Office, 1897.

Baker, Ella. "Bigger Than a Hamburger." *Southern Patriot,* May 1960. https://www.crmvet.org/docs/sncc2.htm, accessed July 9, 2018.

Ball, Charles. *Slavery in the United States: A Narrative of the Life and Adventures of Charles Ball.* New York: John S. Taylor, 1837.

Barbot, Jean. *A Description of the Coasts of North and South-Guinea.* London, 1702.

Bellagamba, Alice, Sandra E. Greene, and Martin A. Klein. *African Voices on Slavery and the Slave Trade, Volume 2.* Cambridge: Cambridge University Press, 2016.

Block, Melissa. Interview with James McWhorter, "The Racially Charged Meaning Behind the Word 'Thug.'" All Things Considered, April 30, 2015. https://www.npr.org/2015/04/30/403362626/the-racially-charged-meaning-behind-the-word-thug, accessed July 13, 2018.

Bosman, Willem. *A New and Accurate Description of the Coast of Guinea.* London: J. Knapton, 1705.

Bowdich, Thomas Edward. *Mission from Cape Coast Castle to Ashantee.* London: Griffin and Faran, 1873.

Brown, Charlotte Hawkins. *The Correct Thing to Do, to Say, to Wear.* New York: G. K. Hall, 1995.

Buist, Erica. "That's Me in the Picture: Hunter Gray Is Attacked at a Civil Rights Protest in Jackson, Mississippi, 28 May 1963." *The Guardian,* March 27, 2015. https://www.theguardian.com/artanddesign/2015/mar/27/hunter-gray-1963-jackson-mississippi-sit-in, accessed on July 9, 2018.

Carmichael, Stokely, with Ekwueme Michael Thelwell. *Ready for Revolution: The Life and Struggles of Stokely Carmichael (Kwame Ture).* New York: Scribners, 2005.

Charles, Dora. *A Real Southern Cook: In Her Savannah Kitchen.* New York: Houghton Mifflin, 2015.

Chicago Commission on Race Relations. *The Negro in Chicago: A Study of Race Relations and a Race Riot.* Chicago: University of Chicago Press, 1922.

Christaller, J. G. *Three Thousand Six Hundred Ghanaian Proverbs,* translated by Kofi Ron Lange. Lewiston, NY: Edwin Mellon Press, 1990.

Cobb, Charles E. "Guns and the Southern Freedom Struggle: What's Missing When We Teach about Nonviolence." *Huffington Post,* September 23, 2014. https://www.huffingtonpost.com/the-zinn-education-project/guns-and-the-southern-fre_b_5868338.html, accessed July 9, 2018.

Davis, Allison, Burleigh B. Gardner, and Mary R. Gardner. *Deep South: A Social Anthropological Study of Caste and Class.* Columbia: University of South Carolina Press, 2009.

De Knight, Freda. *A Date with a Dish: A Cook Book of American Negro Recipes.* New York: Hermitage Press, 1948.

Dollard, John. *Caste and Class in a Southern Town.* Madison, WI: University of Wisconsin Press, 1989.

Douglass, Frederick. *The Life and Times of Frederick Douglass.* Boston: DuWolf & Fiske, 1892.

———. *Narrative of the Life of Frederick Douglass, Written by Himself.* Boston: Anti-Slavery Office, 1845.

Drake, St. Clair, and Horace Cayton. *Black Metropolis: A Study of Negro Life in a Northern City.* Chicago: University of Chicago Press, 1993.

Du Bois, W. E. B. *Economic Co-Operation among Negro Americans.* Atlanta: Atlanta University Press, 1907.

———. "Food." *The Crisis,* August 1918, 165.

———, ed. *The Health and Physique of the Negro America.* Atlanta: Atlanta University Press, 1906.

———, ed. *The Negro in Business.* Atlanta, GA: Atlanta University, 1899.

———. *The Philadelphia Negro.* New York: Shocken Books, 1967.

———. Review of *Race Traits and Tendencies of the American Negro* by Frederick L. Hoffman. *Annals of the American Academy of Political and Social Science* 9 (January 1897): 127–33.

———. "Segregation." *Crisis,* January 1934, 20.

Dunbar-Nelson, Alice. *Give Us Each Day: The Diary of Alice Dunbar-Nelson,* edited by Gloria T. Hull. New York: W. W. Norton, 1984.

Dunn, Arlene (Wilgoren). "My Arkansas Journey." In *Arsnick: The Student Nonviolent Coordinating Committee in Arkansas,* edited by Jennifer Jensen Wallach and John A. Kirk, 160–65. Fayetteville, AR: University of Arkansas Press, 2011.

Edge, John T., and Tunde Wey. "Who Owns Southern Food?" *Oxford American,* June 3, 2016. https://www.oxfordamerican.org/magazine/item/870-who-owns-southern -food, accessed July 27, 2018.

Elie, Lolis Eric. "On Marcus Samuelsson and Red Rooster: What It Means to Be a Harlem Restaurant." *Serious Eats,* July 2, 2012. https://newyork.seriouse-ats.com/2012/07/marcus-samuelsson-eddie-huang-yes-chef-red-rooster-harlem .html#comments-119569, accessed July 12, 2018.

———. "The Soul of a New Cuisine." *Gourmet,* October 2000. http://www.gourmet .com.s3-website-us-east-1.amazonaws.com/magazine/2000s/2000/10/newcuisine .html, accessed July 12, 2018.

Ellison, Ralph. *Invisible Man.* New York: Vintage Books, 1995.

Eltis, David, et al. *The Transatlantic Slave Trade Database.* http://www.slavevoyages .org, accessed September 17, 2018.

Equiano, Olaudah. *The Interesting Narrative of the Life of Olaudah Equiano or Gustavus Vassa, the African.* London, 1790.

Falconbridge, Alexander. *An Account of the Slave Trade on the Coast of Africa.* London, 1788.

Fisher, Abby. *What Mrs. Fisher Knows about Old Southern Cooking, Soups, Pickles, Preserves, Etc.* San Francisco: Women's Cooperative Printing Office, 1881.

Foner, Laura. "Arkansas SNCC Memories." In *Arsnick: The Student Nonviolent Coordinating Committee in Arkansas*, edited by Jennifer Jensen Wallach and John A. Kirk, 148–54. Fayetteville, AR: University of Arkansas Press, 2011.

Fortune, T. Thomas. "The Present Relations of Labor and Capitol (1896)." In *Lift Every Voice: African American Oratory, 1787–1900*, edited by Philip S. Foner and Robert J. Branham, 649. Tuscaloosa, AL: University of Alabama Press, 1997.

Fulton, Alvenia M. *Vegetarianism: Fact or Myth? Eating to Live.* Chicago: B.C.A. Publishing, 1978.

Garvey, Marcus. "Articles by Marcus Garvey." In *Marcus Garvey, Life and Lessons: A Centennial Companion to the Marcus Garvey and Universal Improvement Association Papers*, edited by Robert A. Hill and Barbara Bair, 35–110. Berkeley, CA: University of California Press, 1987.

———. "Lesson 15: Personality." In *Marcus Garvey, Life and Lessons: A Centennial Companion to the Marcus Garvey and Universal Improvement Association Papers*, edited by Robert A. Hill and Barbara Bair, 283. Berkeley, CA: University of California Press, 1987.

Gaskins, Ruth. *A Good Heart and a Light Hand: Ruth L. Gaskins' Collection of Traditional Negro Recipes.* New York: Simon and Schuster, 1968.

Gerarde, John. *The Herball or Generall Historie of Plantes.* London: John Norton, 1597.

Gobineau, Arthur de. *The Inequality of Human Races*, translated by Adrian Collins. London: Heinemann, 1915.

Green, Victor. *The Negro Traveler's Green Book* (Spring 1956). http://library.sc.edu/digital/collections/greenbookmap.html, accessed July 27, 2018.

Gregory, Dick. *Dick Gregory's Natural Diet for Folks Who Eat: Cookin' with Mother Nature.* New York: Harper and Row, 1973.

Gregory, Dick, and Shelia P. Moses. *Callus on My Soul: A Memoir.* Atlanta, GA: Longstreet Press, 2000.

Griffin, John Howard. *Black Like Me.* New York: Signet, 1976.

Harlan, Louis R., and Raymond W. Smock, eds. *The Booker T. Washington Papers, Volume 5.* Urbana: University of Illinois Press, 1976.

———. *The Booker T. Washington Papers, Volume 9.* Urbana: University of Illinois Press, 1980.

———. *The Booker T. Washington Papers, Volume 11.* Urbana: University of Illinois Press, 1981.

Harper, A. Breeze. *Sistah Vegan: Black Female Vegans Speak on Food, Identity, Health, and Society.* Herndon, VA: Lantern Books, 2009.

Hawkins, Joseph. *A History of a Voyage to the Coast of Africa and Travels into the Interior.* Philadelphia, 1797.

Hilliard, David, ed. *The Black Panther Party: Service to the People Programs.* Albuquerque, NM: University of New Mexico Press, 2008.

Hoffman, Frederick L. *The Race Traits and Tendencies of the American Negro.* New York: Macmillan, 1896.

Huang, Eddie. "Marcus Samuelsson's Overcooked Memoir Makes His Pricey Harlem Discomfort Food Hard to Swallow." *New York Observer*, June 25, 2012. http://

observer.com/2012/06/marcus-samuelssons-overcooked-memoir-prompts-a-new -look-at-his-pricey-harlem-discomfort-food/, accessed July 27, 2018.

Jackson, Chris. "Reverse Migration." *The Atlantic*, January 10, 2011. https://www .theatlantic.com/national/archive/2011/01/reverse-migration/69233/, accessed July 27, 2018.

Jacobs, Harriet. *Incidents in the Life of a Slave Girl, Written by Herself.* Boston, 1861.

Johnson, Charles S., Edwin R. Embree, and W. W. Alexander. *The Collapse of Cotton Tenancy: Summary of Field Studies and Statistical Surveys, 1933–35.* Chapel Hill: University of North Carolina Press, 1935.

Jones, LeRoi (Amiri Baraka). *Home: Social Essays.* New York: Akashi Classics, 2009.

King, Ed, and Trent Watts. *Ed King's Mississippi: Behind the Scenes of Freedom Summer.* Jackson: University Press of Mississippi, 2014.

Lee, Don L. (Haki Madhubuti). *From Plan to Planet: Life Studies: The Need for Afrikan Minds and Institutions.* Detroit: Broadside Press, 1973.

McKinney, Emma, and William McKinney. *Aunt Caroline's Dixieland Recipes: A Rare Collection of Choice Southern Dishes.* Chicago: Laird & Lee, 1922.

Mendes, Helen. *The African Heritage Cookbook.* New York: The Macmillan Company, 1971.

Moody, Anne. *Coming of Age in Mississippi: The Classic Autobiography of Growing Up Poor and Black in the Rural South.* New York: Dell, 1992.

Muhammad, Elijah. *How to Eat to Live, Book No. 1.* Phoenix, AZ: Secretarious MEMPS Publications, 1967, 4–5.

———. *How to Eat to Live, Book No. 2.* Phoenix, AZ: Secretarious MEMPS Publications, 1972, 107.

———. *Message to the Blackman in America.* Atlanta, GA: Messenger Elijah Muhammad Propagation Society, 1965.

Murray, Pauli. "A Blueprint for First Class Citizenship." *The Crisis*, November 1944.

Northup, Solomon. *Twelve Years a Slave.* Auburn, NY: Derby and Miller, 1853.

Obama, Barack. *The Audacity of Hope: Thoughts on Reclaiming the American Dream.* New York: Broadway Books, 2007.

Oladipo, Gloria. "Decolonizing Veganism to Make It More Accessible and Less Racist." *AfroPunk*, November 1, 2017. http://afropunk.com/2017/11/decolonizing-veganism-make-accessible-less-racist/, accessed July 13, 2018.

Parker, Idella, with Mary Keating. *Idella: Marjorie Rawlings's "Perfect Maid."* Gainsville, FL: University of Florida Press, 1992.

Powdermaker, Hortense. *After Freedom: A Cultural Study of the Deep South.* New York: Viking Press, 1939.

Preacely, Peggy Trotter. "It Was Simply in My Blood." In *Hands on the Freedom Plow: Personal Accounts by Women in SNCC*, edited by Faith S. Holsaert, Martha Prescod, Norman Noonan, Judy Richardson, Betty Garman Robinson, Jean Smith Young, and Dorothy M. Zellner, 163–71. Urbana: University of Illinois Press, 2010.

Rambeau, Janie Culbreth. "Ripe for the Picking." In *Hands on the Freedom Plow: Personal Accounts by Women in SNCC*, edited by Faith S. Holsaert, Martha Prescod,

Norman Noonan, Judy Richardson, Betty Garman Robinson, Jean Smith Young, and Dorothy M. Zellner, 91–99. Urbana: University of Illinois Press, 2010.

Randolph, Mary. *The Virginia Housewife; Or, Methodical Cook.* Baltimore: John Plaskitt, 1836.

Rattray, R. Sutherland. *Ashanti Proverbs: The Primitive Ethics of a Savage People.* Oxford: Clarendon Press, 1916.

Russell, Malinda. *Domestic Cook Book: Containing a Careful Selection of Useful Recipes for the Kitchen.* Ann Arbor, MI: William L. Clements Library, 2007.

Samuelsson, Marcus. *The Soul of a New Cuisine: A Discovery of the Foods and Flavors of Africa.* New York: Houghton Mifflin, 2006.

Samuelsson, Marcus, with Veronica Chambers. *Yes, Chef: A Memoir.* New York: Random House, 2013.

Shaw, Nate, and Theodore Rosengarten. *All God's Dangers: The Life of Nate Shaw.* New York: Knopf, 1974.

Snelgrave, William. *A New Account of Some Parts of Guinea, and the Slave Trade.* London, 1734.

Spillers, Hortense. *Black, White, and in Color: Essays on American Literature and Culture.* Chicago: University of Chicago Press, 2003.

Terrell, Mary Church. "The Black Mammy Monument (1923)." In *From Megaphones to Microphones: Speeches of American Women, 1920–1960,* edited by Sandra J. Sarkela, Susan Mallon Ross, and Margaret A. Lowe, 15. Westport, CT: Praeger, 2003.

———. *A Colored Woman in a White World.* New York: G. K. Hall & Co., 1996.

———. "The Woman's World." *The Colored American,* March 17, 1900, 6.

Terrill, Tom E., and Jerrold Hirsch, eds. *Such as Us: Southern Voices of the Thirties.* New York: W. W. Norton, 1979.

Terry, Bryant. "The Problem with 'Thug' Cuisine." CNN, October 10, 2014. https://www.cnn.com/2014/10/10/living/thug-kitchen-controversy-eatocracy/, accessed July 13, 2018.

Twitty, Michael W. *The Cooking Gene: A Journey through African American Culinary History in the Old South.* New York: Amistad, 2017.

———. "Rules of Engagement: Food Journalism in a Multicultural America." *Gravy* (Spring 2017). https://www.southernfoodways.org/rules-of-engagement-food-journalism-in-a-multicultural-america/, accessed July 12, 2008.

Virey, Julien-Joseph. *A Natural History of the Negro Race,* translated by J. H. Guenebault. Charleston, SC: D. J. Dowling, 1837.

Washington, Booker T. "Chicken, Pigs, and People." *The Outlook* 68 (May 1901): 291–300.

———. *Up from Slavery.* Garden City, NY: The Country Life Press, 1901.

Washington, Margaret Murray. "We Must Have a Cleaner Social Morality." In *Lift Every Voice: African American Oratory, 1787–1900,* edited by Philip S. Foner and Robert J. Branham, 867–68. Tuscaloosa, AL: University of Alabama Press, 1997.

White, Annette Jones. "Finding Form for the Expression of My Discontent." In *Hands on the Freedom Plow: Personal Accounts by Women in SNCC,* edited by Faith

S. Holsaert, Martha Prescod, Norman Noonan, Judy Richardson, Betty Garman Robinson, Jean Smith Young, and Dorothy M. Zellner, 100–18. Urbana: University of Illinois Press, 2010.

Williams, Martha McCulloch. *Dishes and Beverages of the Old South.* New York: McBride Nast & Co., 1913.

Woodall, John. *The Surgions Mate: The First Compendium on Naval Medicine, Surgery and Drug Therapy, 1617*, edited and annotated by Irmgard Muller. Basel, Switzerland: Birkhauser, 2016.

Works Progress Administration. *Slave Narratives: A Folk History of Slavery in the United States with Interviews from Former Slaves, Volume II*, Arkansas Narratives Part 1. Library of Congress: Washington, DC: 1941.

———. *Slave Narratives: A Folk History of Slavery in the United States with Interviews from Former Slaves, Volume II*, Arkansas Narratives Part 5. Library of Congress: Washington, DC: 1941.

———. *Slave Narratives: A Folk History of Slavery in the United States with Interviews from Former Slaves, Volume IX*, Mississippi Narratives. Library of Congress: Washington, DC: 1941.

———. *Slave Narratives: A Folk History of Slavery in the United States with Interviews from Former Slaves, Volume XI, Part II*, North Carolina, Library of Congress: Washington, DC: 1941.

Wright, Richard. *Black Boy: A Record of Childhood and Youth.* New York: Harper Perennial, 2007.

———. *12 Million Black Voices.* New York: Basic Books, 2002.

Yeargen Kaiser, Inez. *Soul Food Cookery.* New York: Putnam, 1968.

SECONDARY SOURCES

Albala, Ken. *Eating Right in the Renaissance.* Berkeley: University of California Press, 2002.

Alpern, Stanley. "The European Introduction of Crops into West Africa in Precolonial Times." *History in Africa* 19 (1992): 13–43.

———. "Exotic Plants of Western Africa: Where They Came from and When." *History in Africa* 35 (2008): 63–102.

Appiah, Kwame Anthony, and Henry Louis Gates Jr., eds. *Africana: The Encyclopedia of the African and African American Experience.* New York: Oxford University Press, 2005.

Bay, Mia. *To Tell the Truth Freely: The Life of Ida B. Wells.* New York: Hill and Wang, 2009.

———. "Traveling Black/Buying Black: Retail and Roadside Accommodations during the Segregation Era." In *Race and Retail: Consumption Across the Color Line*, edited by Mia Bay and Ann Fabian, 15–33. New Brunswick, NJ: Rutgers University Press, 2015.

Beardsley, Edward H. *A History of Neglect: Health Care for Blacks and Mill Workers in the Twentieth-Century South.* Knoxville: University of Tennessee Press, 1987.

Bégin, Camille. *Taste of the Nation: The New Deal Search for America's Food.* Urbana: University of Illinois Press, 2016.

Bentley, Amy. *Eating for Victory: Food Rationing and the Politics of Domesticity.* Urbana, IL: University of Illinois Press, 1998.

Berlin, Ira. *The Making of African America: The Four Great Migrations.* New York: Penguin Books, 2010.

———. *Many Thousands Gone: The First Two Centuries of Slavery in North America.* Cambridge: Harvard University Press, 1998.

Biltekoff, Charlotte. *Eating Right in America: The Cultural Politics of Food and Health.* Durham, NC: Duke University Press, 2013.

Blassingame, John. *The Slave Community: Plantation Life in the Antebellum South.* New York: Oxford University Press, 1972.

Bloom, Joshua, and Waldo E. Martin Jr. *Black Against Empire: The History and Politics of the Black Panther Party.* Berkeley, CA: University of California Press, 2016.

Bobrow-Strain, Aaron. *White Bread: A Social History of the Store-Bought Loaf.* Boston: Beacon Press, 2013.

Carney, Judith A. *Black Rice: The African Origins of Rice Cultivation in the Americas.* Cambridge: Harvard University Press, 2001.

Carney, Judith A., and Richard Nicholas Rosomoff. *In the Shadow of Slavery: Africa's Botanical Legacy in the Atlantic World.* Berkeley: University of California Press, 2009.

Carpenter, Stephanie A. "At the Agricultural Front: The Women's Land Army during World War II." PhD Dissertation, Iowa State University, 1997, 274–76.

———. *On the Farm Front: The Women's Land Army in World War II.* DeKalb, IL: University of Northern Illinois Press, 2003.

Carson, Clayborne. *In Struggle: SNCC and the Black Awakening of the 1960s.* Cambridge, MA: Harvard University Press, 1995.

Civitello, Linda. *Cuisine and Culture: A History of Food and People, Second Edition.* Hoboken, NJ: John Wiley and Sons, 2008.

Coates, Ta-Nehesi. "Slavery Made America: The Case for Reparations." *Atlantic Monthly,* June 24, 2014. https://www.theatlantic.com/business/archive/2014/06/slavery-made-america/373288/, accessed September 17, 2018.

Coe, Andrew. *Chop Suey: A Cultural History of Chinese Food in the United States.* Oxford: Oxford University Press, 2009.

Cohen, Lizabeth. *Making a New Deal: Industrial Workers in Chicago, 1919–1939.* Cambridge: Cambridge University Press, 1990.

Conrad, David Eugene. *The Forgotten Farmers: The Story of Sharecroppers in the New Deal.* Westport, CT: Greenwood Publishers, 1965.

Cooley, Angela Jill. "Freedom's Farms: Activism and Sustenance in Rural Mississippi." In *Dethroning the Deceitful Pork Chop: Rethinking African American Foodways from Slavery to Obama,* edited by Jennifer Jensen Wallach, 199–214. Fayetteville, AR: University of Arkansas Press, 2015.

———. *To Live and Dine in Dixie: The Evolution of Urban Food Culture in the Jim Crow South.* Athens, GA: University of Georgia Press, 2015.

Covey, Herbert C., and Dwight Eisnach. *What the Slaves Ate: Recollections of African American Foods and Foodways from the Slave Narratives.* Santa Barbara, CA: ABC CLIO, 2009.

Cronon, E. David. *Black Moses: The Story of Marcus Garvey*. Madison: University of Wisconsin Press, 1955.

Crosby, Alfred W. *The Columbian Exchange: Biological and Cultural Consequences of 1492*. Westport, CT: Greenwood, 1972.

Cumo, Christopher. *The Ongoing Columbian Exchange: Stories of Biological and Economic Transfer in World History*. Santa Barbara, CA: ABC-CLIO, 2015.

Curtin, Philip D. *The Atlantic Slave Trade: A Census*. Madison: University of Wisconsin Press, 1969.

Daniel, Pete. *Breaking the Land: The Transformation of Cotton, Tobacco and Rice Cultures since 1880*. Urbana: University of Illinois Press, 1985.

———. *The Shadow of Slavery: Peonage in the South, 1901–1969*. Urbana: University of Illinois Press, 1990.

Dantzig, Albert van, and Willem Bosman. "Willem Bosman's 'New and Accurate Description of the Coast of Guinea': How Accurate Is It?" *History in Africa* 1 (1974): 101–8.

Daponte, Beth Osborne, and Shannon Lee Bade. "The Evolution, Cost, and Operation of the Private Food Assistance Network." Institute for Research on Poverty Discussion Paper No. 1211-00. https://www.irp.wisc.edu/publications/dps/pdfs/dp121100.pdf, 6, accessed July 10, 2018.

David, Paul A., Herbert G. Gutman, Richard Sutch, Peter Temin, and Gavin Wright. *Reckoning with Slavery: A Critical Study of the Quantitative History of American Negro Slavery*. New York: Oxford University Press, 1976.

Davidson, Alan, and Tom Jaine, eds. *The Oxford Companion to Food and Drink, Second Edition*. Oxford: Oxford University Press, 2006.

Davis, David Brion. "The Impact of British Abolitionism on American Sectionalism." In *In the Shadow of Freedom: The Politics of Slavery in the National Capitol*, edited by Paul Finkelman and Donald R. Kennon, 19–36. Athens: Ohio State University Press, 2011.

Deetz, Kelley Fanto. *Bound to the Fire: How Virginia's Enslaved Cooks Helped Invent American Cuisine*. Lexington, KY: University Press of Kentucky, 2017.

Demar, George E. "Negro Women Are American Workers, Too." *Opportunity*, April 1943, reprinted in *Bitter Fruit: African American Women in World War II*, edited by Maureen Honey, 104–7. Columbia, MO: University of Missouri Press, 1999.

Devlin, Paul. "Lillian Harris Dean." In *Harlem Renaissance Lives*, edited by Henry Louis Gates Jr. and Evelyn Brooks Higginbotham. New York: Oxford University Press, 2009.

Dick, Bruce Allen. "A Forgotten Chapter: Richard Wright, Playwrights, and the Modern Theater." In *Richard Wright in a Post-Racial Imaginary*, edited by William E. Dow, Alice Mikal Craven, and Yoko Nakamura, 179–96. New York: Bloomsbury, 2014.

Diner, Hasia. *Hungering for America: Italian, Irish, and Jewish Foodways in the Age of Migration*. Cambridge, MA: Harvard University Press, 2003.

Dirks, Robert T., and Nancy Duran. "African American Dietary Patterns at the Beginning of the 20th Century." *Journal of Nutrition* 31, no. 7 (July 2001): 1881–89.

Dittmer, John. *Local People: The Struggle for Civil Rights in Mississippi.* Champaign-Urbana, IL: University of Illinois Press, 1995.

Dormon, James M. "Shaping the Popular Image of Post-Reconstruction American Blacks: The 'Coon Song' Phenomenon of the Gilded Age." *American Quarterly* 40 (1988): 450–71.

Dougan, Michael B. *Arkansas Odyssey.* Little Rock, AR: Rose Publishing, 1994.

Downs, Jim. *Sick from Freedom: African-American Illness and Suffering during the Civil War and Reconstruction.* New York: Oxford University Press, 2012.

Du Bois, W. E. B. *Black Reconstruction in America, 1860–1880.* New York: Free Press, 1998.

Earle, Rebecca. *The Body of the Conquistador: Food, Race and the Colonial Experience in Spanish America, 1492–1700.* Cambridge: Cambridge University Press, 2012.

Eden, Trudy. *The Early American Table: Food and Society in the New World.* DeKalb: Northern Illinois University Press, 2008.

Edge, John T. *The Potlikker Papers: A Food History of the Modern South.* New York: Penguin Press, 2017.

Elias, Megan J. *Food in the United States, 1809–1945.* Santa Barbara, CA: ABC-CLIO, 2009.

———. "Summoning the Food Ghosts: Food History as Public History." *Public Historian* 34, no. 2 (Spring 2012): 13–29.

Eltis, David, Philip Morgan, and David Richardson. "Agency and Diaspora in Atlantic History: Reassessing the African Contribution to Rice Cultivation in the Americas." *American Historical Review* 112, no. 5 (December 2007): 1329–58.

Engelhardt, Elizabeth S. D. *A Mess of Greens: Southern Gender and Southern Food.* Athens, GA: University of Georgia Press, 2011.

Evans, Amy C. "Introduction: Hot Tamales and the Mississippi Delta." Southern Foodways Alliance. http://www.southernfoodways.org/interview/hot-tamales-the-mississippi-delta/, accessed September 17, 2018.

Fage, J. D. "Hawkins' Hoax? A Sequel to 'Drake's Fake.'" *History in Africa* 18 (1991): 83–91.

Fennell, Christopher F. "Early African America: Archeological Studies of Significance and Diversity." *Journal of Archeological Research* 19, no. 1 (March 2011): 1–49.

Ferguson, Jeffrey. *The Sage of Sugar Hill: George S. Schuyler and the Harlem Renaissance.* New Haven, CT: Yale University Press, 2005.

Ferris, Marcie Cohen. *The Edible South: The Power of Food and the Making of an American Region.* Chapel Hill: University of North Carolina Press, 2016.

———. *Matzoh Ball Gumbo: Culinary Tales of the Jewish South.* Chapel Hill, NC: University of North Carolina Press, 2010.

Fite, Gilbert C. *Cotton Fields No More.* Lexington: University of Kentucky Press, 1984.

Fogel, Robert William, and Stanley Engerman. *Time on the Cross: The Economics of American Negro Slavery.* Boston: Little, Brown, and Company, 1974.

Foner, Eric. *A Short History of Reconstruction, Updated Edition.* New York: Harper Perennial, 2015.

Freedmen, Paul. *Ten Restaurants That Changed America.* New York: Liverwright Publishing, 2016.

Gee, Denise. "The Gospel of Great Southern Food." *Southern Living,* June 1996, 126–28.

Genovese, Eugene. *Roll, Jordan, Roll: The World the Slaves Made.* New York: Vintage, 1976.

Gibbs, Tyson, Kathleen Cargill, Leslie Sue Lieberman, and Elizabeth Reitz. "Nutrition in a Slave Population: An Anthropological Examination." *Medical Anthropology* 4, no. 2 (1980): 175–262.

Gilmer, Robert A. "Native American Contributions to African American Foodways: Slavery, Colonialism, and Cuisine." In *Dethroning the Deceitful Pork Chop: Rethinking African American Foodways from Slavery to Obama,* edited by Jennifer Jensen Wallach, 17–30. Fayetteville: University of Arkansas Press, 2015.

Gilroy, Paul. *The Black Atlantic: Modernity and Double Consciousness.* Cambridge, MA: Harvard University Press, 1993.

Gomez, Michael. *Exchanging Our Country Marks: The Transformation of African Identities in the Colonial and Antebellum South.* Chapel Hill: University of North Carolina Press, 1998.

Gordan, Jessica. *Collective Courage: A History of African American Cooperative Economic Thought and Practice.* University Park: The Pennsylvania State University Press, 2014.

Gowdy-Wygant, Cecilia. *Cultivating Victory: The Women's Land Army and the Victory Garden Movement.* Pittsburgh: University of Pittsburgh Press, 2013.

Grant, Colin. *Negro with a Hat: The Rise and Fall of Marcus Garvey.* New York: Oxford University Press, 2008.

Green, Rayna. "Mother Corn and Dixie Pig: Native Food in the Native South." In *The Larder: Food Studies Methods from the American South,* edited by John T. Edge, Elizabeth Engelhardt, and Ted Ownby, 155–65. Athens: University of Georgia Press, 2013.

Greenberg, Cheryl Lynn. *To Ask for an Equal Chance: African Americans in the Great Depression.* Lanham, MD: Rowman & Littlefield, 2009.

Greene, Alison Collis. "'Human Beings Do Not Behave Like Test Tube Experiments': Dorothy Dickens and the Science of Home Economics in Mid-Twentieth Century Mississippi." *Journal of Mississippi History* 75, no. 1 (Spring 2013): 5–13.

Grossman, John R. *Land of Hope: Chicago, Black Southerners, and the Great Migration.* Chicago: University of Chicago Press, 1989.

Grubbs, Donald H. *Cry from the Cotton: The Southern Tenant Farmers' Union and the New Deal.* Chapel Hill: University of North Carolina Press, 1971.

Hall, Gwendolyn Midlo. *Slavery and African Ethnicities in the Americas: Restoring the Links.* Chapel Hill: University of North Carolina Press, 2007.

Hall, Robert L. "Africa and the American South: Culinary Connections." *Southern Quarterly* 44, no. 2 (Winter 2007): 19–52.

———. "Food Crops, Medicinal Plants, and the Atlantic Slave Trade." In *African American Foodways: Explorations of History and Culture,* edited by Anne L. Bower, 17–44. Urbana: University of Illinois Press, 2007.

Hordeman, Nicholas P. *Shucks, Shacks, and Hominy Blocks Corn as a Way of Life in Pioneer America* (Baton Rouge: Louisiana State University Press, 1981), 149–50.

Harding, Vincent. *There Is a River: The Black Struggle for Freedom in America.* New York: Houghton Mifflin, 1981.

Harris, Jessica. *High on the Hog: A Culinary Journey from Africa to America.* New York: Bloomsbury, 2011.

———. "Three Is a Magic Number." *Southern Quarterly* 44, no. 2 (2007): 9–15.

Harris, Sara. *Father Divine: Holy Husband.* Garden City, NY: Doubleday & Company, 1953.

Haynes, Elizabeth Ross. "Negroes in Domestic Service in the United States." *Journal of Negro History* 8, no. 4 (1923): 384–442.

Heimann, Jim, ed. *Menu Design in America.* Berlin: Taschen, 2011.

Herskovits, Melville. *The Myth of the Negro Past.* Boston: Beacon Press, 1990.

Hess, Karen. *The Carolina Rice Kitchen: The African Connection.* Columbia, SC: University of South Carolina Press, 1998.

Heywood, Linda M., and John K. Thornton. *Central Africans, Atlantic Creoles, and the Foundations of the Americas.* Cambridge: Cambridge University Press, 2007.

Hilliard, Kathleen. *Masters, Slaves, and Exchange: Power's Purchase in the Old South.* New York: Cambridge University Press, 2014.

Hilliard, Sam Bowers. *Hog Meat and Hoecake: Food Supply in the Old South, 1840–1860.* Athens: University of Georgia Press, 2014.

Hoekstra, Dave. *The People's Place: Soul Food Restaurants and Reminiscences from the Civil Rights Era to Today.* Chicago: Chicago Review Press, 2015.

Hogan, Wesley. *Many Minds, One Heart: SNCC's Dream for a New America.* Chapel Hill: University of North Carolina Press, 2009.

Holloway, Joseph E. "Africanisms in African American Names in the United States." In *Africanisms in American Culture*, edited by Joseph E. Holloway, 82–110. Bloomington: Indiana University Press, 2005.

Holt, Sharon Ann. *Making Freedom Pay: North Carolina Freedpeople Working for Themselves.* Athens: University of Georgia Press, 2000.

Honey, Maureen. *Bitter Fruit: African American Women in World War II.* Columbia, MO: University of Missouri Press, 1999.

Horowitz, Roger. *Putting Meat on the American Table.* Baltimore: Johns Hopkins University Press, 2006.

Horwitz, Tony. "The Mammy Washington Almost Had." *The Atlantic*, May 31, 2013. https://www.theatlantic.com/national/archive/2013/05/the-mammy-washington-almost-had/276431/, accessed September 18, 2018.

Hunter, Tera. *To 'Joy My Freedom: Southern Black Women's Lives and Labors after the Civil War.* Cambridge, MA: Harvard University Press, 1998.

Hurt, R. Douglas. *American Agriculture: A Brief History.* West Layfayette, IN: Purdue University Press, 2002.

Jeffries, John W. "Mobilization and Its Impact." In *World War II and the American Home Front*, National Parks Service. https://www.nps.gov/nhl/learn/themes/wwii homefront.pdf, 9-49, accessed June 20, 2018.

Jones, Jacqueline. *Labor of Love, Labor of Sorrow: Black Women, Work, and the Family from Slavery to the Present.* New York: Basic Books, 1985.

Joyner, Charles. *Down by the Riverside: A South Carolina Slave Community.* Urbana: University of Illinois Press, 1984.

Kahan, Benjamin. "The Other Harlem Renaissance: Father Divine, Celibate Economics, and the Making of Black Sexuality." *Arizona Quarterly: A Journal of American Literature, Culture, and Theory* 65, no. 4 (Winter 2009): 37–61.

Kelley, Robin D. G. *Freedom Dreams: The Black Radical Imagination.* Boston: Beacon Books, 2003.

———. *Race Rebels: Culture, Politics, and the Black Working Class.* New York: Free Press, 1996.

Kiple, Kenneth F., and Brian T. Higgins. "Mortality Caused by Dehydration during the Middle Passage." *Social Science History* 13, no. 4 (January 1989): 420–37.

Kiple, Kenneth F., and Virgina Himmelsteib King. *Another Dimension to the Black Diaspora: Diet, Disease, and Racism.* Cambridge: Cambridge University Press, 1981.

Kiple, Kenneth, and Virginia H. Kiple. "Slave Child Mortality: Some Nutritional Answers to a Perennial Puzzle." *Journal of Social History* 10, no. 3 (Spring 1977): 284–309.

Kirby, Jack Temple. *Rural Worlds Lost: The American South, 1920–1960.* Baton Rouge, LA: Louisiana State University Press, 1986.

Kiuchi, Toru, and Yoshinobu Hakutani. *Richard Wright: A Documented Chronology, 1908–1960.* Jefferson, NC: McFarland, 2014.

Kolb, Carolyn, and C. Paige Gutierrez. "Gumbo." In *The New Encyclopedia of Southern Culture, Volume 7, Foodways,* edited by John T. Edge, 177–79. Chapel Hill: University of North Carolina Press, 2007.

La Fleur, J. D. *Fusion Foodways of Africa's Gold Coast in the Atlantic Era.* Leiden: Brill, 2012.

Lam, Francis. "Edna Lewis and the Black Roots of American Cooking." *New York Times,* October 28, 2015. https://www.nytimes.com/2015/11/01/magazine/edna-lewis-and-the-black-roots-of-american-cooking.html, accessed July 10, 2018.

Levenstein, Harvey. *Revolution at the Table: The Transformation of the American Diet.* Berkeley: University of California Press, 2003.

Lichtenstein, Nelson. "Labor and the Working Class in World War II." In *World War II and the American Home Front,* National Parks Service. https://www.nps.gov/nhl/learn/themes/wwiihomefront.pdf, 8-103, accessed June 20, 2018.

Litoff, Judith Barrett. "Southern Women in a World War." In *Remaking Dixie: The Impact of World War II on the American South,* edited by Neil R. McMillan, 56–69. Jackson, MS: University Press of Mississippi, 1997.

Litoff, Judy Barrett, and David C. Smith. "To the Rescue of the Crops: The Women's Land Army during World War II." *Prologue* 25, no. 4 (Winter 1993). http://www.archives.gov/publications/prologue/1993/winter/landarmy.html, accessed June 20, 2018.

Littlefield, Daniel C. *Rice and Slaves: Ethnicity and the Slave Trade in Colonial South Carolina.* Urbana: University of Illinois Press, 1981.

Litwack, Leon. *Been in the Storm So Long: The Aftermath of Slavery.* New York: Knopf, 1979.

———. *Trouble in Mind: Black Southerners in the Age of Jim Crow.* New York: Vintage, 1999.

Lively, Janice Tuck. "Lillian Harris Dean." *Encyclopedia of the Harlem Renaissance*, edited by Cary D. Wintz and Paul Finkelman, 298–99. New York: Routledge, 2004.

Long, Ereven J. "The Agricultural Ladder: Its Adequacy as a Model for Farm Tenure Research." *Land Economics* 26, no. 3 (August 1950): 268–73.

Luster, J. Michael. "Persimmons." In *The New Encyclopedia of Southern Culture: Foodways*, edited by John T. Edge, 221. Chapel Hill: University of North Carolina Press, 2007.

Maddox, Gregory. *Sub-Saharan Africa: An Environmental History*. Santa Barbara, CA: ABC-CLIO, 2006.

Mallipeddi, Ramesh. "'A Fixed Melancholy': Migration, Memory, and the Middle Passage." *The Eighteenth Century* 55, no. 2 (2014): 235–53.

Mandelblatt, Bertie R. "'Beans from *Rochel* and Manioc from *Prince's Island*': West Africa, French Atlantic Commodity Circuits, and the Provisioning of the French Middle Passage." *History of European Ideas* 34, no. 4 (2008): 411–23.

Manring, M. M. *A Slave in a Box: The Strange Career of Aunt Jemima*. Charlottesville: University of Virginia Press, 1997.

Martin, Tony. *Race First: The Ideological and Organizational Struggles of Marcus Garvey and the Universal Negro Improvement Association*. Dover, MA: The Majority Press, 1976.

Martinez, Elizabeth. *Letters from Mississippi: Reports from Civil Rights Volunteers and Freedom School Poetry of the 1964 Freedom Summer*. Brookline, MA: Zephyr Press, 2007.

May, Vanessa. "'Obtaining a Decent Livelihood': Food Work, Race, and Gender in W. E. B. Du Bois's *The Philadelphia Negro*." *Labor: Studies in Working-Class History of the Americas* 12, no. 1–2 (2015): 115–26.

Meacham, Ellen B. *Delta Epiphany: Robert F. Kennedy in Mississippi*. Jackson, MS: University Press of Mississippi, 2018.

McAdam, Doug. *Freedom Summer*. New York: Oxford University Press, 1990.

McEyla, Micki. *Clinging to Mammy: The Faithful Slave in Twentieth-Century America*. Cambridge, MA: Harvard University Press, 2007.

McGee, Holly Y. "It Was the Wrong Time, and They Just Weren't Ready." In *Arsnick: The Student Nonviolent Coordinating Committee in Arkansas*, edited by Jennifer Jensen Wallach and John A. Kirk, 35–53. Fayetteville, AR: University of Arkansas Press, 2011.

McMann, James C. *Maize and Grace: Africa's Encounter with a New World Crop, 1500–2000*. Cambridge: Harvard University Press, 2005.

———. *Stirring the Pot: A History of African Cuisine*. Athens: Ohio University Press, 2009.

McMillen, Matt. "Beef." In *The New Encyclopedia of Southern Culture: Foodways*, edited by John T. Edge, 26–27. Chapel Hill: University of North Carolina Press, 2007.

McMillan, Neil R. *Dark Journey: Black Mississippians in the Age of Jim Crow*. Urbana: University of Illinois Press, 1990.

McWilliams, James. *A Revolution in Eating: How the Quest for Food Shaped America*. New York: Columbia University Press, 2005.

Meier, August. "Whither the Black Perspective in Afro-American Historiography?" *Journal of American History* 70, no. 1 (June 1983): 101–5.

Miller, Adrian. *Soul Food: The Surprising Story of an American Cuisine, One Plate at a Time.* Chapel Hill: University of North Carolina Press, 2017.

Miller, Richard E. *The Messmen Chronicles: African Americans in the U.S. Navy, 1932–1943.* Annapolis, MD: Naval Institute Press, 2004.

Mintz, Sidney W., and Richard Price. *The Birth of African-American Culture: An Anthropological Perspective.* Boston: Beacon Press, 1992.

Mitchell, William Frank. *African American Food Culture.* Westport, CT: Greenwood Press, 2009.

Moore, Christopher Paul. *Fighting for America: Black Soldiers—the Unsung Heroes of World War II.* New York: One World Ballentine Books, 2005.

Morehouse, Maggi M. *Fighting in the Jim Crow Army: Black Men and Women Remember World War II.* Lanham, MD: Rowman & Littlefield, 2000.

Morgan, Philip. "The Ownership of Property by Slaves in the Mid-Nineteenth-Century Low Country." *Journal of Southern History* 49, no. 3 (August 1983): 399–420.

———. *Slave Counterpoint: Black Culture in the Eighteenth Century Chesapeake and Lowcountry.* Chapel Hill: University of North Carolina Press, 1998.

Mustakeem, Sowande M. *Slavery at Sea: Terror, Sex, and Sickness in the Middle Passage.* Urbana, IL: University of Illinois Press, 2016.

Nembhard, Jessica Gordon, *Collective Courage: A History of African American Cooperative Economic Thought and Practice* (University Park: The Pennsylvania State University Press, 2014), 104–5.

Nordahl, Darrin. *Eating Appalachia: Rediscovering Regional American Flavors.* Chicago: Chicago Review Press, 2015.

Northrup, David. "The Compatibility of the Slave and Palm Oil Trades in the Bight of Biafra." *Journal of African History* 17, no. 3 (1976): 353–64.

Nwokeji, G. Ugo. *The Slave Trade and Culture in the Bight of Biafra.* Cambridge: Cambridge University Press, 2010.

Opie, Frederick Douglass. *Hog and Hominy: Soul Food from Africa to America.* New York: Columbia University Press, 2008.

———. *Southern Food and Civil Rights: Feeding the Revolution.* Charleston, SC: American Palate, 2017.

Osseo-Asare, Fran. *Food Culture in Sub-Saharan Africa.* Westport, CT: Greenwood Press, 2005.

Otto, John Solomon, and Augustus Marion Burns III. "Black Folks and Poor Buckras: Archeological Evidence of Slave and Overseer Living Conditions on an Antebellum Plantation." *Journal of Black Studies* 14, no. 2 (December 1983): 185–200.

Ownby, Ted. *American Dreams in Mississippi: Consumers, Poverty, and Culture, 1830–1998.* Chapel Hill, NC: University of North Carolina Press, 1999.

Payne, Charles. *I've Got the Light of Freedom: The Organizing Tradition and the Mississippi Freedom Struggle.* Berkeley, CA: University of California Press, 2007.

Petty, Miriam J. Petty. *Stealing the Show: African American Performers and Audiences in 1930s Hollywood.* Berkeley: University of California Press, 2016.

Phillips, John Edward. "The African Heritage of White America." In *Africanisms in American Culture*, edited by Joseph E. Holloway, 372–96. Bloomington: Indiana University Press, 2005.

Pilcher, Jeffrey M. *Que Vivan Los Tamales!: Food and the Making of Mexican Identity*. Albuquerque: University of New Mexico Press, 1998.

Poe, Tracy. "The Origins of Soul Food in Black Urban Identity: Chicago, 1915–1947." *American Studies International* (February 1999): 4–32.

Poppendieck, Janet. *Breadlines Knee-Deep in Wheat: Food Assistance in the Great Depression*. Berkeley, CA: University of California Press, 2014.

Postma, Johannes. *The Dutch in the Atlantic Slave Trade, 1600–1815*. Cambridge: Cambridge University Press, 1990.

Primiano, Leonard Norman. "'And as We Dine, We Sing and Praise God': Father and Mother Divine's Theologies of Food." In *Religion, Food, and Eating in North America*, edited by Benjamin Zeller, Marie Dallam, Reid Neilson, and Nora Rubel, 42–67. New York: Columbia University Press, 2014.

Purdue, Theda. *Cherokee Women: Gender and Culture Change, 1700–1835*. Lincoln: University of Nebraska Press, 1998.

Raine, Howell. *My Soul Is Rested: Movement Days in the Deep South Remembered*. New York: Penguin, 1983.

Ransby, Barbara. *Ella Baker and the Black Freedom Movement: A Radical Democratic Vision*. Chapel Hill: University of North Carolina Press, 2005.

Ranson, Roger L. "The Economics of the Civil War." EH.net. http://eh.net/encyclopedia/the-economics-of-the-civil-war/, accessed September 17, 2018.

Rawley, James, and Stephen D. Behrendt. *The Transatlantic Slave Trade: A History*. Lincoln: University of Nebraska Press, 2005.

Rediker, Marcus. *The Slave Ship: A Human History*. New York: Penguin Books, 2007.

Ritterhouse, Jennifer. *Growing Up Jim Crow: How Black and White Southern Children Learned Race*. Chapel Hill: University of North Carolina Press, 2006.

Rogers, Kim Lacy. *Life and Death in the Delta: African American Narratives of Violence, Resilience, and Social Change*. London: Palgrave, 2006.

Rothstein, Richard. *The Color of Law: A Forgotten History of How Our Government Segregated America*. New York: Liveright, 2017.

Rountree, Helen C. *The Powhatan Indians of Virginia: Their Traditional Culture*. Norman: University of Oklahoma Press, 1989.

Ruhn, Muriel. "My Most Humiliating Jim Crow Experience." *Negro Digest*, September 1945, reprinted in reprinted in *Bitter Fruit: African American Women in World War II*, edited by Maureen Honey, 337–38. Columbia, MO: University of Missouri Press, 1999.

Rushdie, Salman. *Imaginary Homelands: Essays and Criticism, 1981–1991*. London: Granta Books, 1991.

Schmidt, Christopher W. *The Sit-Ins: Protest and Legal Change during the Civil Rights Era*. Chicago: University of Chicago Press, 2018.

Seibart, Gerhard. "Sao Tome and Principe: The First Plantation Economy in the Tropics." In *Commercial Agriculture: The Slave Trade and Slavery in Atlantic Africa*, edited by Robin Law, Suzanne Schwarz, Silke Strickrodt, 54–78. Woodbridge, Suffolk: James Currey, 2013.

Semmes, Clovis. "The Role of African American Health Beliefs and Practices in Social Movements and Cultural Revitalization." *Minority Voices* 6 (1990): 45–57.

Shapiro, Laura. *Perfection Salad: Women and Cooking at the Turn of the Century.* Berkeley: University of California Press, 2009.

Sharpless, Rebecca. *Cooking in Other Women's Kitchens: Domestic Workers in the South, 1865–1960.* Chapel Hill, NC: University of North Carolina Press, 2010.

———. "Neither Friends nor Peers: Idella Parker, Marjorie Kinnan Rawlings, and the Limits of Gender Solidarity at Cross Creek." *Journal of Southern History* 78, no. 2 (May 2012): 327–60.

Singleton, Theresa. "The Archeology of Slave Life." In *Images of the Recent Past: Readings in Historical Archaeology*, edited by Charles E. Orser Jr., 141–61. Walnut Creek, CA: Altamira, 1996.

Smallwood, Stephanie E. *Saltwater Slavery: A Middle Passage from Africa to American Diaspora.* Cambridge, MA: Harvard University Press, 2007.

Smith, Andrew F. "Peanuts." In *The Oxford Companion to American Food and Drink*, edited by Andrew F. Smith. New York: Oxford University Press, 2007.

———. *Peanuts: The Illustrious History of the Goober Pea.* Urbana: University of Illinois Press, 2007.

Spencer, Colin. *British Food: An Extraordinary Thousand Years of History.* New York: Columbia University Press, 2002.

Stampp, Kenneth. *The Peculiar Institution: Slavery in the Ante-Bellum South.* New York: Knopf, 1956.

Steckel, Richard H. "A Peculiar Population: The Nutrition, Health, and Mortality of American Slaves from Childhood to Maturity." *Journal of Economic History* 46, no. 3 (September 1986): 721–41.

———. "Women, Work, and Health under Plantation Slavery." In *More Than Chattel: Black Women and Slavery in the Americas*, edited by David Barry Gasper and Darlene Clark Hine, 43–60. Bloomington, IN: Indiana University Press, 1996.

Stein, Judith. *The World of Marcus Garvey: Race and Class in Modern Society.* Baton Rouge, LA: Louisiana State University Press, 1986.

Sterner, Richard. *The Negro's Share: A Study of Income, Consumption, Housing, and Public Assistance.* New York: Harper & Brother's, 1943.

Sutch, Richard. "The Care and Feeding of Slaves." In *Reckoning with Slavery: A Critical Study of the Quantitative History of American Negro Slavery*, edited by Paul A. David, Herbert G. Gutman, Richard Sutch, Peter Temin, and Gavin Wright, 231–301. New York: Oxford University Press, 1976.

Taylor, Eric Robert. *If We Must Die: Shipboard Insurrections in the Era of the Transatlantic Slave Trade.* Baton Rouge: Louisiana State University Press, 2009.

Theophano, Janet. *Eat My Words: Reading Women's Lives through the Cookbooks They Wrote.* New York: St. Martin's, 2003.

Thornton, John. *Africa and Africans in the Making of the Atlantic World, 1400–1800, Second Edition.* Cambridge: Cambridge University Press, 1998.

Tipton-Martin, Toni. *The Jemima Code: Two Centuries of African American Cookbooks.* Austin, TX: University of Texas Press, 2015.

Townsend, Jacinda. "How the *Green Book* Helped African-American Tourists Navigate a Segregated Nation." *Smithsonian Magazine*, April 2016. https://www .smithsonianmag.com/smithsonian-institution/history-green-book-african-ameri-can-travelers-180958506/, accessed July 27, 2018.

Tuttle, William M. "The American Family on the Home Front." In *World War II and the American Home Front*, National Parks Service. https://www.nps.gov/nhl/learn/ themes/wwiihomefront.pdf, 50–79, accessed June 20, 2018.

Twitty, Michael W. "Gardens." In *World of the Slave: Encyclopedia of the Material Life of Slaves in the United States*, edited by Martha B. Katz-Hyman and Kym S. Rice, 245–50. Santa Barbara, CA: Greenwood, 2011.

Van Deburg, William L. *New Day in Babylon: The Black Power Movement and American Culture, 1965–1975.* Chicago: University of Chicago Press, 1992.

Veit, Helen Zoe. *Modern Food, Moral Food: Self-Control, Science, and the Rise of Modern American Eating in the Early Twentieth Century.* Chapel Hill: University of North Carolina Press, 2013.

Waibel, Leo. "The Political Significance of Tropical Vegetable Fats for the Industrial Countries of Europe." *Annals of the Association of American Geographers* 33, no. 2 (June 1943): 118–28.

Walker, Juliet E. K., ed. *Encyclopedia of African American Business History.* Westport, CT: Greenwood Press, 1999.

———. *The History of Black Business in America: Capitalism, Race, Entrepreneurship.* New York: Macmillan Library Reference, 1998.

Wallach, Jennifer Jensen. *Every Nation Has Its Dish: Black Bodies and Black Food in Twentieth-Century America.* Chapel Hill: University of North Carolina Press, 2019.

———. "Food and Race." In *The Routledge History of American Foodways*, edited by Michael D. Wise and Jennifer Jensen Wallach, 293–310. London: Routledge, 2016.

———. *How America Eats: A Social History of US Food and Culture.* Lanham, MD: Rowman & Littlefield, 2013.

———. "How to Eat to Live: Black Nationalism and the Post-1964 Culinary Turn." https://southernstudies.olemiss.edu/study-the-south/how-to-eat-to-live/, accessed July 10, 2018.

Walton, Becca. "C. O. Chinn." In *The Mississippi Encyclopedia*, edited by Ted Ownby, Charles Reagan Wilson, Ann J. Abadie, Odie Lindsey, James G. Thomas, 208. Jackson: The University Press of Mississippi, 2017.

Ward, Jerry W., and Robert J. Butler, eds. *The Richard Wright Encyclopedia.* Westport, CT: Greenwood, 2008.

Washburn, Patrick S. "The Pittsburgh *Courier*'s Double V Campaign in 1942." *American Journalism* 3, no. 2 (2013): 73–86.

Watson, Bruce. *Freedom Summer: The Savage Season of 1964 That Made Mississippi Burn and Made America a Democracy.* New York: Penguin Books, 2011.

Watts, Jill. *God, Harlem U.S.A.* Berkeley, CA: University of California Press, 1995.

Weisbrot, Robert. *Father Divine and the Struggle for Racial Equality*. Urbana, IL: University of Illinois Press, 1983.

Whayne, Jeannie. *A New Plantation South: Land, Labor, and Federal Favor in Twentieth Century Arkansas*. Charlottesville: University of Virginia Press, 1996.

Whit, William C. "Soul Food as Cultural Creation." In *African American Foodways: Explorations of History and Culture*, edited by Anne L. Bower, 45–58. Urbana: University of Illinois Press, 2007.

Wilkerson, Isabel. *The Warmth of Other Sons: The Epic Story of America's Great Migration*. New York: Vintage, 2011.

Williams-Forson, Psyche. *Building Houses Out of Chicken Legs: Black Women, Food, and Power*. Chapel Hill: University of North Carolina Press, 2006.

———. "Chickens and Chains: Using African American Foodways to Understand Black Identities." In *African American Foodways: Explorations of History and Culture*, edited by Ann L. Bower, 126–38. Urbana: University of Illinois Press, 2007.

———. "Take the Chicken Out of the Box: Demystifying the Sameness of African American Culinary Heritage in the U.S." In *Edible Identities: Food as Cultural Heritage*, edited by Rhonda L. Brulotte and Michael A. Di Giovine, 93–108. New York: Routledge, 2016.

Williamson, Samuel H., and Louis P. Cain. "Measuring Slavery in 2016 Dollars." Measuringworth.com. https://www.measuringworth.com/slavery.php#foot2, accessed September 17, 2018.

Wilson, Charles Reagan. "Biscuits." In *The New Encyclopedia of Southern Culture: Foodways*, edited by John T. Edge, 122–25. Chapel Hill: University of North Carolina Press, 2007.

———. "Cornbread." In *The New Encyclopedia of Southern Culture: Foodways*, edited by John T. Edge, 152–54. Chapel Hill: University of North Carolina Press, 2007.

———. "Pork." In *The New Encyclopedia of Southern Culture: Foodways*, edited by John T. Edge, 88–92. Chapel Hill: University of North Carolina Press, 2007.

Wilson, Mary Tolford. "Peaceful Integration: The Owner's Adoption of His Slaves' Food." *Journal of Negro History* 4, no. 2 (1964): 116–27.

Witt, Doris. "The Intersections of Literary and Culinary Studies." In *African American Foodways: Explorations of History & Culture*, edited by Anne L. Bower, 101–25. Urbana: University of Illinois Press, 2007.

Wood, Peter H. *Black Majority: Negroes in Colonial South Carolina*. New York: Alfred A. Knopf, 1974.

Wright, Clarissa Dickson. *A History of English Food*. London: Random House UK, 2011.

Yentsch, Anne. "Excavating the South's African American Food History." In *African American Foodways: Explorations of History and Culture*, edited by Anne L. Bower, 59–100. Urbana: University of Illinois Press, 2007.

Zanger, Mark H. "Cassava." In *The Oxford Companion to American Food and Drink*, edited by Andrew F. Smith. New York: Oxford University Press, 2007.

Ziegelman, Jane, and Andrew Coe. *A Square Meal: A Culinary History of the Great Depression*. New York: Harper, 2016.

Index

Depression and, 113–14; segregation in, 89–90; servants in, 119–20; "victory gardens" in, 116–18, *118*; WLA in, 115–16

WPA. *See* Works Progress Administration

Wright, Chester, 120

Wright, Ella, 73

Wright, Marian, 132

Wright, Richard, 64, 73, 94, 106

yams, 13–14, 30, 165n6

Yentsch, Anne, 72

Young Negroes' Cooperative League (YNCL), 112

Zippert, John, 132

About the Author

Jennifer Jensen Wallach is the author or editor of several books about African American and food history, including *How America Eats: A Social History of U.S. Food and Culture*. She teaches history at the University of North Texas.